MAN TO MAN

MAN TO MAN

AFRICAN AMERICAN VOICES ON FAITH, WISDOM, AND PERSEVERANCE

Lee N. June, PhD, General Editor
Christopher C. Mathis Jr., PhD, General Editor
Matthew Parker Sr., Consulting Editor

Man to Man: African American Voices on Faith, Wisdom, and Perseverance
© 2025 by Institute for Black Family Development

Requests for permission to quote from this book should be directed to: Permissions Department, Our Daily Bread Publishing, PO Box 3566, Grand Rapids, MI 49501; or contact us by email at permissionsdept@odbm.org.

Bible permissions statements can be found on page 327.

Interior design by Michael J. Williams

ISBN: 978-1-64070-292-9

Library of Congress Cataloging-in-Publication Data Available

Printed in the United States of America
25 26 27 28 29 30 31 32 / 8 7 6 5 4 3 2 1

Contents

Preface

MATTHEW PARKER SR., MA, HONORARY DOCTORATE

Three times a year all your men must appear before the
LORD your God at the place he will choose: at the Festival
of Unleavened Bread, the Festival of Weeks and the Festival
of Tabernacles. No one should appear before the LORD
empty-handed: Each of you must bring a gift in proportion
to the way the LORD your God has blessed you.

Deuteronomy 16:16–17

In the Old Testament nation of Israel, the men gathered together
three times a year to pray for the men, women, and children of
the nation; to fellowship; and to share resources. That powerful
example illustrates what I pray this book will be to our brothers.
Many of the men who contributed to this book have played a role
in my life as prayer partners, mentors, and leadership coaches . . .
even in my discipline. These men helped heal me and increase my
understanding of God's principles. I believe that readers of these
chapters will have a similar opportunity to glean from these men
what it means to be a man of God as we reflect on what it means
to be a husband, father, and leader.

My life experiences are similar to many of the stories shared
by these writers. My story starts November 14, 1945, when my
father, with his love for my mother, Ruth Spann Parker, gave life

to me. When I was three years old, my mother died in childbirth, and my father did what he could to provide the basic needs of shelter, food, and clothing. Those simple acts laid the foundation for my future as a man, husband, and father.

In 1968, I met the late African American evangelist and thought-leader Rev. Dr. Tom Skinner, who laid critical ministry skills on the foundation my father had established: leadership, networking, and organizational development. Then in 1971, I met Dr. Lloyd Blue, who became my "father in the faith," and with his wife, Tressie Blue, pointed me toward the next leg of my life journey. His commitment to evangelize and disciple men, especially men of African descent, became my commitment as well. I am grateful for all the men who have had an impact on my life and grateful, too, to know many of the writers in this book. I trust the book will be an encouragement to all who read it.

Introduction

LEE N. JUNE, CTS, MML, PHD
CHRISTOPHER C. MATHIS JR., MDIV, PHD

This book is aimed toward African American men but is for anyone who seeks new insights into the essence of African American Christian men across generations and our lifespan. Whether you are churched or unchurched, a professional, a lay leader, or someone who wants to explore the full range of African American male culture, this book is for you. You will find fresh insights, affirmations, support, and workable solutions that help the reader transcend the challenges of African American manhood to fulfill its rich promise for life's adversities, challenges, and opportunities.

Biblically and academically sound, this book is multifaceted. First, you hear the voices of scholars, educators, community leaders, pastors, professionals, and youth speaking to areas of life that are critical for godly success. Second, the authors, African American men and one African American woman, offer advice and uncover the essence of all that makes the Christian African American man—one who has endured hardships and made major contributions in his community, American society, and the world. The contributions of these authors and their voices are intended to fill a void in the literature that too often ignores African American men, their contributions, and their voices.

Amid the challenges still facing today's African American males in the early part of the twenty-first century, there is much hope and there are many successes. In this completely revised edition of

Men to Men (1996), Black scholars, professionals, practitioners, and youth share personal and practical insights into what it takes to succeed in all avenues of manhood, from family to faith, finances to career, and the criminal justice system to the educational setting. Whether you are a pastor, educator, counselor, lay leader, or simply someone concerned with how to apply your faith to turn life's hurdles into opportunities, this book gives you proven perspectives that can spark success and growth in your own and others' lives.

We draw on the expertise and wisdom of twenty-two individuals from a variety of fields. This includes older men, such as Dr. Lloyd Blue Sr., Dr. Henry Allen, Dr. Lee N. June, Dr. Ken Staley, Claude L. Dallas Jr., Dr. Lonnie J. Chipp III, attorney Kenneth L. McDaniels, Karl I. Bell, Rev. Joseph Williams, Dr. Michael Lyles Sr., Rev. Ron Mosby, and Rodney S. Patterson, MA. We also include younger men such as Dr. Christopher C. Mathis Jr., Rev. Michael T. Westbrook, Rev. Lenroy Jones, Dr. Kevin L. Jones, Amod Field, Michael Lyles II (joint with his wife, Kristina J. Lyles), Tim Herd, Dr. Kenneth D. Russell, Dr. Patrick L. Stearns, and Brian L. June. All share practical advice on topics of vital interest.

In-depth, biblical, encouraging, and based on twenty-first-century scholarship and personal experiences, this book shows how one can avoid the pitfalls associated with Black manhood to achieve spiritual, personal, and social prosperity. As was the first edition, this book is a companion to *Woman to Woman*, edited by Drs. Norvella P. Carter, Quinita Ogletree, and Kamala Williams with Karon Parker as consulting editor. A special thanks to Joyce M. Dinkins for her suggestions for improvement and meticulous editing of early versions of this manuscript.

Part 1: Developing Life-Enhancement Skills

To thrive as men and Christians, there are numerous areas that one must master and control. Some of these critical life-enhancement skills are discussed in this section that contains seven chapters.

Chapter 1. Integrity: A Necessity—Lee N. June, CTS, MML, PhD

The Bible tells us that the Lord orders the steps of a good man. Yet, there are many situations in which we may stray, and as a result, our witness for God as salt and light is compromised. This chapter challenges readers to do all they can to walk upright and offers tips for doing so. Such a journey can start at an early age and continue throughout one's lifespan.

Chapter 2. Cultivating: Greatness in the Valleys of Disappointment—Henry L. Allen, PhD

Many individuals (young and old) in the Bible and in the society in which we live have had disappointments and failures. This chapter reminds us that greatness can flow from being in valleys of disappointment and can become a stepping stone for success and greatness.

Chapter 3. Stewardship: Generate Wealth with Biblical Values—Karl I. Bell, MBA

African Americans are beginning to accumulate wealth. However, too many men are still not managing their finances as well as they can and would like to. This chapter explores how one can, from a biblical perspective, accumulate and maintain wealth for oneself and future generations.

Chapter 4. Bond: With a Purpose on Purpose—Rodney S. Patterson, MA

Women typically bond with each other easier and often do so better or differently than men. But it is also critical that men of all ages form and maintain productive relationships with each other. This chapter, written by a pastor and diversity consultant expert, shares tidbits from ongoing groups and shows the difficulties and the necessary steps to bonding. It also challenges the church community to do more in this area by bonding with the purpose of eliminating racism and creating racial reconciliation.

Chapter 5. Discover: Finding Our Life's Calling—Lenroy Jones, MA

Finding a career direction and life calling, given the array of possibilities, can be a daunting task. New career possibilities are surfacing at a rapid rate. Drawing on the expertise gained from years in the field of career development and ministry, this chapter discusses how to approach planning and manage the many steps that follow on the path toward one's calling.

Chapter 6. Perspective: Maintaining a Kingdom Mind—Ron Mosby, BA

How do individuals of all age groups during a period of postmodernity develop and maintain a kingdom perspective? That is, how does one be in the world but not of the world. This chapter, written by a pastor, explores how to do this effectively.

Chapter 7. Health: Becoming an Expert on Our Wellness—Michael R. Lyles Sr., MD

It is critical that we pay attention to our health. Men are especially prone to neglect this area of our lives. Dr. Michael Lyles Sr., a psychiatrist, challenges and shows us how to become an expert on our health. He also shares his personal story with health issues.

Part 2: Mentoring and Guiding the Next Generation

If we are to improve our society and maximize opportunities for young men, we must be laser focused on maximizing the potential of our young men and women. In this section, five chapters focus on how to perform this daunting, but rewarding task.

Chapter 8. Passage: Navigate Christ-Centered Covert Connections on Campus—Dr. Kevin L. Jones, PhD

Many of our future leaders come from college campuses. How does a Black male maximize this experience and remain Christ-centered? A college professor in teacher education shares his insights, perspectives, and his personal journey through the educational system while offering tips with particular focus on how to make Christian connections and utilize them during this period of life.

Chapter 9. Relate: Choosing Role Models Wisely—Tim Herd, MSEd, MA

Young men are bombarded with images and public figures. How then does one choose who to emulate in dress, speech, and morals?

This chapter, written by a graduate student, shares his life journey thus far in how he chooses role models and offers helpful tips to others who are traveling and or will travel the same road.

Chapter 10. Reflect: Developing Spiritual Self-Defense Tactics— Patrick L. Stearns, MFA, PhD

Life brings many challenges. Just like a game of sports, one must employ offensive as well as defensive tactics. This chapter, written by a college professor, identifies areas men of all ages face and offers proactive, spiritual self-defense strategies for effective living. He revisits his younger self and discusses what he could have done better, as well as reflecting on what younger people can do differently in the future so as not to have too many regrets.

Chapter 11. Mentor: Serve Others' Success—Christopher C. Mathis Jr., MDiv, PhD

Successful men often have people who have guided them along the way. In this chapter you'll find a discussion on how to maximize the mentoring process of young African American men for later success. In doing so, the author, a college administrator and pastor, shares his personal experiences of being mentored and challenges others to take advantage of both being mentored and mentoring others.

Chapter 12. Engage: Stepping Up during Your Child's K–12 Journey—Amod Field, MAS

Since most all of our young men go through the K–12 school system, what can we—students, parents, grandparents, guardians, school personnel, etc.—do to maximize this experience? For too many of our young men, the K–12 experience is often a negative one. A school principal shares his perspective on what needs to and can be done to make it a mostly positive experience.

Part 3: Strengthening Relationships within Families

In the twenty-first century the family remains the most critical unit in society. What are some areas that must be addressed for continued success? Five critical areas for strengthening families and family lives are discussed in this section.

Chapter 13. Hear: Attending to Young Black Males' Voices—Lee N. June, CTS, MML, PhD

In a focus group, six young Black men share their hopes, dreams, and needs for the future. These are voices we must listen to, heed, and incorporate in our decision making in the present and the future.

Chapter 14. Not Alone: Parenting a Child with Special Needs— Michael R. Lyles II, JD; and Kristina J. Lyles, JD

Many of us care for or have cared for a child with special needs. Such a situation brings challenges but also great joy. This husband-and-wife team share their personal journey in parenting a child with special needs. Like seasoned storytellers, they take the reader through their experiences.

Chapter 15. Prosper: Growing Generations with Biblical Values— Claude L. Dallas Jr., MS, MA

Not only is parenting a skill that men need, but there is also the increasing need for skills in how to effectively grandparent. Both parenting and grandparenting skills are discussed in this chapter by this grandfather.

Chapter 16. Balance: Balancing Family and Career—Ken Staley, MDiv, DD

In effective families, men must not only pursue their career, but they must not neglect their family responsibilities. This chapter is written by someone who has had success in both his career—engineering and pastoring—and with his family. Tips on how to balance a career and family are presented.

Chapter 17. Love: Ways to Romance Your Wife—Lloyd C. Blue Sr., DMin

Dr. Blue, who has been married for sixty-eight years to the same woman as of this writing, shares one of the secrets of longevity in marriage—how to keep the love life burning throughout the span of marriage. This seasoned and now retired pastor and husband views romancing as one of the keys for men who are Christian and married.

Part 4: Dealing with the Criminal Justice Systems

In the twenty-first century, Black males continue to be significantly overrepresented in the criminal justice system. In part 4, two men, a lawyer and a survivor of the criminal justice system, offer their insights and strategies for avoiding arrest and prison. Drawing on their significant knowledge and experience, they also offer advice on how to maintain hope for those already in the system and how to succeed post incarceration.

Chapter 18. Survive: Avoiding Arrest and Prison—Kenneth L. McDaniels, LLM, JD

We constantly see in media the arrests and brutality inflicted on many African American males. What do we need to tell and teach African American males, particularly young men, about avoiding arrest and prison? A lawyer and prosecutor shares his perspectives and experiences. Preventive steps are emphasized.

Chapter 19. Thrive: Overcoming Prison like Joseph—Joseph Williams, MA

There can be a successful transition from prison to being productive in society. An individual who has made this journey successfully, and has devoted his life to helping others do the same, tells his story and provides transferable tips.

Part 5: Facing Contemporary and Future Challenges

As we advance further into the twenty-first century, some old challenges continue, and new ones arise. Three pressing contemporary challenges are discussed in this section. Specifically addressed are the world of technology; issues related to diversity, equity, and inclusion; and a specific challenge and message to young Black males.

Chapter 20. Navigate: The World of Technology—Michael T. Westbrook, MA and Brian L. June, MML, MS

Technology is here to stay and is constantly escalating within society. Today's challenge is how to maximize the potential of the powerful technological tools for success. Written by a Gen Xer and a Boomer, a pastor and a member of a church audiovisual team share their personal experiences and give tips on ways to maximize these essential tools of technology within the church setting.

Chapter 21. Interrogate: What to a Black Man Is a White Evangelical Education—Dr. Kenneth D. Russell, MDiv, PhD

Many Black men study at predominantly White Christian oriented institutions of higher education. Many often find the approaches of these institutions in covering and discussing issues relating to Black people as problematic. The author shares his personal experiences navigating these institutions. He also discusses the role of Critical Race Theory, and other Crit areas that are too often misunderstood and maligned.

Chapter 22. Closing: A Letter to Young Black Men—Lonnie J. Chipp III, MA, Honorary Doctorate

Black men attend church services at rates less than Black women. They also face many life struggles. An experienced pastor shares a message he feels that Black men, particularly young Black men, need to hear.

PART 1

DEVELOPING LIFE-ENHANCEMENT SKILLS

1

Integrity

A Necessity

LEE N. JUNE, CTS, MML, PHD

Then the LORD said to Satan, "Have you considered
my servant Job? There is no one on earth like him; he is
blameless and upright, a man who fears God and shuns
evil. And he still maintains his *integrity*, though you incited
me against him to ruin him without any reason."
Job 2:3 (emphasis added)

The *integrity* of the upright guides them, but the
unfaithful are destroyed by their duplicity.
Proverbs 11:3 (emphasis added)

Introduction

What is one of the most important personal characteristics we
can possess and seek to maintain in life? A characteristic that is
difficult, if not impossible, to regain once lost? Many seek first
to achieve fame or to be successful in a general sense. There is
nothing wrong with the aspiration to become successful as long it
is anchored in or undergirded by something and someone beyond
the self, that is, God.

Integrity in Everyday Life

Integrity is a word frequently used in our world today. If one were to go to a bookstore or browse the internet for books on integrity or books that have the word *integrity* in their title, several would appear. Such titles include *The Road to Character* by David Brooks; *The Price of Principle: Why Integrity Is Worth the Consequences* by Alan Dershowitz; *Integrity: The Courage to Meet the Demands of Reality* by Henry Cloud; *Integrity and God's Man: The Foundation and Formation of Integrity* by John W. Tucker; and *Leading with Integrity: Competence with Christian Character* by Fred Smith and David L. Goetz. Some of these books discuss integrity in a general sense; others address integrity from a religious or spiritual perspective.

Society often considers integrity to be a virtue. For example, positive psychology advocates certain virtues that should be encouraged, whether in a religious context or not, for the overall benefit and well-being of society. Positive psychology's mission, according to the book *The Psychology of Religion* by Ralph Hood and others, is "the scientific study of the 'good life'—that is, what works, what is improving, what its capacities are, what makes people authentically happy."[1] While integrity is not explicitly listed as one of the virtues of positive psychology, honesty is. Other core virtues of positive psychology mentioned by Hood and his coauthors are wisdom, courage, humanity, justice, transcendence, temperance, and self-control.[2] This list of virtues has deep roots in Christianity.

What Integrity Is

The American Heritage College Dictionary defines *integrity* as "(1) steadfast adherence to an ethical code; (2) the state of being unimpaired, soundness; (3) the quality or condition of being whole or undivided; completeness." Their synonym for *integrity* is *honesty*.[3]

Merriam-Webster's online dictionary indicates synonyms and antonyms of integrity:

1: firm adherence to a code of especially moral or artistic values: INCORRUPTIBILITY

2: an unimpaired condition: SOUNDNESS

3: the quality or state of being complete or undivided: COMPLETENESS

Synonyms: character, decency, goodness, honesty, morality, probity, rectitude, righteousness, rightness, uprightness, virtue, and virtuousness.

Antonyms (opposite in meaning): badness, evil, evildoing, immorality, iniquity, sin, villainy, and wickedness.[4]

From a biblical standpoint, *Holman Illustrated Bible Dictionary* defines *integrity* as the "faithful support of a standard of values."[5] The authors note that there are terms in the Bible which occur in parallel to integrity such as *righteousness, uprightness, without wavering,* and *blameless.* Old Testament individuals the authors designate as having these characteristics include Noah (Genesis 6:9), Abraham (Genesis 17:1), Jacob (Genesis 25:27), Job (Job 1:1, 8; 2:3), and David (1 Kings 9:4). They further note that in the New Testament, the word sometimes translated as *integrity* occurs only in Titus 2:7 (as translated in the NRSV and NIV), and this is in regard to teaching.

The New Strong's Exhaustive Concordance of the Bible lists sixteen occurrences of the word *integrity* as translated in the King James Version of the Bible. All of these are found in the Old Testament. Integrity is therein defined as "completeness."[6] While the word *integrity* is not found in the New Testament in the King James Version, the idea of integrity continues in the New Testament in the concepts "perfection" (maturity) and "blameless."

Nelson's New Illustrated Bible Dictionary defines and says the following about the word *integrity.*

Honesty, sincerity, singleness of purpose. In the Old Testament, Noah (Gen 6:9), Abraham (Gen 7:1), Jacob (Gen 25:27), David (1 Kings 9:4), and Job (Job 1:1, 8; 2:3, 9; 4:6; 27:5; 31:6) were called people of integrity. Although Jesus did not use the word integrity, he called for purity of heart (Matt 5:8) and purity of motive (Matt 6:1–6).[7]

The *Africa Bible Commentary*, likewise, notes the importance of integrity by highlighting its centrality in Job's life.[8]

Why is integrity the lead chapter in this book, a book written primarily to men from men? While integrity is important for all, we have seen too many men face a situation where their promising careers and positive reputations were tested. Too often they failed the test, and their integrity was destroyed, tarnished, or diminished. I believe that this can and must be avoided if we want to have a cadre of mighty men of valor in the remainder of this century and beyond. Integrity must be visible in all areas of our lives and is paramount to the chapters covered in this book, in our families, in mentoring others, in our careers, in our finances, and more.

One must, however, distinguish between failures, setbacks, and losing one's integrity. Failure, as some writers have pointed out, if properly dealt with, can be a prelude to success.[9] A setback, likewise, if managed correctly, can be merely a temporary pause along one's road to success. To maintain integrity, one must possess the proper tools that can help a person to avoid threats and practice resilience, that is, the ability to bounce back. Just as there are numerous examples of failures and setbacks that did not lead to losing integrity, there are many examples of resilience amid failures and setbacks. Think for a moment and identify individuals you know who have bounced back. What are some of the defining characteristics of such individuals?

A Deeper Biblical Perspective with Examples

While striving for and maintaining integrity is paramount, it cannot be our God, nor is it the source of salvation. The biblical source of salvation is stated in Ephesians 2:8–10. Thus, mature Christians place integrity in its proper perspective.

> For it is by grace you have been saved, through faith—and this is not from yourselves, it is the gift

of God—not by works, so that no one can boast. For we are God's handiwork, created in Christ Jesus to do good works, which God prepared in advance for us to do.

Thus, the Christian seeks for and maintains integrity because this is God's expectation for those who are saved, since "we are God's handiwork, created in Christ Jesus to do good works" (v. 10).

What men of the Bible come to your mind as men of integrity? For me, the first person who comes to mind is Job. Job is described by God to Satan as a person of integrity. In this instance, we might say that God was bragging on Job that he had integrity and would maintain it even when tested by Satan. As Job was attacked, his wife, observing what was happening, suggested that holding on to his integrity was not worth the cost, given the horrendous attacks by Satan and the results that were occurring. Her words to him were "Curse God and die!" (Job 2:9). Yet, while Job was not fully aware of all that was happening to him, and without proper support from his wife and friends, he held on to his integrity. As men, this is what we must strive to do. Our relationship with God must remain preeminent even when we face trials and tribulations.

Nelson's New Illustrated Bible Dictionary also mentions Noah, David, and Jacob as men of integrity.[10] In Genesis 6:9, Noah is described as "a righteous man, blameless among the people of his time, and he walked faithfully with God." Noah's life was one of obedience to God and he sought to do what God had assigned him to do. This is the hallmark of integrity.

As described in the case of Noah, we see that the idea of blamelessness is associated with integrity. What does *blameless* mean? This is a requirement specified for bishops in 1 Timothy 3:2 as translated in the King James Version. The word for blameless is translated "be above reproach" in the New International Version. It carries the idea of "to be unaccused." When I think of this concept, I often say that one cannot control what one is accused of, but one can control whether one is guilty. To have integrity and to be blameless mean that a person is living a lifestyle wherein they are in a right relationship with God and are not practicing sin whereby others can legitimately bring a charge against them.

It does not mean that one has never sinned. In the case of Noah, while he obeyed God, he was not perfect as defined in our English language, as the incident of his drunkenness later in life shows.

David is also mentioned by *Nelson's New Illustrated Dictionary* as a person of integrity. Their reference to David in this manner is in 1 Kings 9:4. The context of this description is when the Lord appeared to Solomon at Gibeon during the dedication of the temple. God said of David to Solomon, "If you walk before me faithfully with *integrity* of heart and uprightness, as David your father did . . ." (emphasis added). This is an especially important description of David, given the known sins that he committed during his lifetime.

When I think of men of integrity in the Bible, beyond those already mentioned, I also think of Joseph, Samuel, Daniel, Shadrach, Meshach, Abednego, and Paul. Joseph faced the temptation of sexual sin initiated by Potiphar's wife. His situation was as follows:

> So Potiphar left everything he had in Joseph's care; with Joseph in charge, he did not concern himself with anything except the food he ate.
>
> Now Joseph was well-built and handsome, and after a while his master's wife took notice of Joseph and said, "Come to bed with me!"
>
> But he refused. "With me in charge," he told her, "my master does not concern himself with anything in the house; everything he owns he has entrusted to my care. No one is greater in this house than I am. My master has withheld nothing from me except you, because you are his wife. How then could I do such a wicked thing and sin against God?" And though she spoke to Joseph day after day, he refused to go to bed with her or even be with her. (Genesis 39:6–10)

Faced with the Joseph situation, what would you have done?

Also, in the case of Samuel, imagine living a life such that you could stand before those in your circle of influence at the end of your life and speak as Samuel did:

Samuel said to all Israel, "I have listened to every-thing you said to me and have set a king over you. Now you have a king as your leader. As for me, I am old and gray, and my sons are here with you. I have been your leader from my youth until this day. Here I stand. Testify against me in the presence of the LORD and his anointed. Whose ox have I taken? Whose donkey have I taken? Whom have I cheated? Whom have I oppressed? From whose hand have I accepted a bribe to make me shut my eyes? If I have done any of these things, I will make it right."

"You have not cheated or oppressed us," they replied. "You have not taken anything from any-one's hand." (1 Samuel 12:1–4)

Yes, one could stand before a group of people and say this, but what makes this incredible regarding Samuel is the people's re-sponse. "You have not cheated or oppressed us," they replied. "You have not taken anything from anyone's hand." The people affirmed his integrity.

Imagine that you are placed in a situation, and you know the behavior that you are about to do or could undertake would compromise your core values, threaten your integrity, and affect your relationship with God. Would you do as Daniel did, when he "resolved not to defile himself with the royal food and wine" (Daniel 1:8)? While this statement by Daniel was made early in his life, he continued to live a life of integrity. Daniel's vow also shows that one can live a life of integrity beginning with and even in youth.

Imagine that you were in a predicament like Shadrach, Meshach, and Abednego. Note how they managed their integrity test.

Furious with rage, Nebuchadnezzar summoned Shadrach, Meshach and Abednego. So these men were brought before the king, and Nebuchadnez-zar said to them, "Is it true, Shadrach, Meshach and Abednego, that you do not serve my gods or worship the image of gold I have set up? Now when you hear the sound of the horn, flute, zither, lyre, harp, pipe and all kinds of music, if you are ready to fall down and worship the image I made, very good. But if you do not worship it, you will be thrown immediately into a blazing furnace. Then what god will be able to rescue you from my hand?" (Daniel 3:13–15)

Faced with this situation, what would you do? Here is what Shadrach, Meshach, and Abednego did:

Shadrach, Meshach and Abednego replied to him, "King Nebuchadnezzar, we do not need to defend ourselves before you in this matter. If we are thrown into the blazing furnace, the God we serve is able to deliver us from it, and he will deliver us from Your Majesty's hand. But even if he does not, we want you to know, Your Majesty, that we will not serve your gods or worship the image of gold you have set up." (Daniel 3:16–18)

Further, imagine that at the end of one's life, you could say as the apostle Paul said in 2 Timothy 4:6–8:

For I am already being poured out like a drink offering, and the time for my departure is near. I have fought the good fight, I have finished the race, I have kept the faith. Now there is in store for me the crown of righteousness, which the Lord, the righteous Judge, will award to me on that day—and not only to me, but also to all who have longed for his appearing.

The ability to say what Paul said after the conversion on the Damascus road is also reflective of having lived a life of integrity.

Responding in the various manners these men did when they were tested or when their lives were at stake reflects a set of principles that they adhered to and were willing to die for. In sum, these principles, indicative of integrity, were

Keeping our relationship with God top priority, even during the most difficult days (Job)

Living a blameless life where no other person can legitimately bring a charge against one (Noah)

Walking faithfully and uprightly before God (David)

Not succumbing to sexual temptations (Joseph)

Not taking anything that does not belong to them, not cheating, not oppressing others, not taking bribes (Samuel)

Not defiling oneself with things of the world (Daniel)

Having absolute trust in God who is with us as Christians, regardless of the circumstances or the outcome (Shadrach, Meshach, and Abednego)

Being willing to stay the course with God amidst a life of horrendous persecutions (Paul)

Tips on Maintaining Integrity

If one of our life goals is to maintain our integrity—to *be* men of integrity—here are some tips and aids that can assist in this endeavor.

Tip one: Do what Scripture tells us to do. For instance, hide the Word of God in your heart: "Thy word have I hid in mine heart, that I might not sin against thee" (Psalm 119:11 KJV). The following Scriptures are suggested as more of life's guideposts.

- Psalm 37:23–24 (God upholds those who delight in Him)
- Psalm 119:105 (God's Word is a lamp and a light)

Study the book of Proverbs and make a list of the passages that you believe can help you to live a life of integrity. You will find many principles laid out in Proverbs. Such principles are too numerous to fully list, but I will share the ones that are extremely helpful to me.

- Proverbs 1:7 (true knowledge begins with reverencing the Lord)
- Proverbs 3:5–6 (trusting, learning from, and submitting to God leads to righteous living)
- Proverbs 4:7 (wisdom and understanding are paramount in life)
- Proverbs 6:16–19 (while God is love and loves, there are things He hates)
- Proverbs 6:32 (adultery is to be avoided)
- Proverbs 9:10 (wisdom begins with reverencing God)
- Proverbs 13:11 (don't be dishonest in matters of money)
- Proverbs 14:12 (everything that appears right is not right)
- Proverbs 15:1, 18 (we need to be gentle in our interactions with others)
- Proverbs 16:7, 18, 25, 32 (God takes pleasure in our right behaviors)
- Proverbs 20:7 (how we live our lives is important)
- Proverbs 21:3 (doing what is right and just is more critical than sacrifice)
- Proverbs 22:1 (our reputation is critical)
- Proverbs 24:1–2 (we must not envy the wicked or desire their company)
- Proverbs 27:1–2 (boasting and self-praise are to be avoided)
- Proverbs 28:13 (secret and unconfessed sin prevent our progress)
- Proverbs 29:11, 18 (the wise person is calm and heeds wisdom)

I am suggesting that we develop a list of Scriptures from the book of Proverbs that can become our life guideposts.

The listing of Scriptures from other parts of the Bible, as guides, is also helpful. Other Scriptures that guide my life are:

- Amos 5:24 (fighting for and promoting justice is pleasing to God)

- Micah 6:8 (God requires us to act justly—do justice, love mercy, and walk humbly with Him)
- Matthew 5:13–16 (remember that we are salt and light in this world)
- Romans 12:1–2 (we are to offer our bodies to God as a living sacrifice and renew our minds rather than being transformed by this world)
- Galatians 5:16 (walking by the Spirit allows us to avoid sin)
- Ephesians 5:23–26 (mutual and proper submission and love are hallmarks of a godly marriage)
- 1 Corinthians 10:13 (God can protect us during temptations)
- James 1:5 (God is the source of wisdom and will give it to us if we ask Him for it)
- 1 John 1:7 (walking in God's light leads to godly fellowship with others)

These are among the main Scriptures that have been helpful to me. I encourage you to make your own list that you feel can help you to develop, practice, and maintain integrity.

Tip Two: Manage the implications and challenges of postmodernity. Philosophers, psychologists, and others have suggested that human beings have lived in three eras regarding how knowledge and beliefs are viewed. These eras have been described as premodernity, modernity, and postmodernity. We are now living in what is called the postmodern era. Postmodernity poses challenges to Christians regarding holding on to their beliefs and principles. For example, according to Brian Zinnbauer, author of "Models of Healthy and Unhealthy Religion and Spirituality," a postmodern approach rejects the idea of revealed truth, asserting that there is no ultimate truth, and that all truths are equally valuable.[11] This is problematic for many in the Christian community. How do we deal with this perspective? Zinnbauer suggests an integrative approach where we accept that there are "multiple truths across multiple dimensions" and that there are "multiple methods, local and universal truths." However, I suggest that for the Christian, the perspective to consider is that there are multiple conceptions of truths, that these perspectives must be acknowledged and respected, but that each of us must hold firm to the belief that is revealed, and ultimate truth—and its source is the Triune God.

Tip Three: Learn from how Jesus dealt with His integrity tests. The Bible records that when Jesus was led into the wilderness by the Spirit to be tested by the devil, He relied on and quoted Scripture in His responses to each of the three temptations. For temptation one, to turn stones into bread when He was hungry, Jesus responded to Satan saying, "It is written: 'Man shall not live on bread alone, but on every word that comes from the mouth of God'" (Matthew 4:4). For temptation two, to throw Himself down from the highest point of the temple so God could rescue Him, Jesus responded that—after Satan misquoted a Scripture—"It is also written: 'Do not put the Lord your God to the test'" (Matthew 4:7). For the third temptation, to bow down and worship Satan in exchange for receiving all the kingdoms of this world and their splendor, Jesus replied, "Away from me, Satan! For it is written: 'Worship the Lord your God, and serve him only'" (Matthew 4:10).

Conclusion

Moving forward, we need a large cadre of men, young and old, who are Christian and who will commit to pursuing and maintaining a life of integrity in their family, in relationship with other men and women, and in their careers. The remaining chapters in this book will help us to seek and maintain integrity, and even more.

As reported on Black Demographics, the 2021 US Census Bureau estimated there are 49,586,352 African Americans in the United States, which is 14.9 percent of the population of the total American population of 331.9 million. This includes those who identify as "Black only" and as "Black in combination with another race."

According to official 2018 estimates from the US Census Bureau, the Black male population in the United States was 21 million in 2018. This is 48 percent of the total Black population, compared to Black females who make up 52 percent of the Black population.[12]

Since Black men are in all areas of society, we need to continue to help raise up a cadre of Black men who are totally committed to Christ and are making living a life of integrity a central goal of life. Imagine 21 million plus Black men in America dedicated to living a life of integrity. With this, God would be well pleased.

NOTES

1. Ralph W. Hood Jr., Peter C. Hill, and Bernard Spilka, *The Psychology of Religion: An Empirical Approach*, 5th ed. (New York: Guilford Press, 2018), 452.

2. Hood, Hill, and Spilka, *The Psychology of Religion*.

3. "Integrity," *The American Heritage College Dictionary* (Boston: Houghton Mifflin, 1993).

4. Merriam-Webster, "integrity," accessed November 1, 2024, https://www.merriam-webster.com/dictionary/integrity.

5. Chad Brand, Charles Draper, and Archie England, eds., *Holman Illustrated Bible Dictionary* (Nashville: Holman Bible Publishers,1998), 827.

6. James Strong, *The New Strong's Exhaustive Concordance of the Bible* (Nashville: Thomas Nelson, 1996).

7. Ronald F. Youngblood, ed., *Nelson's New Illustrated Bible Dictionary* (Nashville: Thomas Nelson, 1995), 602.

8. Tokunboh Adeyemo, *Africa Bible Commentary* (Grand Rapids, MI: Zondervan, 2006).

9. Henry Allen, "Risk and Failure as a Prelude to Success," in *Men to Men: Perspectives of Sixteen African-American Christian Men*, ed. Lee N. June and Matthew Parker (Grand Rapids, MI: Zondervan, 1996).

10. Youngblood, *Nelson's New Illustrated Bible Dictionary*, 602.

11. Brian J. Zinnbauer, "Models of Healthy and Unhealthy Religion and Spirituality," in *APA Handbook of Psychology, Religion, and Spirituality*, ed. K. Pargament (Washington, DC: American Psychological Association, 2013), 73.

12. "Black Male Statistics," Black Demographics, accessed February 3, 2025, www.blackdemographics.com/population/black-male-statistics.

2

Cultivating
Greatness in the Valleys of Disappointment

HENRY L. ALLEN, PHD

Those who are wise will shine like the brightness
of the heavens, and those who lead many to
righteousness, like the stars for ever and ever.

Daniel 12:3

Introduction

Before he died, Dr. Martin Luther King Jr. emphasized the greatness of serving others within and outside African American communities. He told us that "everybody can be great, because everybody can serve." However, our service and rewards can be thwarted by wrong perspectives about or responses to our valleys of disappointment, traumas, and unexpected setbacks. Using biblical insights and sociological perspectives, this chapter intends to encourage generations of African American men to value the learning that comes from our valleys of disappointments. By faith and humility, we can overcome disappointments and achieve greatness through the Lord's love, truth, power, wisdom, and goodness.

Exploring recent generations of African American men involves many resources, including film media. One of my favorite film series has always been Alex Haley's monumental story *Roots*, probably because it was televised in the year I graduated from my undergraduate studies.[1] As a sociologist, I became fascinated by how tribal societies could survive environmental woes and unexpected situations. Because generations matter, the tribal griot was a pivotal figure in African societies, trusted to share the intragenerational struggles and intergenerational challenges traced by that tribe of origin—by memory. He would tell the story orally, no matter the time involved. Everyone was enraptured by learning about the ancestors. To translate into sociological jargon, the griot elaborated the historical, social, economic, political, familial, cultural, and religious events of note for society. In the next few pages, I attempt to do the same in a conversational, and at times challenging, tone as an elder sharing wisdom and advice to those who listen.

My Early Life

My life began in 1955, so my generation includes my elders who experienced the Great Northern Migration, Civil Rights Era, Sidney Poitier, Willie Mays, Bill Russell, Nat King Cole, Sammy Davis Jr., and many others. My heroes were Kareem Abdul Jabbar, Dr. Martin Luther King Jr., Motown's Marvin Gaye, James Brown, Gladys Knight, and that great pantheon of 1970s soul music too amazing to account here. From this social foundation until the end of the 1970s, I experienced the Black Power Movement, school desegregation, identity formation, the Vietnam War, basketball, football, Black radio, church, and all the youthful accruements of socialization as a male within a relatively homogenous Black suburb. As an emerging sociologist, I always loved books and frequented libraries as a hobby. One adolescent hero for me was W. E. B. Du Bois.

My Later Life

Since that period, I have witnessed in this nation periods of White backlash related to criminal stereotypes, hostility toward effective affirmative action, symbolic racism, evangelicalism, political conservatism, urban decay, and internal fragmentation in African

American communities in Illinois, Minnesota, Michigan, and New York—along with a host of other states I visited as a college or university professor throughout my career across four decades. Therefore, I have been socialized by my children (and now by my grandchildren) and students to engage recent generations typified by rap music, hip-hop, President Obama, prosperity gospel, the Black Lives Matter and Me Too social movements, along with the explosion of sports, entertainment, and commercial media as well as the digital revolution. TikTok, Snapchat, Instagram, and Facebook (among others) now pervade human consciousness and communication. Computers, social media, cell phones, video games, and other technologies saturate the social and cultural landscape, near and far. Meanwhile, wars, violence, sophistry, duplicity, drugs, police murders, mass shootings, political corruption, sex trafficking, immigration woes, insurrection, sabotage, pandemics, epidemics, cryptocurrencies, environmental disasters, and death are regular realities. Marvin Gaye's epic album *What's Going On?* still echoes across generations tethered epistemologically and spiritually to an evolving ball of confusion. Anomie is *en vogue* like a perpetual fashion icon in music, expression, and behaviors. Black fatigue is a genuine reality. So are the indelible, multifaceted traumas we face together over generations in this two-faced, unstable society with many tongues.

On the positive side, my contemporary vantage point has been embellished as well as enriched by marriage to a virtuous Liberian woman, her large family, and pan-African concerns for Liberia, Ethiopia, Ghana, and other African societies. My Christian faith has been enlarged exponentially by all these phenomena. For brevity's sake, with this background exposition, let us now begin our journey probing the ongoing plight of African American men. Invariably, this chapter will focus on intersecting core issues or items that incorporate but transcend particular generations. How then do we cultivate greatness in the valleys of disappointment with reverent and humble intentionality?

As authentic, genuine disciples of Jesus Christ (see Revelation 2:8–11, the letter to genuine disciples suffering persecution), we must always remember that *agape* (unconditional) love, hope, mercy, and forgiveness are key components energizing our lives, relationships, work, ministry, leisure, and development. We must incorporate spiritual intelligence with practical competencies involving resilience, empathy, social capital, emotional intelligence, excellence, social intelligence, tacit knowledge, intuition, and improvisation into a symphony of our diasporic humanity. Using ongoing personal assessments, practical therapies, and other community resources in our toolboxes, we must daily inculcate a habitual SWOT analysis to probe our predicaments (S: strengths, W: weaknesses, O: opportunities, T: threats) by (1) featuring our intergenerational assets, (2) accentuating various coping strategies, and (3) transforming our failures, mistakes, and weaknesses with divine medicine or professional expertise. Thus we can overcome the pathological obstacles that threaten our self-efficacy, families, finances, and future. Resurrection power awaits us. As Psalm 75 clearly reminds us, with our sovereign, almighty God we must expect the unexpected (Isaiah 43:18–19).

Cultivating Greatness by Dealing with Internal Traumas and External Toxins

Sociologists understand that every macro level social system contains destructive, lethal components that mitigate against biblical standards of love and justice. Any astute scientific observer without ethnocentric nationalistic preferences can easily recognize that the bulk of the United States' populace has a moronic ignorance about the traumas inflicted upon African Americans across generations, notwithstanding any sanctioned remedies and all superficial political policies.[2] Few are mature and honest enough to face the undeniable truth, disregarding ideological fantasies. Moreover, some uncouth citizens and political demagogues even relish such foolishness, celebrating the mythologies of racism as if they were sacred rudiments of life. They deny the contaminated atrocities such as kidnapping, slavery, rape, oppression, contract labor, prejudice, lynching, discrimination, and theft. We routinely observe the missteps of the dominant populace as micro-aggressions, implicit biases and their deadly consequences that proliferate decades after civil rights legislation and judicial remedies have targeted the collective conscience. The radioactive, subliminal conditions spawning Black Lives Matter are ubiquitous in the imperial psyche.

We must decisively reiterate the following hard truths, even if these are unpopular or controversial to many. First, involuntary immigrants were tortured and enslaved to build this capitalistic enterprise. Secondly, this colonial nation of voluntary and involuntary immigrants (despite the optimistic rhetoric of liberty and equality) has not insured a society of wisdom and respect for those it enslaved across centuries. Crimes against humanity are yet to be adjudicated. Even worse, uninformed citizens blame dilapidated neighborhoods, poverty, and moral turpitude on us, ignoring how those culpable and complicit generated this ecology. Those who have benefited from this pathology have attempted to disregard the truth because it makes them uncomfortable. Funny how seldom these indecent occupants realize that African Americans have been in a perpetual state of discomfort throughout their involuntary sojourn in this country. Perhaps our humanity and pain matter less?

Scholars have pinpointed how social forces have shaped the individual opportunities of African Americans. Legal scholar Richard Rothstein, in his paradigmatic book *The Color of Law*, has refuted such bogus, insensitive thinking.[3] He provides empirical evidence of how law, politics, policing, housing, and economics enhanced racial segregation, showing that African Americans have suffered much more toxic trauma than those who choose comfort over truth. Invariably, African American men always inherit an entangled sociological mess. No number of sentimental platitudes or patriotic slogans can assuage this complicated predicament with its external and internal contours. Remedies have never been isomorphic (that is, one-to-one correspondence between the two sets) with the atrocities levied against African Americans. Altogether, we face a powerful waterfall of disappointments and traumas akin to Niagara Falls. No amount of fake bravado can sustain us in this quagmire. Pursuing vanity is an empty choice (as Solomon told us long ago in the book of Ecclesiastes).

Unfortunately, with a few exceptions, this structural situation is longitudinal in nature and scope. During the 1960s, two African American social psychologists, William Grier and Price M. Cobbs, wrote a poignant book about our plight entitled *Black Rage*.[4] This book connected our traumas to hypertension, morbidity, stress, and other maladaptive structural conditions imposed by our toxic society. More recently, Dr. Mary-Frances Winters has updated our plight in her book *Black Fatigue*.[5] Despite the many decades between them, both monographs indicate that African Americans confront a tangled pathology of rigged opportunities in a land of systemic neglect and denial. Moreover, since the COVID-19 global pandemic, the National Academies of Science, Engineering, and Medicine have devoted systematic scientific scrutiny to all the ways that diversity, equity, and inclusion involve anti-Black racism.[6]

Assessing and Addressing Our Predicament in the Twenty-First Century

Collectively, this social research paints a precarious picture. For some fortunate elites, it is the best of times, while too many others remain stuck in decaying neighborhoods under the glue of a racist vortex. More than fifty years after affirmative action policies emerged, African Americans face far too many stressors and traumas and too few doctors, lawyers, scientists, mathematicians, and other professionals. Last hired, first fired. We are the disproportionate victims of hate crimes and maniacal schemes. Poor schools. Violent streets. Hypersegregation, all while dying far too often in the armed services defending this nation. Sports and entertainment avenues of social mobility warp our vocational aspirations. Pets are treated with greater empathy than police criminals treat us. Anti-Black racism is still the radioactive toxin that acts as a vampire against our vitality and longevity. White backlash seldom ceases to explode as a nuclear threat to our existence via its terrorism, vandalism, violence, and subterfuge. The daily bombardment of dominant group images (Whiteness) in media and the deluge of ostentatious motifs pollute our developmental consciousness as the famous Doll Study indicates.[7] In this study, Black children, due to societal discriminations and limitations occurring at the time, identified with and chose White dolls rather that those representing their racial or ethnic identity. Maladaptive social forces are continuously at pandemic levels for so many of our weak, needy ones as was the case in the days of Ezekiel's prophecy (Ezekiel 34). Meanwhile, our detractors flood the information landscape with nonsense. Rapacious creditors and imposters vanquish too many of us; they are thieves coming to do like Satan does—"steal, kill, and destroy" (John 10:10). Satan and his minions are always busy working against us as others watch like Amalekites and do nothing.

The perennial plight of African Americans is to have one foot in the hope of a more perfect union, and the other foot in the tragic realities of systemic neglect and unrealistic denials. We teeter on the seesaw from assimilation to pluralism. Disengagement and disaffection can realistically result from the anomie (social instability and breakdown) of our predicament. As African American men in every generation, we must heal our bruised egos from all external assaults and internalized degradations. We seek nurture, beauty for ashes (Isaiah 61:3), a healing balm from the distortions of our identity and humanity. Shaped by the ontology of slavery, segregation, and emasculation, we must repel the social and psychological forces of idiocy so typical of the worst moral or spiritual contaminants in this society. We cannot overcompensate for the pandemic of ignorance directed toward us. Media stereotypes of criminality, irresponsibility, indolence, savagery, and indecency are fabrications that have infected far too many of us across decades. Like the apostle Paul urged, we must nullify "vain imaginations" (false pretenses) and all ideas that assault our dignity (2 Corinthians 10:3–5). Some places of oasis can be found in the therapies of church, education, science, community, and spirituality. Our ongoing search for solace takes us well beyond the predictable hypocrisies and ongoing injustices of this nation. We cannot afford to suffer fools gladly, in or beyond the church. Generations of lives are at stake.

What then are the transcendent challenges facing every generation of African American men? Our abbreviated SWOT analysis ought to begin here. Every generation embarks upon a quest for meaning (*Why am I here?*) to understand the purpose of life and its complexities or complications. Finding our unique place and contributions within and beyond a many-tongued society is an obvious quest, formally (overtly) and informally (covertly). On the visible level, we must develop and use our God-given talents or abilities to the maximum. There is no excuse for underachievement or misguided competencies, as Matthew 25:14–30 attests so well. The Lord of glory detests laziness and superfluous excuses from anyone. We must continue to pursue innovations wherever and whenever possible. On the covert level, our behind-the-scenes efforts must be stellar (Proverbs 21:21; Romans 14:17), starting with godly character (Psalm 15; James 3:13–18). We must embrace Psalm 90:12–17, Matthew 25:40, and Galatians 6:7–10 as our moral foundations.

Every generation seeks innovation or uniqueness, producing its own imprint in space and time, in culture and society. Sociologists target diversity, meaning, communications, and consciousness as markers along these lines as generations adapt to sociocultural environments plus existing opportunities. Thus, every cohort must simultaneously coordinate and generate its internal and external milieus. Stimuli abound as society reproduces itself via media, family structures, sexuality, music, entertainment, popular culture, ideologies, technology, rituals, and spirituality.

We can often monitor evolution in music: from Motown to Beyoncé. We see this evolution in sports: from Kareem Abdul Jabbar to LeBron James. We see it in families: from single-wage earners to dual-career earners, from large families to small families. We see it in social spaces: from urban to suburban. We see it in technology: from landlines to cell phones. We see it in life: from old-school to chic. Generational change is everywhere, overtly and covertly. Recall how society has changed from analog computing to digital platforms, from digital to quantum technologies. Wow! If only our character competencies were as robust as our ongoing contributions to the materialism of capitalism. Striking a healthy balance between consumption and production is prudent.

Yet throughout history, males control the biological seeds of civilizations, while disproportionately affecting the spiritual, moral, and material foundations of society. This structural capacity has been a sacred responsibility since creation. However, this inevitable reality is not a justification for abusing women and children via pathologies of narcissism, Machiavellianism, or psychopathy. It is not an excuse for sexism or violence against women. It does not give a rapacious sanction to engage in paranoid or predatory violence, with preemptive behaviors. Men have the greatest opportunity to do good, to make the world a better place, if they adopt a biblical masculinity instead of the abnormal corruptions of society. Verbal attacks are not sanguine. We reap what we sow. Rebutting all negative distractions, personal mistakes, unrecognized pitfalls, or addictions, including pornography, drugs, and immorality, is forever an epic struggle to guide strong, biblical marriages and families (Genesis 18:19). Intercession in prayer is mandatory! Asking for forgiveness and inculcating mercy is imperative.

The Lord unleashes unimagined spiritual acumen and resilient vision to those who are eager to reject bitterness and fatalism. Our disappointments and traumas are the atomic energy that will propel us forward toward empathy and justice. They can give us irreplaceable joy as we tenaciously overcome obstacles or constraints. African American men can rise to be vital spiritual warriors in the Lord's army. We can be devoted priests for our families. We can be servant-kings imitating our Messiah. We can be wise and thoughtful ambassadors (Proverbs 29:7). We can be bold prophets to our misguided society. We can nurture ourselves and others with gentleness. We can always act as a refuge for those less fortunate than we are, especially on a global scale. The power of the Lord is released whenever we show mercy to others (Luke 6:36–38). We are tested by the perfunctory and popular, by the vile and vulgar. Thus, we cannot accept being the best of the worst or relax as the worst of the best whenever we engage the world.

Fortifying Our Resilience

How then can African American men handle cultivating greatness in the midst of the aforementioned onslaught? Let us start by cultivating spiritual resilience with a robust faith that implements genuine salvation while demonstrating redemption (Proverbs 21:21; Romans 14:17). Let us recognize how popular culture, humanistic tropes, sophistry, and science are entangled with church differentiation. Let us move from self to groups to our social networks, communities, organizations, institutions, and social systems, whether heterogenous or homogenous. Let us seek persistent learning and evaluations as we dedicate ourselves to continuous improvement—to be our best always no matter what difficulties we face. Let us emasculate the pervasive racist weaponry designed to destroy us (John 10:10). We can heal from bruised egos the way David vanquished Goliath.

Psalm 23 is a spiritual path of serenity and quietness for every soul who seeks the Lord. First, we acknowledge our helplessness like sheep as we rest in the Lord's sovereignty and care (Proverbs 16:9). We adjust our desires to be thankful for the simple treasures of life: health, family, safety, and refreshment. We use our Sabbaths to retool our worship and dedication each week. We restore ourselves for every battle with the faith of Caleb (Numbers 14:8–9). We relish a divine destiny above and beyond our plight in society (Daniel 2:20–23). We ingest the Word of the Lord (Psalm 119), seeking His strategic plan (Isaiah 61).

In the process, we must redefine greatness as the Lord does in addressing the seven churches in the book of Revelation (Revelation 1–3). Each church had issues, struggles, and challenges to overcome. Some scholars think that these churches represent patterns or types; others favor seeing them as embodiments of ages or eras. Our Lord nonetheless commended them for whatever good they produced and cited disciplinary measures where needed before postulating a reward for overcoming. Like the church at Smyrna (Revelation 2:8–11), African American men can overcome (Romans 8). Our legacy demonstrates survival in the face of imperialism and injustice (Psalm 124). Matthew 25:40 is our mantra within this colonial republic.

Like Moses, we must endure and prosper in our struggles in this society (Psalm 90). We use every tool to discover our talents and spiritual gifts (Romans 12). We yield to Adonai's extra curriculum in the classroom of hard knocks (1 Corinthians 13:11–13)! We anticipate and accept His threshing process (Isaiah 41:10–20). Our weaknesses or poverty teaches us to cling to Him severely (Psalm

15). We can watch as the Lord guides us from the desperation plus depravity of our ashes and disappointments to the beauties of His reign everywhere on the globe. His kingdom will ultimately prevail (2 Thessalonians 1). Like Job, we yield (Job 1:21).

On the Positive Power of Failures

There is great resurrection power in learning humbly from our failures or mistakes (Isaiah 40:31). Our Lord often uses prolonged adversity to strengthen us and to give wisdom for our endurance (James 1:1–5). Like an athlete who routinely lifts heavy weights, our spiritual capacity is enlarged as He transforms our weakness into strength (2 Corinthians 12:9–10). Pain can be a master teacher. Many biblical examples illustrate this pattern in recovering from disappointments or failures. Adam failed. Noah failed. Abraham failed, as Jacob surely did on many occasions. Samson failed. Moses failed. Joshua failed. Saul failed. David failed. Solomon's failures wrecked the kingdom of Israel. Yet, the Lord's redemptive plan incorporated these traumatic mistakes in His everlasting mercies.

Peter and the disciples had failures of faith at several times, culminating in abandoning the Lord of glory at His weakest point (Matthew 26:56; Mark 14:50). Anyone who carefully reads the book of Acts—and the entire New Testament, for that matter—can detect failures in the church: neglecting widows, showing partiality, squabbles, immorality, materialism, and so on. Sinful folly guarantees failure. In my own life, I have experienced financial failures, professional missteps, marital discord, arrogant pride, stubbornness, abusive speech, criminal impulses, sexism, prejudice, moral failures, hypocrisy, and atheistic flirtations. My lifelong valleys of trauma and disappointments led me to confess and forsake these ungodly attributes (Romans 5:1–21). Confessing known sin from every aspect of my life has had a therapeutic effect, freeing me to fulfill my destiny with divine purposes and excellence. My problems and struggles have ushered in opportunities to receive and experience awesome resurrection power (Psalm 142:7), as I have relinquished control and confessed my lawlessness before my almighty God (Isaiah 9:6–7). Like a jet lifting off the earth via powerful air currents, my valleys have caused me to soar across the planet in His goodness. For example, several times I had to experience tangibly the unexpected humiliation of downward mobility (for family reasons) only to exceed all my initial pre-conceptions for success in the valleys I inhabited throughout my career (Proverbs 15:33; 21:22, 30–31; 22:29).

Even in culture and society, we can observe how individuals who overcome disappointments can soar to new heights of achievement or innovation. Sidney Poitier could barely read or write, but with dedicated effort he became an international sensation as a global actor. Barack Obama failed in a low-level election but persevered to become president of the United States. Berry Gordy failed before becoming a pathbreaking change agent in establishing Motown. The Temptations, the Supremes, and other musical acts failed miserably before winning stellar status. Steve Jobs and Bill Gates failed before becoming wealthy patrons. Doug Williams failed before becoming a Super Bowl champion quarterback. As a youngster, Michael Jordan was cut from his basketball team only to emerge as one of the greatest basketball icons ever.

In the academy, mathematician John Nash failed before becoming a Nobel Laureate. Even Joe Biden failed several elections before becoming president of the United States in his senior years. Many skeptics thought Albert Einstein was a failure until his ideas were proven to transform the entire world's scientific paradigm. Go figure! Alex Haley failed as a writer many times before his epic book transformed our sense of African American identity forever. These are just a few of myriad possible stories of those who overcame the valleys of disappointment in their lives. Hope elevates all who trust God for good things because He is so gracious and merciful. Resilience is surely a gift of God!

How Disappointments Produce Precious Opportunities

What lessons can we learn and cherish in responding correctly to our valleys of disappointment? Celebrate your uniqueness. First and foremost, I advise every man to anchor your primary mindset emotions in biblical truth (Psalm 119) to routinely avoid foolishness and superficiality to the extent possible, especially in this era of social media and mass media (Proverbs 26:4–5).

Paul understood this (Romans 12; 2 Corinthians 10:3–5). Iron sharpens iron (Proverbs 27:17). We must sanitize and refute all the foul sensory data that anchors us in worldly vanities (1 John 2:15–17). The wounds of trauma and disappointments allow humility, mercy, and grace to flourish in our souls (Psalm 16:11).

These learning modules teach us to cling decisively to the Lord of hosts (Psalm 46). They cleanse and sanctify our thoughts, motives, and ambitions. They reflect Mark 10:45 and the pruning process (John 15:1–20), bringing authenticity to our worship and witness. They lead us to new vistas and horizons, thereby enlarging us for service (Psalm 4:1). My valleys have led me to the apex of law enforcement within the FBI academy to excursions at the University of Oxford, to Athens, Toronto, Vienna, and Japan. My healed wounds have expanded my sympathies for world societies, giving me exponential empathy for the weak and innocent in every sociological domain. Success has been redefined away from wealth, status, power, beauty, corruption, and commercial vanities toward validated truth. The journey has been spectacular in the Lord. No one can predict what the Lord can and will do for African American men who serve Him sacrificially in spirit and truth. The race of life is not given to the swift, the braggart, or the hypocrite, but to those who endure to the end (Galatians 6:9–10).

The great artist of soul music Curtis Mayfield reminded us so well that there is no room for a hopeless sinner who would hurt all humankind for selfish benefit. We must be ready to have pity on those whose chances grow thinner because there is no hiding place against the kingdom stone (Daniel 2). Various rap and hip-hop artists have pinpointed these recurrent injustices for current cohorts. They serve as the griots of our times, teaching us to maintain our grip on what is most important about life. Celebrities spark and fade. Longevity and vitality energize vision across generations of African Americans because the Word and will of the Lord of hosts is forever, even beyond His creation (Matthew 5:17–18).

As one who grew up in relative poverty with three autistic siblings, I can certify that we can excel beyond inner-city blues, suburban blahs, and rural ignominy. The only one stopping us is the one we notice in the mirror. We must wait in anticipation with tenacious faith. We discount our Lord when we succumb to our valleys of disappointment, robbing Him of resurrected glory.

Steps toward Cultivating Greatness

Over the years, I have found the following items helpful in rebounding from valleys of disappointment and traumas. First, we must constantly remember how and why Jesus faced sinful pathologies (Isaiah 53). This meditative activity of contrition and cleansing helps us to observe the unleashing of the Holy Spirit and wisdom in our lives (Proverbs 4:20–27). As mentioned already, we must covenant to embrace biblical godliness, not convenient worldliness (1 John 2:15–17). Here, we must inculcate biblical and common revelation as Paul urged (Philippians 4:8). Too many Christians are anemic, either too steeped in secular knowledge or too irrelevant with superficial biblical tropes. Daniel is an exemplar for any complex society (Daniel 6).

As African American men we must remember and learn the best strategic, adaptable lessons from our elders (Titus 2). That means avoiding arrogance, autocracy, hypocrisy, and heresies (Matthew 23). That entails encouraging yourself when facing Goliaths, backstabbers, and fraudsters (1 Samuel 30). Our reward is inculcating the best of His kingdom rule and reign (Romans 14:17), giving us a global kingdom vision (Psalm 67; Isaiah 61:11) as we are cultivating a beautiful mind (2 Timothy 1:7).

Like Job, we observe that traumas and disappointments are inevitable in life (Job 12:13–25). Consequently, there has always been variation and differentiation regarding the life experiences of African American males. This observation is axiomatic. These inevitable social forces cannot be denied or truncated into simplistic solutions. Thus, we must anticipate struggles and troubles, calling upon the Lord (Psalm 116). Next, we must prepare robustly to benefit from every valley of disappointment (Proverbs 24:15–16), being enlarged like King David by our distresses (Psalm 4:1). Thirdly, we must forever build upon the redemptive suffering and resilience of our enslaved ancestors, generation by generation, looking forward to kingdom justice (Isaiah 61). Wisely, we must cultivate opportunities for mentorship and sponsorship (Titus 2; Proverbs 11:30; Psalm 133; Luke 6:36–38) in the spirit of the saints of all eras.

More technically or professionally, for academics, we must activate or establish the frontiers of mathematics and science. Hebrews 11:3 indicates that invisible ideas are essential to creating inventions that preserve and enhance our lives. In this era, vast internet resources, libraries, and educational institutions can shepherd our development with social capital, social intelligence, and practical competencies. For me, the Public Broadcasting Service has always been a staple of ingenuity and growth. Lastly, we must always be proactive in adapting to the woes and vicissitudes of global capitalism within and beyond national boundaries (Daniel 2:20–23). Covert operations and propaganda must be exposed. Many African nations could profit from our sustained attention and professional services as their emerging populations seek to flourish (Matthew 25:40).

Conclusion

Our valleys of disappointment can usher us into unfathomable greatness no matter our circumstances (1 Thessalonians 4:13–18). Biblical wisdom empowers us; sociological analyses liberate us. Whether targeted at individual, group, network, community, organizational, or institutional levels, we remain a vital part of this social system. Our destiny has fluidity and flux. Diversity matters, along with social exchanges, conflicts, and truth. Ignoring our plight only dooms the nation. Yet, our ultimate hope is always in a heavenly King and His regime (Psalm 110).

Because we study how tangible contingencies operate and how history structures outcomes in social systems, sociologists are not sentimental or sanctimonious about the fate of African Americans in the United States. Intellectually, in this country where popular sovereignty (history) delegates authority, citizens fly at very different altitudes in grasping the rigor of evidence and explanations (Proverbs 9:4; 14:15, 18; 21:11; 22:3). Assuming a posture of scientific skepticism, we are thus quite wary of popular platitudes, political machinations, sophistry, optimistic prognostications, and religious fervor. The epidemic of wickedness, duplicity, and backstabbing directed against African American men will probably continue as ongoing spiritual warfare. We can prepare ourselves with Ephesians 6:10–18, which instructs us on how to deal with it effectively. Police murders, gang violence, unemployment woes, mass incarceration, and other disturbances will not dissipate as long as the church and populace lack the volition and expertise needed to govern in a complex society. Few positive scenarios are palpable, despite the rhetoric of many pundits, icons, or benefactors. I sincerely wish it were otherwise.

Nonetheless, the weak solidarity so typical of this colonial society's inherited infrastructure cannot invalidate our intergenerational destinies. The increase of mixed ethnicities (biracial or multiracial) makes addressing our unique, aggrieved concerns much more complicated. Sadly, the petulant interests of waves of recent voluntary immigrants may undercut our historic contributions or agendas. In short, we must make the world a better place utilizing our personalized engagement with the key insights delineated above. Integrity, excellence, challenge, and support are the moral contours of our ongoing journey as African American men in the twenty-first century. In this era of global realignment, we must remain vigilant in reducing our internal and external vulnerabilities as well as the distorted stigmas projected toward us. As in the past, the nefarious escapades linked to counter-intelligence will likely be directed against us as we ascend among the nations. Simultaneously, we must have fun and treasure joyfully the preciousness of every life in our community to avoid becoming an endangered species. Let us boldly go wherever the Lord assigns us. Thanks to everyone dedicated to this robust agenda (John 16:33).

NOTES

1. Alex Haley, *Roots: The Saga of an American Family* (New York: Doubleday,1976).

2. Henry L. Allen, "Scientific Literacy and the Future of Ethnic Minority Groups in the United States: The Unfinished Civil Rights Movement," *Athens Journal of Social Sciences* 5, no. 2 (2018): 133–50, 10.30958 /ajss.5-2-1, https://www.athensjournals.gr/social/2018-5-2-1-Allen.pdf.

3. Richard Rothstein, *The Color of Law: A Forgotten History of How Government Segregated America* (New York: Liveright, 2017).

4. William H. Grier and Price M. Cobbs, *Black Rage* (New York: Bantam, 1968).

5. Mary-Frances Winters, *Black Fatigue: How Racism Erodes the Mind, Body, and Spirit* (Oakland, CA: Berrett-Koehler, 2020).

6. C. T. Laurencin, C. P. Jones, and L. M. Holden, eds., *The State of Anti-Black Racism in the United States: Reflections and Solutions from the Roundtable on Black Men and Black Women in Science, Engineering, and Medicine: Proceedings of a Workshop* (Washington, DC: National Academies Press, 2023).

7. Kenneth B. Clark, *Dark Ghetto: Dilemmas of Social Power* (New York: Harper and Row, 1965).

3

Stewardship

Generate Wealth with Biblical Values

KARL I. BELL, MBA

The wise have wealth and luxury, but
fools spend whatever they get.
Proverbs 21:20 NLT

Introduction

In today's fast-paced and materialistic world, the pursuit of
wealth can become a singular focus, detached from the values
that guide our lives. The path to wealth and thus generational
wealth starts with a simple truth we all know but sometimes fail
to implement. We must start by spending less than we earn over
an extended period of time and prudently allocate the excess
funds. However, for those who seek to align their lifestyle of
spending and consumption with biblical principles, the journey
toward income generation and generational wealth takes on a
deeper purpose—one rooted in faith, stewardship, and the desire
to make a positive impact on the world around us. In order to
change the economic and wealth status of African Americans,
there must be a change in how we view money, economics, and
wealth. According to DeForest Soaries in his book *dfree: Breaking
Free from Financial Slavery*, "Our attitude must change if we are
to follow through and change behaviors and habits that continue
to jeopardize our financial health."[1]

Long-Term Planning

The process of generating wealth is a long-term commitment to a plan of spending less than is earned, growing income, and investing. In the movie *Coming to America*, the character played by Eddie Murphy uses a Frederick Nietzsche quote that says, "He who would learn to fly one day must first learn to walk and learn . . . ; one cannot fly into flying." Eddie Murphy uses Nietzsche's quote to acknowledge the long-term planning necessary to reaching a particular goal. The effort to spend less than the income received is easier for some than for others and often requires a long-term plan to increase the level of income to meet this objective. Management of expenses is sometimes a quicker route to making sure there is a surplus of income at the end of each month. We have all heard the phrase "keeping up with the Joneses" as a metaphor for frivolous spending that leads to overspending and "bad debt." In general, "bad debt" is any debt acquired to finance our social lifestyle. This would include debt to finance vacations, clothing, entertainment, or "nights on the town." There is, on the other hand, "good debt": educational debt that leads to higher-income opportunities or debt to purchase income-producing properties that will lead to higher income. These will not only pay off the debt incurred but also provide a surplus to enhance your lifestyle and contribute to others.

The Bible provides invaluable wisdom and guidance on managing wealth, investing wisely, and cultivating a mindset of abundance. It offers a holistic perspective that encompasses financial success, moral integrity, and the responsibility to use our resources for the greater good. By integrating biblical values into our financial decisions and actions, we can create a sustainable and fulfilling path to both personal prosperity and generational wealth. These concepts are not common in all communities and require professional assistance and additional education on money matters. We can start by having a simple conversation with a knowledgeable friend, local banker, or financial adviser. The path to surplus income and wealth transfer is a long journey; "get rich quick" opportunities are not the answer.

Why "Get Rich Quick" Is Not the Answer

"Get rich quick" schemes have been around since the dawn of time. Most of them represent some type of financial fraud designed to relieve us of our hard-earned money and enrich someone else. Most are soon discovered and dissolved into yesterday's news, only to be revived with a new and appealing twist that appeals to humanity's interest in getting a lot for a little.

Several characteristics can help identify these types of schemes. The first and largest red flag is the promise of large returns with little to no risk. Investing is risky and there is never a guarantee of returns. Investing follows the rule, "The higher the returns, the higher the risk." Anything to the contrary should be approached with skepticism.

Biblical Principles of Financial Stewardship

Stewardship is at the core of the biblical approach to wealth creation. As believers, we understand that everything we have—our skills, talents, resources, and opportunities ultimately belong to God. We are merely entrusted with these blessings during our time on earth, and it is our responsibility to manage ourselves wisely.

In the book of Proverbs, we find numerous teachings on the importance of diligence, integrity, and a disciplined work ethic. Scripture reminds us that diligent hands lead to wealth and that our labor should be dedicated to serving both God and others. By aligning our work with our God-given purpose and focusing on providing value to those around us, we can lay a solid foundation for income generation.

Investing with Biblical Values

Another key aspect of creating income and generational wealth through biblical values is investing. As the Bible encourages believers to be wise stewards of their financial resources, Scripture advises us to apply the principle of diversification and cautions us against reckless speculation. This stewardship encompasses more than income generation and our investment decisions but also includes how we spend and save our resources. Proverbs 21:20

advises us against squandering wealth but instead encourages the accumulation of resources for future needs. Through sound financial planning, prudent investment strategies, and a long-term perspective, we can multiply our resources and create a foundation of financial security for ourselves and future generations. However, biblical investing goes beyond financial gains alone; this emphasizes investing in enterprises that align with our values and contribute to others' well-being too. This may involve supporting businesses that prioritize ethical practices, promote social justice, or provide products and services that enhance people's lives. By investing in businesses that align with biblical values, we can create a positive impact on society while growing our wealth. There are several faith-based investment companies and vehicles available through the internet. Please, before pursuing any investment opportunity, perform your due diligence and/or consult with your personal financial adviser when making decisions.

Generational Wealth and Legacy

Beyond personal financial success, the biblical perspective on the world also places great emphasis on generational wealth and the concept of leaving a legacy. "A good person leaves an inheritance for their children's children" (Proverbs 13:22). This passage highlights the importance of long-term thinking and passing down financial wisdom to future generations. In the United States, proper transfer of wealth requires proper documentation.

We have all heard of wills and trusts but most fail to have these documents created and executed. Without these documents, estates must go through probate to have assets distributed. Absent instructions by the deceased, assets will be distributed by formulas that vary depending on the state. Generational wealth is not limited to material possessions but encompasses a broader sense of inheritance—values, character, faith, and work ethic. By instilling biblical principles of natural stewardship in our children and grandchildren, we equip them with tools to navigate the complexities of wealth responsibility and continue the cycle of abundance and impact.

African American Wealth and Debt

Understanding historical Black-White gaps in income, wealth, and education requires an understanding of the complex relationship between regional inequality, race, and policies at the local, state, and national levels. Systematic exploitation of labor and legislated exclusion from economic opportunity have suppressed African American income, asset accumulation, and wealth creation. African American household wealth is reported at approximately 13 percent of White household wealth. It has been noted that racial gaps in wealth cannot be attributed simply to the differences in household savings habits or cash-flow management issues but are outcomes of public policy decisions ranging from the New Deal to the formation of Social Security that excluded many occupations held by African Americans.[2] Despite these historical facts, there are still ways to earn and keep generational wealth. We have already discussed the practice of spending less than you earn and investing.

One of the largest withdrawals from your income is taxes. There are rules in the world of taxes that all should know. The United States has a tax system that does not tax all income the same. At this writing, the current tax code taxes earned income (job and annual interest income) at its highest level; taxable income from investments (stocks, bonds, etc.) at lower levels; your assets held longer than one year and inherited wealth at even lower levels.

African Americans' Wealth Statistics

Over the past fifty years, the unemployment rate of African Americans in the United States has consistently been approximately double the unemployment rate of White Americans.[3] Even in a good economy, when White Americans are experiencing unemployment rates of 3 percent, African Americans are experiencing rates of approximately 6 percent. This disparity is greater during periods of economic downturn, with African American unemployment reaching the mid-teens and African American youth unemployment of more than 20 percent. Therefore, these youth are three times more likely to live in poverty than are White American youth. The median wealth (wealth defined as the value of all family assets less than the total of all family debt) of African American families is approximately $17,000, which is less than one-tenth of White American families, who have a median wealth of $171,000. These wealth statistics are reflected in home ownership, as 73 percent of White American families own their homes while only 42 percent of African American families own their homes.[4] In order to improve the economic well-being of African American families, we must learn more about how to manage our financial resources, discover better ways of managing our income and expenses, and teach our youth about wealth versus consumption.

Youth Income and Wealth

In his book *Say Yes to No Debt* (the updated version of *dfree*), Soaries states, "You must examine the psychology of your spending habits and explore the emotions attached to money-related matters."[5] Oftentimes, African American youth are encouraged to seek materialistic things. This concept stems from the misunderstanding of *value*. The more things one obtains or possesses, the more potential value they are able to create. While things hold utility, making them useful in society, the thing itself actually has no true intrinsic value. Actually, one could argue that the true value can be found in what made that thing possible in the first place. To better understand this concept, let's consider an apple. An apple has apparent value because it provides nourishment, important nutrients, and is a food source for millions of people around the world. The apple, however, can only be made possible by harvesting from the tree, making the tree a vital part of the process. The tree, on the other hand, is only made possible by the seed that was planted to give it life. In this chain of events, is the apple, tree, or seed most important? Well, the answer to this question would depend on the perspective instilled into the youth. In this example, let's consider three different perspectives: consumer, saver, and investor.

To the first type, the *consumer* perspective, this shiny, delicious, and readily available apple would represent the cars, clothes, jewelry, or toys that some youth often fantasize about or obsess after, believing those things will bring happiness and create true value. As history has proven, all those things eventually depreciate or lose their foreseen value as soon as they are obtained, if not after a few months of ownership. Even with the apple, once it is consumed, it no longer has any value to provide. This consumer mindset is embedded into a person's mindset as a direct by-product of the mindsets in their immediate circles of influence. Naturally, this consumer mindset can lead to a relentless cycle of financial disparity and hardship.

The *saver* perspective, however, would look past the apple as having intrinsic value and only view it as a by-product of the tree, the true source of value. In this example the tree represents a job, a career, or a stream of income that has the potential to produce monetary value. The tree, like a job or career, has the ability to sustain itself for a longer period of time and as a result can produce more fruit. This mindset normally allows individuals to experience moments of financial flexibility without reaching the ultimate potential of financial freedom. Usually, this mindset is taught to middle-class youth or to youth blessed to be exposed to certain principles through the educational system or other outside influences.

The third perspective, *investor*, would consider the apple a by-product, the tree an avenue or means, and the seed as the true source of value. The seed represents knowledge, opportunity, and trust. With every seed, one needs to understand how to plant it and when to plant it, and also to believe that what they planted will bear fruit. Youth who receive this perspective understand that *true value* creates wealth. They would view this seed as an opportunity to plant multiple trees as they harvest additional seeds from other apples, allowing them to create a forest full of trees bearing fruit. This concept signifies the idea of developing multiple streams of income, so wealth creation is never solely dependent on one source. In addition, they understand the power of a network and the need to scale manpower to take care of all the trees, harvest the apples, and have a distribution channel to sell them. Without the proper network, none of this would be feasible, reinforcing the concept that one's net worth can be defined by their network.

The key concepts that are important to gain from this illustration are:

1. Currency in and of itself is useless if it doesn't create additional opportunities to create more currency or buying power. View currency as a tool, not as the goal.

2. Sustainable value does not come from materialistic things; rather, wisdom, understanding, opportunities, and biblical principles are the sources.

3. Every person has something that can be leveraged to create opportunities—talents, skills, relationships, currency, personality. It is critical to practice patience and surround oneself with the right influences to discover these opportunities.

4. Multiple streams of income are necessary to create the financial freedom needed to experience and enjoy wealth.

5. Wealth has spiritual, mental, physical, and emotional aspects that all need to be understood and explored in order to create and maintain wealth.

When considering mindsets or perspectives for youth, another helpful illustration is the use of one hundred dollars. A poor person views one hundred dollars as an opportunity to buy or consume one hundred dollars' worth of things. The rich person views the one hundred dollars in segments: a portion of it should be saved, a portion should be consumed, and a portion should go toward the settlement of different types of outstanding debt. The wealthy individual views the one hundred dollars as an opportunity to grow that amount to one thousand dollars over a period of time. For the wealthy person, it's never an issue of affordability, but rather how they use their creativity to generate a revenue stream to purchase that item in the most efficient way. By managing the purchase process, the wealthy not only discover ways to reduce the overall cost of the item but also make the purchase in the most tax-efficient way that can reduce the cost even further.

Taxation Considerations

While many individuals are familiar with having to *pay* taxes, very few are familiar with how to *plan for* taxes. Oftentimes, taxation is a reactive conversation that occurs at the end of the year or after an event or circumstance has occurred. Sadly, a lack of planning prior to the taxable event strips the individual of significant opportunities and benefits. Although most individuals try to earn as much money as possible and hope to pay less in taxes, without proper tax planning, they will most likely pay more taxes in a given year than someone who has planned.

The United States tax code taxes various types of income differently and at different rates. Therefore, as shown in the example that follows, the same amount of income earned in different categories results in different net income retained. The two broad categories of taxation are referred to as Ordinary Income (income from working wages, salaries, commissions, and interest earned on bank deposits) and Capital Gains Income or Passive Income (income generated from assets held more than one year, such as stocks, bonds, real estate, and other investments). For example, in the above section, three different perspectives (Poor, Rich, and Wealthy) were mentioned to identify various mindsets. As it relates to taxation, these mindsets could also apply, illustrating how taxation magnifies the Black-White income and wealth gaps.

The *Poor* perspective, driven by materialistic values, will primarily earn most income as ordinary income. Ordinary income is subject to the highest income tax rates. The *Rich* will generally have income from both ordinary income and capital gains income, while the *Wealthy* will generate their income primarily from capital gains.

The *Rich* perspective often incorporates a mixture of common tax-planning strategies, allowing for some reductions to ordinary income and leaving the primary amount of income classified as ordinary. These tax-planning strategies often are driven by employers who offer tax-deferred retirement plans, charitable contributions, healthcare saving accounts, or other tax-deductible employee benefits that will help to reduce ordinary income. In this perspective, individuals are attempting to reduce their ordinary income through tax deductions as opposed to recategorizing.

The *Wealthy* perspective is primarily focused on income recategorization as opposed to simply reducing ordinary income. This perspective utilizes the tax law to create opportunities for their potential ordinary income to flow through to business entities, investments, trusts, or other vehicles to recategorize it to capital gains or passive income. Capital gains and passive income are beneficial, not just because of the lower potential tax rates, but also for the ability to defer potential taxes, if not eliminate tax exposure completely. For example, $100,000 taxed as ordinary income would generally create a tax liability for a single tax filer of $24,000 (based on the 2023 tax brackets at 24 percent). If, however, this $100,000 could be categorized as long-term capital gains, it would generally create a tax liability for a single tax filer individual of $15,000 (based on the 2023 long-term capital gains tax rate at 15 percent). This would create a tax savings of $9,000. Having exposure to these tax strategies and vehicles can often create a significant difference in the amount of time it takes to generate, produce, and protect generational wealth. Seeking advice from a tax professional can assist in planning and reducing taxes, therefore increasing family income and wealth.

Conclusion

Creating income and generational wealth from a biblical perspective offers a profound opportunity to align our financial pursuits with our faith and values. By embracing the principles of stewardship, diligent work, wise investing, and a focus on generational legacy, we can build a prosperous and purpose-driven financial future.[6] As we embark on this journey, it is important to remember that our ultimate goal is not just personal enrichment but the greater good and the advancement of God's kingdom on earth. By remaining faithful to biblical values and seeking to use our wealth for the betterment of others, we can experience true abundance and leave a lasting legacy.

NOTES

1. DeForest B. Soaries Jr., *dfree: Breaking Free from Financial Slavery* (Grand Rapids, MI: Zondervan, 2011), 60.

2. Emily Moss, Kriston McIntosh, Wendy Edelberg, and Kristen Broady, "The Black-White Wealth Gap Left Black Households More Vulnerable," Brookings, December 8, 2020, https://www.brookings .edu/articles/the-black-white-wealth-gap-left-black-households-more -vulnerable/.

3. "The Economic State of Black America 2020," Joint Economic Committee, February 14, 2020, https://www.jec.senate.gov/public /index.cfm/democrats/2020/2/economic-state-of-black-america-2020.

4. Bradley L. Hardy, Trevon D. Logan, and John Parman, "The Historical Role of Race and Policy for Regional Inequality," The Hamilton Project, Brookings, September 28, 2018, 1023, https://www .brookings.edu/articles/the-historical-role-of-race-and-policy-for -regional-inequality/.

5. DeForest B. Soaries, *Say Yes to No Debt: 12 Steps to Financial Freedom* (Grand Rapids, MI: Zondervan, 2015), 4. I only briefly discussed the subject of being debt free. If you are looking for more details on this subject, you should consult Soaries's book.

6. For a more comprehensive and detailed prescription on building wealth in a biblical way and creating a strategy for taking control of your personal finances, I refer you to Dr. Soaries's book *Say Yes to No Debt*.

4

Bond

With a Purpose on Purpose

RODNEY S. PATTERSON, MA

There is neither Jew nor Gentile, neither slave nor
free, nor is there male and female, for you are all one
in Christ Jesus. If you belong to Christ, then you are
Abraham's seed, and heirs according to the promise.

Galatians 3:28–29

Introduction

When men bond with a purpose, something significant can happen.
When the purpose is to address racism and to bring reconciliation to their immediate environments and within their personal
relationships, this bonding helps us successfully deal with our
racist past.

Men Bonding with a Purpose, on Purpose

Dwain approached me two years ago following the murder of
George Floyd in 2020 and said, "Man, I need your help."[1] Dwain
was one of a few Black partners at an executive search firm. "Of
course. Whatever you need," I replied. It was two weeks after
the killing of George Floyd. The whole world needed help. News
stories around the globe served as evidence of this reality.

"I've had six White partners in the firm approach me—all

separately," Dwain sighed heavily. "They want me to help them make sense of all this. I'm trying to make sense of it my own self. And some of them I'm not even that close to. Man, I'm not even sure how to respond to these guys."

Dwain's situation is not unique. If I had a dollar for every White person who called me for advice or out of concern in the aftermath of the George Floyd incident, I'd be rich. Clearly a conversation was needed. Weeks later, I led a six-week workshop on *Dissecting Race and Racism* for Dwain and his colleagues. Before beginning the experience, I sent Dwain the outline of each session. He knew it would take them to some deep, emotional places. He had warned the guys.

"Dwain," I asked, "What did you tell those guys that made them say yes?" "I told them, I'm glad you wanna do something, but I need you to understand this. First, you gotta make a serious commitment. Don't start up, then bail out when it gets hard and heavy. We're either gonna end up hating each other and never speak to one another again, or we'll come out as brothers forever. We'll be closer than we've ever been to any other colleague or each other.

"Man, each of them said, 'I'm in.'" Dwain smiled. "So, let's rock 'n' roll, baby."

None of them had any idea how intense things would get. I'm sure they had no plans to express the level of vulnerability they would display with one another. But it got pretty deep in less than six weeks. Most of the sessions were on Zoom, as this was during the height of COVID-19 and its debilitating impact on gathering in person. But that didn't curb the intensity.

Session three was when it all broke loose. It started with me showing them an emotional dialogue from the movie *The Color of Fear*. I asked them one simple question: "Who do you most relate to in this film and why?"[2]

Dwain jumped in first. "I relate most to the brother who was finally able to tell those White guys how he really felt. Man, it seemed like he had that stuff bottled up in him for a long time. He couldn't take it anymore. I feel like that every d—— day in this firm. Y'all all walk around me, and you see how successful

I am." Dwain breathed deeply. "But you have no idea what it takes to make it happen. In fact . . ." Tears began to well up in the corners of both of his eyes. He paused for ten seconds, but it felt like ten minutes. He took three hard and deep breaths. Then he continued, tears streaming down his left cheek.

"In fact, some of you have been the main culprits. I wonder if you think what I do doesn't even matter. Trey, I remember like it was yesterday when you asked me about a year ago, *'Dwain, why do you even focus on that diversity search stuff? That's just a waste of time, Dude!'* I carry crap like that around every day. I suck it up and make my numbers. And you see my success. But you don't know my pain."

On this particular day, Justin, another White colleague, was in the same room as Dwain. He'd gone to Dwain's house to be on the Zoom call together. Dwain leaned back in his chair and a few more tears rolled down his cheeks. Justin picked up his chair and moved closer, next to Dwain. Justin just sat next to him, in silence. Tears started rolling down Justin's cheeks as well.

Several of the other men started tearing up. The Zoom room got so quiet, I could hear the mouse on the cotton ball on the floor, in the corner of my office. Dwain's White colleagues in the room opened up to a new conversation.

"Dwain, that was a piercing blow," Trey said with a tone of remorse. "To know that I said something like that to you that's had that kind of lingering impact," Trey paused with his hand to his heart, "is deeply disturbing for me." We could feel Trey's regret in his words. "I'm tired of showing up as that kind of person."

The healing exchange continued. For the first time, Dwain said everything that needed to be said about the impact he'd experienced over the years from Trey's behavior. To Trey's credit, he sat and took it. The exchange shifted the demeanor of both men. The whole team emerged as a different group. For months after this session, other colleagues at the firm were amazed at the shift on this team.

Most especially, Trey's transformation captured their attention. Trey's past behavior had earned him the reputation as the tough guy of the firm. He's a "tell it like it is" guy. The challenge with "tell it like it is" is that our reality is often informed by our assumptions. While candor was one of Trey's strengths, his assumptions caused this strength to operate as a double-edged sword. Trey was still a force to be reckoned with. The awakened new level of intelligence he acquired during the six weeks made him more insightful. He became a self-aware tough guy.

Some people refer to a situation like this as a display of unconscious bias. My work in corporate environments involves addressing situations like these when they occur and teaching people how to navigate through them successfully. Doing so in this situation allowed Trey to enhance his collegial relationships and earn record revenue.

My work as a clergyperson feels quite different and, in many ways, more rewarding. In those circles, I refer to it as racial reconciliation. I raise attention to it in this chapter because I believe the six men bonded like never before, and they continue to meet regularly to this day. What I most appreciate about what this situation reveals is how well bonding with a purpose, on purpose can manifest within secular, corporate settings. Consider what might occur when bonding takes place within the body of Christ. How much more powerful might the results become for those involved in the experience?

The Need for a Call to Action

This chapter is meant to serve as a call to action for people in general and men in particular. The reason I am focusing specifically on men is because men took the role of leadership in creating a racialized, thus racist society. Religious scholar Willie Jennings points out the pivotal position men were in when slaves were brought to Portugal and how Christianity was used to justify and rationalize racist ideologies and practices. During that time, those Prince George encountered who were Black or very dark-skinned were perceived to be most unlikely to convert to Christianity and those considered White or light-skinned were viewed in the opposite way. The role men played in the development of racist ideologies is captured and chronicled throughout Jennings's work.[3]

The role women played was almost nonexistent. Women are by

no means exonerated, yet their role was not nearly as significant or pivotal as the role of men. The work of Stephanie Jones-Rogers in her book, *They Were Her Property: White Women as Slaveowners in the American South*, depicts how complicit women were in the development of racism.[4] Men, however, gave birth to the concept of race and perpetuated the systemic manifestation of the "ism" far more than women.

Now, men must assume a leadership position in repairing what has been broken for centuries. Doing so will require establishing strong bonds and solid collaboration across racialized lines. By racialized lines, I refer to the fictitious lines of demarcation, manufactured based upon the mythical concept of race, to arbitrarily distinguish people from one another. We now look at what is required to remove the fictitious man-made lines.

Catalytic Conversions

In her book *Roadmap to Racial Reconciliation 2.0*, Brenda Mc-Neil writes about the impact of catalytic conversion experiences on people and the essential part they play on the road to racial reconciliation. She describes them as "painful but necessary experiences that happen to individuals and organizations and serve to jump-start the reconciliation process."[5] McNeil mentions John Paul Lederach's expression of a catalytic event, stating:

> John Paul Lederach, a Mennonite scholar and peace practitioner, refers to catalytic events as "turning points." He suggests that they are unexpected moments when new life is infused into the "barren" space of a conflict situation and that these unexpected moments make it possible for constructive change to take place.[6]

McNeil then uses the apostle Paul's conversion experience in Acts 9 as a biblical example of what a catalytic conversion looks like in the spiritual realm.[7] Many will recall that Paul was named Saul prior to his conversion, and he was notorious for having Christians killed due to his disbelief in and denouncing of Jesus

Christ. Yet, on the Damascus road he encountered a light from heaven and the voice of Jesus inquiring about why Saul was persecuting Him. Saul temporarily lost his sight. That catalytic conversion changed Saul forever and as a sign, his name was changed from Saul to Paul.

Joshua Reichard explains something very similar to a catalytic conversion in his description of the three critical components of the learning process.[8] Reichard shares that the first key component of the learning process is considered a significant experience. Something or someone is considered significant to us based upon our personal connection. That could be simply because we decided to purchase a new, blue Toyota Prius. On purchasing the vehicle, we now notice every other blue Toyota Prius on the road; prior to our purchase, the same make and model car remained insignificant.

McNeil's dissection of a catalytic conversion more poignantly explains what occurred between Dwain and his colleagues. While their experience seemed quite significant, the six-week sessions allowed them to "move from the isolation and stagnation of life, in their respective, homogeneous groups and break through into a new reality."[9]

My Personal Catalytic Experience

In the fall of 1979, shortly after I entered my junior year of undergraduate school at Valparaiso University (VU), I had my most frightening encounter with blatant racism.

Men were always the culprit whenever I experienced extremely racist encounters. Such was the case this time as well. My classmate and I decided to stroll from the new portion of campus to the old campus section. On a warm, breezy spring evening we passed the VU gymnasium to our right, the landmark dividing the new portion of campus from the old. Just then, a black 1980 Chevy Monte Carlo slowly pulled up to the stop sign across the street from us.

Slowly, the electric-powered window on the driver's side descended. Peering at us from within the car was a young White man who appeared to be in his mid-twenties. With a frowned face, turned up nose, and eyes that seemed ablaze, he leaned out the window toward us. He then scoffed at us in a husky tone saying, "I smell something really nasty. You better fear the Klan, cause we're here to kill you." The wheels of the car spun and screeched fast and furiously, as he and his front-seat passenger sped off, descending the hill behind us, heading in the opposite direction.

Less than thirty seconds later, the same black Monte Carlo sped up the hilly street directly in our pathway from behind. They proceeded to drive up on the sidewalk, attempting to run us down. I pushed my classmate down the grassy hill adjacent to us. Quickly following her, we ran as fast as we could. We maneuvered through the dark field of grass and into a nearby parking lot. We frantically entered the Student Union Center building, just about two hundred yards away. Immediately, we called the police and the vice president of student affairs. That unforgettable experience remains etched in my memory, reminding me of the horror of racist attacks and the lingering impact they leave. The same event jump-started my commitment to rid the world of racism.

Things Must Change

Stories like mine are all too familiar, way too frequent, and are not just a thing of the past. Racism is alive and well. I encountered the racist Klansmen in the spring of 1979. Over forty years later, we still hear similar stories. Just recently, CNN Reporters Eric Levenson, Sara Smart, Nouran Salahieh, Isabel Rosales, and Andy Rose released a story about a White gunman who took the lives of three Black individuals at a Jacksonville, Florida, Dollar General store.[10] Before Ryan Palmeter entered the Dollar General store, he was disallowed entry at a nearby campus, Edward Waters University. Palmeter was unwilling to identify himself to a campus security officer, who then denied him access.

In another account, church members of the Mother Emanuel Methodist Church of Charleston, South Carolina, welcomed the likes of twenty-one-year-old Dylann Roof into their faith community. Dylan, a young White man, then murdered nine parishioners, firing off seventy-four rounds of artillery. Their only "crime" was handing him a Bible and being Black worshipers. Stories like these have become too exhausting to list and too numerous to retell.

The undeniable racist acts of violence perpetrated by callous men reveal the résumé of hatred that begs the attention of sober, like-minded men, bonded together by a common purpose and a passion to bring true reconciliation to the nation.

Men tend to bond easily around specific tasks rather than for simple, social connections. They rarely connect just to talk and catch up or hang out. Men coalesce around a purposeful activity, even if the primary reason is entertainment-driven.[11] In this chapter, my desire is to inspire men to bond intentionally and strategically around a significant cause, which requires our uncompromising attention and effort, to eradicate racism once and for all. Since men are primarily responsible for initiating and perpetuating the existence of racism, men must grab the reins of leadership not from but with dynamic women who are making significant advancements, specifically within the body of Christ.

A Lifelong Veteran

The accomplishments of trailblazers like Pastor John M. Perkins and numerous others go far from unnoticed. Born in 1930, John Perkins has seen quite a bit of racism. As a clergyman, he dedicated much of his life's work and ministry to eradicating racism. The website JohnMPerkins.com reveals the following about him: Dr. John Perkins is the author of books entitled *Let Justice Roll Down*, *One Blood*, *He Calls Me Friend*, and *Count It All Joy*. He also published a magazine called *Urban Family Magazine*. Born during the 1930s, a descendant of sharecroppers in Jackson, Mississippi, Perkins managed to serve as counselor to six US Presidents on issues related to race and civil rights.

After befriending a former KKK member responsible for attempting to bomb a Jewish leader, Perkins later founded the Christian Community Development Association (CCDA). The organization grew from thirty-seven members to some sixty-eight hundred individuals and six hundred churches, institutions, and businesses in more than one hundred cities across the country. Resulting from his life's work is a powerful six-part, self-paced course offered through Moody Bible Institute. *One Life Well Lived* contains six course topics and offers a certificate upon completion.[12]

This course is offered as a place to begin a personal journey and is for those seeking guidance from a life-long veteran associated with racial reconciliation.

Promise Keeping

Additionally, the efforts originating in the Promise Keepers movement remain noteworthy. We would be remiss if we failed to mention the pioneering work of these men and their movements in historical times. Daniel Silliman tells of the work of the organization and the efforts of Coach Bill McCartney to address racism since the inception of Promise Keepers.[13] Long before Deion "Primetime" Sanders became Head Coach of the Colorado Buffalos, McCartney was not only leading his team but also leading thousands of men into stadiums across the country to walk more closely with the Lord Jesus Christ. Close comrades of McCartney suggested that effort during a funeral service at a Black church in Boulder, Colorado. He felt led by the Holy Spirit to ignite an effort with a Christ-centered focus. The first gathering drew over 4,000 participants; the second event garnered more than 50,000 men in 1991.

Promise Keepers inspired men to adhere to several promises, with Promise Number Six tethering the men to a true commitment to racial reconciliation. In theory, Promise Six was admirable and ambitious. The problem was the promise lacked a process. Silliman, quoting Mark Pollard, sums things up best: "You can't have a reconciliation moment without a reconciliation process."[14] Worse yet, by 1997, the organization began a swift disintegration, marked by the laying off of all 345 staffers.

Although some staff were eventually brought back, the organization was never the same. Tensions ensued due to some board members, staffers, and general members believing Promise Keepers focused too heavily on racial reconciliation. While Promise Keepers still remains in existence, the emphasis on racial reconciliation has significantly shifted. Following the murder of George Floyd, Promise Keepers did manage to launch a Promise Six Sunday.

Eliza Griswold, a contributing writer at *The New Yorker* wrote the following about Promise Keepers and other historical efforts:

Over the next two decades, racial reconciliation moved away from efforts to combat institutional racism and focused instead on addressing personal feelings about race. This focus sits more easily with the theological underpinnings of evangelical Christianity, which emphasize a believer's personal relationship with Jesus and portray sin and salvation as matters of personal choice. Today, the reconciliation movement centers around gimmicky one-off events, like pulpit-swaps, in which Black and white pastors switch congregations. Conversations about race are reduced to "relational" confessionals, often one-sided chats in which white Christians share the ways in which they've committed the sins of racism, and Christians of color are cast in the role of confessors, required to hear and then to absolve their white counterparts.[15]

Real, sustainable transformation will require more than what the past has offered. One essential component needed involves how racial reconciliation is defined.

The Spark That Ignites

I believe the efforts of Promise Keepers fell short because they lacked a process for transformation to advance the work of the catalyst conversion experience. McNeil mentions catalytic events as "turning points."[16] The turning point ignites the process, but a turning point without a process leaves transformation to chance.

A Promise Keepers stadium event could very well serve as a catalytic conversion and the next steps beyond the mountaintop experience determine what follows. Brenda McNeil suggests, "Even when there is significant desire for peace and reconciliation, it's incredibly challenging to change our entrenched cycles in order to allow for the possibility of new relationships. We are so accustomed to our own social circles and homogeneous units."[17] Racial reconciliation involves a process—specifically, a process that leads to bonding.

McNeil further suggests that part of the problem with creating true racial reconciliation stems from failing to recognize what reconciliation really means. She points out in her book *Roadmap to Reconciliation 2.0* how a plethora of leaders and practitioners attending a conference on the subject lacked a common definition themselves.[18] She says reconciliation must contain repentance, justice, and forgiveness; yet more is also required.

McNeil defines reconciliation as "an ongoing spiritual process, involving repentance, forgiveness, and justice, which restores broken relationships and systems, to reflect God's original intention for all creation to flourish."[19] Additionally, McNeil noted, "Reconciliation is possible only if we approach it primarily as a spiritual process that requires a posture of hope in the reconciling work of Christ, and a commitment from the church to both be and proclaim this type of reconciled community."[20]

Where Do We Go from Here?

Racial reconciliation will not occur by happenstance nor coincidence. Racial reconciliation requires intentional action on the part of the people desirous of undergoing a transformation process. In her book, *Be the Bridge*, Latasha Morrison wrote about bringing together several friends to discuss the film *The Color Purple*.[21] They continued meeting for a monthly dialogue about the realities of racism and how to address its impactful manifestation in their own lives. During their meetings, Morrison taught groups of ethnically diverse women about racism within the church and Christian faith. Their beginning efforts served as a catalytic conversion toward establishing the Be the Bridge movement.

Morrison states, "If we come together in the posture of humility, we can start to bridge the racial divide, a bridge that lifts up marginalized voices, a bridge that is about equity of marginalized voices, not equality." Unveiling the impact of internalized racism, Morrison also shares how colorism fueled the schism between W. E. B. Du Bois and Marcus Garvey. Instead of bonding as brothers fighting against the reality of racism, their inability to bond prevented them from making combined and even more significant strides. Their fixation on colorism resulted in what

William Lynch captures in his letter, depicting how divisive and negatively impactful internalized forms of racism are, even to the victims of the social disease.

I was inspired by both the scholarly work of Morrison and her practical work in establishing a formidable movement of racial reconciliation-seeking advocates. The first Be the Bridge group included members of Morrison's close circle of friends, consenting to meet at the African American Cultural and Heritage Facility in Austin, Texas. Her original intent was not to start a movement but to meet as friends committed to the dialogue. One thing led to another. Since that time, Be the Bridge groups have formed nationally and internationally, utilizing curriculum developed by Morrison.

One noteworthy church Morrison has mentioned is The Family Church in Gainesville, Florida. The church leadership and staff not only created a group of their own, they also developed a four-week discipleship group focused on racial reconciliation, hired an African American executive pastor, and partnered with another local church to launch a Be the Bridge group. Inspiring stories like these bring the blueprint spoken of by Salter McNeil to fruition.

A few years ago, I made some effort to bring churches of mixed racial and ethnic heritage together for a series of sessions related to dissecting race and racism. The first effort included a congregation located in Libertyville, Illinois, coupled with our inner-city, Chicago-based congregation. We met four times for dialogue in a workshop-style experience and also conducted a joint worship service. Some of the sessions were held in Libertyville and some at the Chicago church location. The idea was to expose members of the congregations to both environments. I considered the experience quite successful, however, sustaining a mutual meeting schedule for all participants became more daunting than anticipated.

The second experience involved bringing together the pastors and congregants of four different churches, all located in downtown Burlington, Vermont. The pastors and congregation members met monthly for six sessions to discuss racism and racial reconciliation. The end goal was to identify a joint project to collectively support, adding both fiscal and human capital from all four congregations. Unfortunately, the COVID pandemic derailed the experience before we completed the cycle. However, participating members still speak fondly of the times. Both experiences provided valuable insights toward creating a new iteration of intentional and strategic gatherings.

Now What?

Like the Rev. Dr. Martin Luther King Jr., I have a dream of creating a racially reconciled nation. After learning about Be the Bridge, I was inspired to become a Bridge Builder. To bring this dream to fruition, I plan to establish four bridge-building groups across the United States, specifically for men. Utilizing the model set forth by Latasha Morrison, my experience pastoring and living in several cities positions me to strategically galvanize potential bridge-building partners in those locales. I plan to work with a team of men coordinating and facilitating groups in Burlington, Vermont; Chicago, Illinois; Lansing, Michigan; and Phoenix, Arizona. I have forged connections within each city and believe groups of men are poised and prepared to engage in life-transforming dialogue. The focus on men is not to intentionally exclude women. As mentioned previously in this chapter, men have been the progenitors and perpetuators of racism in the world. Men must assume the reins of leadership and responsibility for course correcting our current situation. The challenge being rendered directly to men is to actively participate in one of the Be the Bridge experiences.

Brenda McNeil provided a clearly delineated roadmap, with sprinklings of thought-provoking exercises to utilize during gatherings.[22] Morrison offered a rinse-and-repeat approach that has been replicated over a thousand times, internationally and across the United States.[23] There is no need to reinvent the process when tried-and-tested methodologies already exist. Sessions will begin and conclude with an in person meeting. The remaining six sessions will occur via a virtual platform. The plan to begin and end sessions in-person will allow the men to facilitate stronger bonding connections and provide for solid closure through physical encounters and interactions.

While virtual experiences have proven successful (especially during the pandemic), in-person experiences arguably more deeply enhance the learning experience. Dwain and his colleagues met during the height of the pandemic without missing a beat. Following their intense, insightful virtual experiences, face-to-face gatherings served as icing on the cake. Two key ingredients needed to heighten success factors are content and approach.

Upskillwise lists some of the pros and cons of both online and in-person learning. According to their research, 70 percent of students believe online classes are better than traditional environments, and 77 percent of academic leadership views online learning as a superior modality.[24] However, the article also reports that direct contact makes asking questions and engaging with others easier and leads to less distractions. Building relationships and friendships is more likely in traditional environments as well. By utilizing both learning modalities, men will encounter the best of both worlds.

Conclusion: The Challenge and Vision

So here is the challenge to you. Men are asked to commit eight weeks to engage in dialogue with other men from diverse backgrounds in hopes of raising their awareness. Beyond greater awareness, the men should anticipate expanding their perspectives and establishing accountability partners for continued personal growth beyond the eight weeks. Men can collectively agree to develop a joint-initiative focused on eradicating racism in their community. Men will know in advance what they are signing up for and the commitment required to complete the journey.

Consider how most men currently spend their time. Many men are into sports that soak up much of their time. Others frequently date. Then, there are others who are extremely occupied with video games as Pew Research Center indicates.[25] The US Bureau of Labor Statistics reports that men spend 5.6 hours per day on leisure and sports activities.[26] Multiplied by seven days, it equals 39.2 hours spent per week and again, multiplied by fifty-two weeks, it totals 2,038 total hours per year. If we request men to commit to two hours per week for eight weeks, that will only subtract sixteen total hours from their significant reservoir of time. Our ultimate goal is to acquire thirty willing participants in each location to sign up for the challenge.

Upon request, I will provide a QR code for those interested in engaging in the work of bonding on purpose, with purpose, to support abolishing racism in our communities. You may sign up to share your interest in joining one of four Be the Bridge groups mentioned earlier in the chapter. Contact me at rpatterson@ thelearnersgroup.com and make the commitment to join the eight-week experience.

Perhaps you're wondering, What difference will it make if only a few men decide to join the four groups? We remember that Jesus recruited twelve men from His surrounding community, and they have continued to multiply and to transform the world. We may not eradicate racism once and for all. However, our efforts will not go unnoticed, and our reach could quite well become exponential. Seek to be one of the thirty men in community. That is our ask of you.

NOTES

1. All names used in describing these group sessions are pseudonyms.

2. Lee Mun Wah, *The Color of Fear*, StirFry Seminars & Consulting, https://www.diversitytrainingfilms.com.

3. Willie James Jennings, *The Christian Imagination: Theology and the Origins of Race* (New Haven, CT: Yale University Press, 2010).

4. Stephanie E. Jones-Rogers, *They Were Her Property: White Women as Slave Owners in the American South* (New Haven, CT: Yale University Press, 2019).

5. Brenda Salter McNeil, *Roadmap to Reconciliation 2.0: Moving Communities into Unity, Wholeness and Justice*, Kindle ed. (Downers Grove, IL: InterVarsity Press, 2020).

6. McNeil, *Roadmap to Reconciliation*, 49.

7. McNeil, *Roadmap to Reconciliation*, 51.

8. Joshua D. Reichard, "From Indoctrination to Initiation: A Non-Coercive Approach to Faith-Learning Integration," *Journal of Education and Christian Belief* 17, no. 2 (2013): 285–99, https://doi.org/10.1177/205699711301700207.

9. McNeil, *Roadmap to Reconciliation*.

10. Eric Levenson, Sarah Smart, Nouran Salahieh, Isabel Rosales, and Andy Rose, "Jacksonville Gunman in Racially Motivated Attack," CNN Wire, August 27, 2023, https://www.cnn.com/2023/08/27/us/jacksonville-florida-shooting-sunday/index.html.

11. Rodney Patterson, "Male Bonding: Men Relating with Men," in *Men to Men: Perspectives of Sixteen African-American Christian Men*, ed. Lee N. June and Matthew Parker (Grand Rapids, MI: Zondervan, 1996).

12. John M. Perkins, *One Life Well Lived*, Moody Publishers, 2023, https://www.johnmperkins.com/one-life-well-lived.html.

13. Daniel Silliman, "Promise Keepers Tried to End Racism 25 Year Ago. It Almost Worked," *Christianity Today*, July/August, 2021, https://www.christianitytoday.com/2021/06/promise-keepers-racial-reconciliation-reconsidered/.

14. Silliman, "Promise Keepers Tried to End Racism 25 Year Ago."

15. Eliza Griswold, "How Black Lives Matter Is Changing the Church," *New Yorker*, August 30, 2020, https://www.newyorker.com/news/on-religion/how-black-lives-matter-is-changing-the-church.

16. McNeil, *Roadmap to Reconciliation*.

17. McNeil, *Roadmap to Reconciliation*.

18. McNeil, *Roadmap to Reconciliation*.

19. McNeil, *Roadmap to Reconciliation*, 26.

20. McNeil, *Roadmap to Reconciliation*, 26.

21. Latasha Morrison, *Be the Bridge: Pursuing God's Heart for Racial Reconciliation* (Colorado Springs: Waterbrook, 2019).

22. McNeil, *Roadmap to Reconciliation*.

23. Morrison, *Be the Bridge*.

24. Catherine Cooke, "In-Person vs. Online Learning Statistics of 2025," Upskillwise, updated February 5, 2025, accessed March 12, 2025, https://upskillwise.com/in-person-vs-online-learning-statistics/.

25. Andrew Perrin, "5 Facts about Americans and Video Games," Pew Research Center, September 17, 2018, https://www.pewresearch.org /short-reads/2018/09/17/5-facts-about-americans-and-video-games/.

26. "Men Spent 5.6 Hours Per Day in Leisure and Sports Activities, Women 4.9 hours, in 2021," US Bureau of Labor Statistics, August 22, 2022, https://www.bls.gov/opub/ted/2022/men-spent-5-6-hours-per -day-in-leisure-and-sports-activities-women-4-9-hours-in-2021.htm.

5

Discover

Finding Our Life's Calling

LENROY JONES, MA

"For I know the plans I have for you," declares
the LORD, "plans to prosper you and not to harm
you, plans to give you hope and a future."
Jeremiah 29:11

When we give up on our dreams, we die while still
alive. If a person is "important" only because of the
uniform he wears, his title, or the office he holds, then his
"importance" is artificial. It is the character that makes
a person valuable, and nobody can give you character;
you must develop it yourself as you walk with God.
Warren W. Wiersbe, *Be Diligent*

Introduction

It's been said that life is a journey, and for many of us, a significant portion is devoted to the pursuit of work. Andrew Naber shared that approximately one-third of our lives is dedicated to our careers.[1] Those years translate to a staggering ninety thousand hours (about ten and a half years) over a lifetime. As the old adage goes, "Find a job you enjoy, and you will never have to work a day in your life." This quote provides valuable insight into the significance of dedicating time, energy, and effort toward prioritizing one's pursuit of a fulfilling career rather than merely settling for a job.

Discovering our life calling, seeking fulfillment and purpose in our chosen paths, becomes ever more essential as we consider questions about our life and our vocation:

Why do you get up in the morning?

What excites you?

Are you happy in the space you are living in today?

What comes easiest to you?

Why are you here today?

What do you want to be when you grow up?

How do you spend your time and impact the people you encounter?

I believe the principles presented in this chapter can apply to everyone.

Do you ever feel lost or need help determining where you're headed? It's a familiar feeling, especially among young adults starting their careers or seasoned adults who have decided to shift to another vocation because they have experienced a good-paying job but simply lack job satisfaction. But don't worry. God has a plan for your life and can guide you in the right direction. Let's explore some tips and strategies grounded in biblical wisdom for discovering our career paths and finding fulfillment in our work.

Keith's Journey to His Life Calling[2]

I remember Keith (not his real name), a close friend from a quaint town nestled between rolling hills and rushing rivers. He was a dreamer. From a young age, Keith felt a magnetic pull toward a purpose, an elusive and alluring life calling. Determined to uncover the true north of his life, Keith embarked on a journey that would transform him in ways he could never have imagined. With a compass inherited from a wise mentor, Keith set out on a path that wound through dense forests and vast meadows. The compass, a trusted guide, pointed unwaveringly toward an elusive destination—the true north of his life calling.

Keith's journey was no sprint; it unfolded like a marathon, each step laden with challenges and victories. At times, the path led

Keith to hilltops where the air was thin, and the view stretched beyond the horizon, offering clarity and inspiration. These were moments of revelation, glimpses into the purpose that beckoned from the distance.

Yet, life's journey is never a straight line, and Keith soon found himself descending into valleys where shadows obscured the path ahead. The valleys were a test of resilience, a reminder that the actual destination could not be reached without navigating the lows and highs. But with the compass in hand, Keith pressed on, guided by an unwavering belief in his calling.

Rivers moved through the landscape with ease and bridges needed to be built or crossed. These rivers symbolized the hurdles and challenges that life inevitably presented. The bridges, products of determination and perseverance, were Keith's tools for overcoming obstacles. Each crossing brought new insights, strength, and the assurance that the actual north was still within reach.

As the journey continued, there were pauses—moments to reflect, recharge, and reassess. These pauses were not detours but essential milestones in the marathon of self-discovery. Keith took on jobs that, though not aligned with his ultimate calling, provided valuable experiences and resources, like pieces of a puzzle contributing to the grand design of his destiny. After all, Keith was a believer who embraced the understanding of Romans 8:28: "We know that in all things God works for the good of those who love him, who have been called according to his purpose." His life's work would all come together and work for his good.

Through the years, the compass remained on Keith's person, a constant reminder of the true north that guided his every step. The journey was not always easy, but the struggles and triumphs shaped Keith into a person of depth and purpose. My friend Keith's story reminds me of Mary Stevenson's version of "Footprints in the Sand." The narrator reflects on a person's life journey with the Lord, observing two sets of footprints during happy times and one set during challenging moments. Feeling abandoned in difficult times, the narrator questions the Lord, who explains that during those challenging periods, He was carrying the narrator.

Ultimately, Keith reached the summit, the culmination of years of dedication and perseverance. North was no longer a distant dream but a tangible reality. As he looked back at the winding path he had traveled, Keith understood that the journey itself was as important as the destination. The journey was a marathon of self-discovery, filled with hilltop and valley experiences, river crossings, and bridges built through resilience. Keith's story became a testament to the enduring power of staying true to one's calling, understanding that the journey is a process, and keeping the compass of true north ever before us.

Prayer and Reflection

The first step in discovering our life calling is to seek God's guidance through prayer and reflection as Proverbs 3:5–6 reminds us: "Trust in the LORD with all your heart; do not depend on your own understanding. Seek his will in all you do, and he will show you which path to take" (NLT). Spend time in prayer, asking God to reveal His plan for your life and guide you in the right direction. For each of us, embarking on our journey to discover our life calling is a deeply personal and spiritual endeavor. Consider reflecting on specific examples that resonate with your values and aspirations to enrich this process. Take moments to ponder about individuals whose life paths align with your deepest convictions, whether they are a mentor, your dad or mom, a historical figure, or someone within your community. Through prayer, seek divine insight and confirmation, asking God for guidance and clarity on your purpose. As you meditate on these examples and engage in sincere conversations with your heavenly Father, trust that God will provide the illumination needed to discern your life calling. The Holy Spirit will counsel you and confirm that you are traveling in the right direction. Consider posing questions such as, *What moments bring me profound joy and fulfillment? In what ways can I contribute to the betterment of others and the world?* This intentional reflection and prayer can be a powerful catalyst in unveiling the path to your life calling, fostering a deeper connection between your aspirations and the divine purpose set before you. These questions can help you stay focused on your goals and direction.

Goals and Values

We must regularly evaluate our aspirations and principles to navigate our life journey successfully. In pursuing a fulfilling life, it is essential to reassess our goals and values regularly. "You can make many plans, but the LORD's purpose will prevail" (Proverbs 19:21 NLT). This biblical insight highlights the importance of aligning our aspirations and principles with God's higher purpose. To successfully navigate our life journey, we must engage in regular self-reflection, evaluating what holds the utmost significance to us personally and professionally. This introspection becomes a compass for our endeavors as it did for Keith. What constitutes our core values? Where do we find genuine joy and fulfillment? Answering these inquiries enriches our self-awareness and serves as a potent strategy for maintaining focus on our overarching purpose and end goal.

A powerful tool for goal development and assessment is adopting SMART goals—a pragmatic approach to purpose-setting designed to heighten the probability of accomplishment. SMART, an acronym denoting *Specific*, *Measurable*, *Achievable*, *Relevant*, and *Time-Bound* goals, furnishes a systematic framework for articulating objectives.[3] This method ensures clarity and realism in our pursuits, transforming vague aspirations into well-defined and actionable items. By incorporating SMART principles into our goal-setting endeavors, we refine our approach and elevate the prospect of realizing our ambitions in facets of our personal and professional lives.

Keith was a professional at a crossroads, yearning to identify his life calling. Keith's core values reflected a deep passion for environmental sustainability and community engagement. He recognized that contributing to meaningful causes and fostering connections with others brought him unparalleled joy. Keith's journey of self-discovery involved identifying his values and actively aligning his pursuits with them.

To assist in this introspective process, it is crucial to consider what constitutes our core values. Where do we find genuine joy and fulfillment? Answering these inquiries enriches our self-awareness and serves as a potent strategy for maintaining focus on our overarching purpose that will get us closer to our life calling.

Fuel for the Spiritual Journey

As we work toward our career goals and seek to secure our life calling, we can see the importance of faith and spiritual growth. "In view of all this, make every effort to respond to God's promises. Supplement your faith with a generous provision of moral excellence, and moral excellence with knowledge, and knowledge with self-control, and self-control with patient endurance, and patient endurance with godliness, and godliness with brotherly affection, and brotherly affection with love for everyone" (2 Peter 1:5–7 NLT).

Here are several suggestions to help maintain a healthy spiritual balance:

1. Daily prayer and devotion. Spending time in prayer and reflection helps foster a deep connection with our faith. It's a moment to express gratitude, seek guidance, and find peace in the presence of our beliefs.

2. Attend a local church weekly. Regular attendance at a local church provides a sense of community and shared worship. It's an opportunity to engage in fellowship, receive spiritual teachings, and participate in ministry activities, if we are able to do so. We also have opportunities to network and perhaps secure a mentor.

3. Seek pastoral counseling when feeling stressed. Pastoral counseling offers a unique blend of spiritual guidance and psychological support. When facing challenges or feeling overwhelmed, seeking counsel from a trusted spiritual leader can provide comfort and perspective.

4. Secure a prayer partner or group. Joining a prayer group or having a prayer partner fosters accountability and shared spiritual growth. It creates a supportive environment where we can pray for each other, share experiences, and strengthen our faith.

5. Dive into self-help books and podcasts grounded in Christian principles. Integrating Christian principles into our personal and professional development through books can be enriching. Reading self-help books or listening to a

podcast with a faith foundation provides insights into applying faith to various aspects of life.

Maintaining a healthy spiritual balance is important, but it is a personal journey, and we may find different practices more beneficial. However, remember that the job search is stressful, and identifying and securing our life call is about our relationship with our heavenly Father. It is wise to be open to exploring various avenues to discover what helps with our spiritual growth.

God-Given Talents and Abilities

This journey to identify one's life calling requires us to know our God-given talents and abilities, as "God has given each of you a gift from his great variety of spiritual gifts. Use them well to serve one another" (1 Peter 4:10 NLT). We should take time to reflect on the skills and talents bestowed on us by God, considering how to leverage them to serve others and positively impact the world.

It's crucial to understand the distinction between soft skills and hard skills. Soft skills center around personal attributes and interactions with others, encompassing qualities like communication, empathy, and adaptability. Examples of soft skills include resilience, public speaking, leadership, emotional intelligence, and critical thinking. On the other hand, hard skills are specific and measurable technical proficiencies, often job-related, such as programming or data analysis. Examples of hard skills include project management, language proficiency, digital marketing, data analysis, and database management. Hard skills are frequently sought across industries due to their broad applicability and impact on job performance. However, it's essential to recognize that specific hard skills may vary based on industry, job role, and technological advancements.

Moreover, the dynamic nature of today's work environment calls for a combination of hard and soft skills. This blend enhances our adaptability and capabilities, and makes each of us a more well-rounded and versatile candidate. As we explore our career paths, consider the harmonious integration of our God-given talents, technical competencies, and interpersonal skills for a fulfilling and purpose-driven professional journey. Make a list of your hard and soft skills. What does your list look like? Start today!

Gaining Experience and Mentorship

Gaining experience in our desired field is vital. In Ecclesiastes 9:10 (NLT), wisdom guides us to put our utmost effort into whatever tasks we undertake: "Whatever you do, do well. For when you go to the grave, there will be no work or planning or knowledge or wisdom." This timeless advice encourages us to work diligently and give our best in all our endeavors.

Over two decades ago, someone sought my counsel and mentorship, embarking on a transformative journey that has propelled him to his current thriving position as the vice president and chief diversity officer at his company. His story echoes the timeless wisdom of Proverbs 15:22 (NLT): "Plans go wrong for lack of advice; many advisers bring success." His path to success involved navigating entry-level positions, assuming a directorship role, and pursuing and securing a master's and doctoral degree, showcasing a commitment to continuous learning and growth. Additionally, this person's global travels have enriched his perspective and contributed to the breadth of his experience. While reflecting on his life's journey, he highlighted the impact of guidance in shaping his career trajectory across diverse roles and fostering his impactful contributions to higher education. His journey underscores the significance of mentors, reinforcing the message that having a mentor is crucial for success—mentors matter! If you still need to secure a mentor, consider adding it to your list of priorities.

Act

The journey to discover our life calling involves more than prayer and reflection; it requires intentional and proactive steps (practical reminders). God reminds us, "So you see, faith by itself isn't enough. Unless it produces good deeds, it is dead and useless" (James 2:17 NLT). Therefore, rather than waiting for our life calling to manifest itself magically, we must take deliberate actions toward our goals.

Here are a few practical suggestions to guide us on this transformative journey and to compel us to action:

Refine your values: Create a list of your values and dive into resources to identify and measure them effectively. Understanding your core values will provide a solid foundation for aligning your life calling with what truly matters. Certainly, values such as integrity, leadership, teamwork, as well as technical understanding and communication skills serve as strong elements of a foundation for personal and professional development. These core qualities can shape how you navigate the journey to discover your calling. What are your core values?

Explore part-time opportunities: Actively search for part-time jobs related to your interests and passions. Practical experience enhances your skills and contributes to your growth, bringing you closer to your calling.

Volunteer purposefully: Compile a list of places to volunteer, ensuring they are connected to areas that resonate with your life calling. Volunteering contributes to meaningful causes and provides hands-on insights into potential career paths.

Incorporating these proactive steps into your quest for purpose demonstrates the vitality of your faith and actively contributes to the process of uncovering your life call. Remember, each intentional action takes you one step closer to fulfilling your unique purpose.

Give

Discovering your life calling is not just about achieving success in your career but also pertains to using your gifts and talents to serve others, pointing to and reflecting glory to God. "Work willingly at whatever you do, as though you were working for the Lord rather than for people. Remember that the Lord will give you an inheritance as your reward, and that the Master you are serving is Christ" (Colossians 3:23–24 NLT). As you pursue your career goals, seek to make a positive impact on those around you and use your work as a means of honoring God.

Engaging in impactful ways to give back to your community and church can significantly enhance the well-being of those around you. First and foremost, dedicating your time as a volunteer to local community organizations and church events allows you to contribute directly to the community's betterment. Whether it's mentoring, tutoring, or organizing activities, offering your skills and services can make a lasting impact on others. Additionally, donating goods or resources, such as food, clothing, or personal care items, helps meet immediate needs and supports vital church programs and community initiatives. Lastly, supporting local businesses strengthens your community's economic fabric and promotes sustainability and growth. By actively participating in these three avenues, you contribute to creating a more vibrant, connected, and supportive community.

Networking

Networking is another critical component to finding our life calling. "As iron sharpens iron, so a friend sharpens a friend" (Proverbs 27:17 NLT). Building relationships with people in our desired field can provide valuable insights and connections. Attend industry events, join professional organizations, and seek out mentors who can offer guidance and support.

Here are a few suggestions for outlets and resources that can aid in good networking and yield successful outcomes:

Attend Networking Events

- Attend industry-specific conferences, seminars, and workshops to connect with professionals in your field.
- Participate in local organizations' company meetups or networking groups to expand your network within your community and stay updated on industry trends.

Utilize Online Platforms

- Create and optimize your LinkedIn profile to showcase your professional experience and connect with others.
- Join relevant LinkedIn groups and actively participate in discussions to engage with professionals with similar interests.

Informational Interviews

- Reach out to professionals in your field and request informational interviews to gain insights into different career paths and industries. Set up informational interviews to learn more about specific roles and industries and to establish valuable connections for your journey.

When conducting informational interviews, ask insightful questions that can provide valuable insights into the industry and profession. Consider asking questions such as

- What skills and experience are essential for success in your role on a day-to-day basis?
- Which aspects of your job do you find most challenging, and how do you navigate them?
- What aspects of your job do you find most enjoyable or rewarding?
- What are the most vital steps someone should take to prepare for a role like yours? Could you share your personal journey and insights on how you obtained your current position?

Securing answers to these questions will provide valuable insight into areas that you have interest in pursuing for your life calling.

Discovery, Evolution, and Resiliency

The journey to discover your life calling will evolve and require resiliency and faith. A determined individual pursuing his life's calling (as in the case of Keith) faces hills and valleys, rivers and bridges along the challenging path to understanding their particular calling, and it's a marathon, not a sprint.

We must understand and embrace the importance of resilience and faith in facing obstacles. The Christian believer is able to do all things through God who strengthens us (Philippians 4:13). This biblical insight encourages us to draw strength from a higher power (God) when navigating life's challenges. Life's calling is not static; it evolves over time, as was the case with Keith.

"Don't copy the behavior and customs of this world, but let God transform you into a new person by changing the way you think. Then you will learn to know God's will for you, which is good and pleasing and perfect" (Romans 12:2 NLT). God advocates for our openness to new opportunities and experiences, fostering personal and professional growth.

During moments of adversity, we can draw inspiration from God's Word assuring us "that God causes everything to work together for the good of those who love God and are called according to his purpose for them" (Romans 8:28 NLT). We can embrace the truth that even setbacks can be woven into a more excellent plan, urging us to maintain faith and trust in God's overarching design.

This holistic narrative with spiritual guidance forms a tapestry of resiliency, adaptability, and unwavering faith in the pursuit of one's life calling. Are you in search of your life's calling? If you have contemplated giving up, you're not alone. As you continue on your journey toward your calling, your name may join the long list of men who nearly surrendered but ultimately succeeded, such as Moses, Gideon, David, Jeremiah, Jonah, Peter, and my personal favorite, Joseph. Some might argue that Joseph had every reason to give up; however, he was destined to fulfill God's plan. Despite being sold into slavery by his brothers, Joseph ascended to become an influential leader in Egypt, playing a crucial role in God's plan to save his family and preserve the bloodline of Jesus Christ. He successfully evolved and we can as well.

Self-Care

Finally, we need to make self-care a priority in the journey. Take time to reflect on these comforting words from Jesus: "Come to me, all of you who are weary and carry heavy burdens, and I will give you rest" (Matthew 11:28 NLT). Make time to recharge and engage in activities that bring you joy and a sense of fulfillment, or just rest. Seek out a network of support from your family, friends, and faith community, and foster connections that provide strength and encouragement. We can't avoid the negative, but we can proactively address negativity and distractions that may divert our focus from daily priorities. We need to remember that exploration and alignment with our life calling is a transformative process, one that holds the potential to impact not just our life but the lives of countless others. As we navigate this journey, assess, and cultivate outlets and environments that contribute to our well-being, we remain alert and productive.

Here are several suggestions to get us started on this exciting experience with self-care in mind:

1. Quality time with loved ones. Spending time with family and friends in a relaxed setting can be enjoyable and restful.
2. Nature walks or hiking. Spending time outdoors, whether it's a leisurely walk in a park or a more adventurous hike in nature, can be both enjoyable and restful.
3. Listen to music or podcasts. Enjoying your favorite music or tuning into interesting podcasts can be a delightful way to unwind.
4. Engage in creative pursuits (art, music, or crafting). Creative activities, such as drawing, painting, playing a musical instrument, or crafting can be both fun and restorative.
5. Stay off the couch: Easier said than done, but it is very important to stay active.

Conclusion

Embarking on the journey to uncover our life calling is a transformative process. This journey is enriched by earnest prayer, self-reflection, dedicated effort, and an unwavering commitment to seek guidance from our heavenly Father. Utilizing our inherent talents, gaining valuable experiences, fostering connections, and staying open to divine direction allow us to discern a career path aligned with our passions, leading to ultimate fulfillment.

As we explore our life calling, we must understand that making mistakes and encountering detours are natural aspects of the journey. Sometimes the path to our ultimate destination is not a straight line but a winding road with unexpected twists and turns. We saw this in the case of Keith. But Keith was a dreamer. Will you dream? Even in uncertainty, we can dream and trust that God is with us and guiding us toward His plan for our lives. Will you trust God? Amidst any uncertainty, we can find solace in the trust that God is present, guiding us toward His intended plan for our lives. In times of doubt, we can turn to God's guidance through reading the Holy Bible and listening to His voice. "For the LORD God is our sun and our shield. He gives us grace and glory. The LORD will withhold no good thing from those who do what is right" (Psalm 84:11 NLT).

The pursuit of our life calling will take time, but with unwavering faith, consistent prayer, and intentional actions, the outcomes will be rewarding. Actively seeking God's counsel, leveraging our unique gifts, seeking wise guidance, and embracing a mindset conducive to continual growth and change enable us to identify a vocational path in harmony with our purpose, fostering fulfillment by discovering our life's calling. Maintaining our focus on God and trusting in His overarching plan for our lives will exceed our expectations.

Remembering that the discovery of our life calling is a journey and a transformative process, underscored by faith and proactive engagement, we must constantly seek God's guidance, employ our gifts and talents, seek wise counsel, and remain open daily to growth and change. This concerted effort will lead us to a career path aligned with our purpose, bringing profound fulfillment. Remembering to center our focus on God and trusting in His more excellent plan for our lives is paramount. "That is what the Scriptures mean when they say, 'No eye has seen, no ear has heard, and no mind has imagined what God has prepared for those who love him'" (1 Corinthians 2:9 NLT). This Scripture underscores the anticipation of unseen blessings in the lives of those who love God. This truth emphasizes the extraordinary nature of God's blessings, extending beyond human understanding and surpassing expectations. The overarching message is that God has orchestrated remarkable outcomes for those devoted to Him, transcending the limits of human perception and expectation. I encourage you to enjoy the journey and to dream as you travel on the road to your life calling.

NOTES

1. Andrew Naber, "One Third of Your Life Is Spent at Work," Gettysburg College, 2007, https://www.gettysburg.edu/news /stories?id=79db7b34-630c-4f49-ad32-4ab9ea48e72b.
2. Keith's story is a composite story of several individuals I have worked with over the years.
3. George T. Doran is credited with creating this acronym in a November 1981 issue of *Management Review*. It has since become a widely used concept.

6

Perspective

Maintaining a Kingdom Mind

RON MOSBY, BA

Tell us therefore, What thinkest thou? Is it lawful to give tribute
unto Caesar, or not? But Jesus perceived their wickedness, and
said, Why tempt ye me, ye hypocrites? Shew me the tribute
money. And they brought unto him a penny. And he saith
unto them, Whose is this image and superscription? They
say unto him, Caesar's. Then saith he unto them, Render
therefore unto Caesar the things which are Caesar's; and unto
God the things that are God's. When they had heard these
words, they marvelled, and left him, and went their way.

Matthew 22:17–22 KJV

Introduction

In the New Testament, the Lord Jesus gave His disciples an imperative: "Seek ye first the kingdom of God" (Matthew 6:33 KJV).
While it is easy to recite, it is much harder to walk out. I was
raised in the African Methodist Episcopal church. Every Sunday,
as part of the service, we would stand and recite what is known
as the Lord's Prayer. I never thought about it at the time, but I
would recite the words "thy kingdom come, thy will be done"
and "for thine is the kingdom" each week. For years, I continued
to recite that prayer, never giving a second thought to what I was
saying. It wasn't until years later when I heard the good news of

the kingdom of God that I pondered what I was saying. I had to ask myself why those words did not have the import to me that they would have had to the disciples of the Lord Jesus? The answer, as I came to learn, was in the fact that I was saying those words as one who lived in a democratic society.

Our Rights in a Democratic Society

In our society, we have several freedoms, one of which is the freedom to choose what religion we want to practice. This is one of the rights enumerated in the US Constitution. Since this is a right, it is granted to each of our nation's citizens at birth. In short, I can choose any religion I feel suits me. Other rights granted to us at birth are the freedom to express our thoughts, ideas, and opinions. These and other rights developed as a result of the original thirteen colonies that were renamed states in order to show independence from England, choosing to rebel against the British monarch.

Why is this important? While in our earthly life we enjoy these freedoms of our democratic society, the renewed mind is striving to be submitted to the Great King of Kings in His kingdom. But how can one submit to a king when one does not know what a kingdom is? How does my mind become free from the right to express my opinion and choose my religion to become loyal to a king? This chapter will be devoted to understanding the differences between a democracy and a kingdom and learning how to renew our minds to serve as citizens of the kingdom of God while living in a democratic society.

The Meaning of a Democracy

What does *democracy* mean? Simply put, democracy means rule by the people. It means that the people decide who will govern. The process of voting is how the collective will of the people is determined. In the United States, we elect our leaders. We elect the people who serve on our local city, village, and township councils; we elect the members of our local school boards; we elect our county and state officials. Finally, we elect our United

States representatives every two years, our nation's president and vice president every four years, and our senators every six years. While our form of government is considered a republic, it still requires a majority of voters to elect a candidate or to pass a decision on an issue.

Typically, citizens refer to this process as politics. The word comes from the Greek word *politika*, which is based on Aristotle's "affairs of the city." It is interesting that two variations of this word occur in the New Testament. Both instances are in Paul's letter to the Philippians. The first instance occurs in Philippians 1:27 KJV: "Only let your conversation be as it becometh the gospel of Christ: that whether I come and see you, or else be absent, I may hear of your affairs, that ye stand fast in one spirit, with one mind striving together for the faith of the gospel."

The phrase "let your conversation be" is from the Greek word *politeuomai*, which means, "to behave as a citizen; or to avail oneself of or recognize the laws." In this case, Paul was instructing the church at Philippi to behave as citizens of the kingdom of God or that our behavior as kingdom citizens ought to be becoming of the gospel of Jesus Christ.

What is politics? In short, politics is citizenship. It is how we conduct our affairs in our country. Politics is much more than simply choosing elected officials; it is recognizing our roles as individuals and carrying out those roles responsibly. Politics, then, consists of the duties and responsibilities that we have as citizens in our society.

Types of Governments

There are many different types of governments in the world, each with their own unique characteristics and systems of governance. Here are some of the most common forms of government:

1. *Democracy:* This is a form of government where power is held by the people. Citizens have a say in how the country is run and elect representatives to make decisions on their behalf.
2. *Monarchy:* In a monarchy, a king, queen, or emperor is

the head of state. The monarch's power may be limited by a constitution or other laws, or the monarch may have absolute power.

3. *Dictatorship:* This is a form of government where power is held by a single person or a small group of people. The ruler usually maintains power through force or intimidation.

4. *Republic:* A republic is a form of government where the people elect representatives to make decisions on their behalf. This is similar to a democracy, but with a focus on representative decision-making rather than direct democracy.

5. *Theocracy:* This is a form of government where religious leaders hold power and make decisions based on religious principles.

6. *Oligarchy:* An oligarchy is a form of government where a small group of people hold power. This can be based on wealth, military power, or other factors.

7. *Anarchy:* This is a state of society where there is no government or ruling authority. Individuals and groups are left to govern themselves.

8. *Federalism:* This is a form of government where power is shared between a central government and regional governments. This can be seen in countries like the United States, Canada, and Australia.

These are just a few of the most common forms of government, and there are many variations and combinations of these systems around the world. Now that we are familiar with the various forms of government, we need to discover how we can live as a citizen of a form of government we have never experienced. Apart from God, this would be impossible. Thankfully, God gave us an example in the apostle Paul.

The Example of the Apostle Paul

What happened with Paul? In Acts chapter 9, Saul, who later became Paul, had an encounter with the resurrected Jesus. In the account, Saul asked only one question: "Who are you, Lord?" When Saul was instructed by Jesus what to do, his response was complete obedience. Obedience is the only response a ruler expects when an order is given. Notice that Saul did not question Jesus. Saul did not ask why, neither did he make any excuse for not carrying out the order. Saul could have easily said, "But I cannot see!" Instead, he endeavored to obey the command of Jesus.

This is a lifestyle that we are unaccustomed to in America. Instead, we are conditioned to question authority. We ask questions like, "Why do I have to do that?" "Why can't someone else do it?" In fact, some people may even label others as cowards for not questioning authority. Yet Paul, a servant of the Lord Jesus, did not murmur or question the instruction he was given. He simply obeyed. Obedience is an essential characteristic of our kingdom's citizenship.

For example, in Paul's first letter to Timothy, Paul gives Timothy a very specific instruction: "I urge, then, first of all, that petitions, prayers, intercession and thanksgiving be made for all people— for kings and all those in authority, that we may live peaceful and quiet lives in all godliness and holiness" (1 Timothy 2:1–2). This exhortation was not a suggestion or a recommendation. It was an instruction that was and is expected to be followed. We don't pray only for the leaders we like. Our prayers are not to be petitions for someone else to be in office. We are not to argue that the election wasn't fair. We don't complain that the person we are praying for wasn't the person we voted for. Doing any of these things is evidence that we are giving precedence to our temporal earthly citizenship.

Needed: A New Mindset as a Christian

So how do we change our mindset? First, we must remember the words of Jesus: "No one can see the kingdom of God unless they are born again" (John 3:3). Religion has taught us that being born again is a process of our choosing or our volition. The truth, however, is that it is not of our choosing. One can no more decide to be born of the Spirit than he or she decided to be born of the flesh. No one chooses to be brought into this world; how then, can that same person decide to be born of the Spirit? If you were unable to decide what your gender was at birth, who your parents were, what nationality you were, all of which are temporal, how do you think that you can choose your eternal citizenship? No person can, of his or her own volition, see the kingdom of God. Jesus was saying that in order to see the kingdom, one must be born of the Spirit or be born again.

Our Citizenship as Christians

Do we have dual citizenship? In Christianity, there is a popular saying that we have dual citizenship, meaning that we belong to two forms of government. We have our temporal citizenship on earth, and we have our eternal citizenship in heaven. However, that is not what Paul stated. Paul stated, with certainty, that we have one citizenship: "But our citizenship is in heaven. And we eagerly await a Savior from there, the Lord Jesus Christ" (Philippians 3:20). Paul concisely states, with certainty, that our citizenship is an eternal citizenship in heaven. This means that all our rights and privileges come from heaven, as well as our duties and responsibilities. While we live on this temporal earth, we are ambassadors, sent from heaven residing in earthly bodies in the land where God has assigned us. While we have been granted the rights and privileges of our earthly government, we partake of them only to the degree that they do not conflict with our heavenly citizenship.

My wife experienced this during a presidential election. Prior to election day, the Holy Spirit told her not to vote for a particular candidate. She did not ask questions, nor did she come to me for advice or clarification. She simply did as she was instructed to do. As it turned out, the person she did not vote for won the election. After the election, she didn't complain that the candidate that she did not vote for won, nor did she question God as to how that candidate got elected. Now, some may question why the Holy Spirit would tell a person to vote in a particular way. They may question if a person actually heard from God because the result wasn't what they expected. It is important to remember that in a kingdom, you don't question the instructions of the king. Your only choice in a kingdom is to obey the king. Our citizenship requires us to obey the voice of God and leave the outcome to Him. Paul had a similar situation in Acts 21:8–13 (NKJV):

> On the next day we who were Paul's companions departed and came to Caesarea, and entered the house of Philip the evangelist, who was one of the seven, and stayed with him. Now this man had four virgin daughters who prophesied. And as we stayed many days, a certain prophet named Agabus came down from Judea. When he had come to us, he took Paul's belt, bound his own hands and feet, and said, "Thus says the Holy Spirit, 'So shall the Jews at Jerusalem bind the man who owns this belt, and deliver him into the hands of the Gentiles.'" Now when we heard these things, both we and those from that place pleaded with him not to go up to Jerusalem. Then Paul answered, "What do you mean by weeping and breaking my heart? For I am ready not only to be bound, but also to die at Jerusalem for the name of the Lord Jesus."

Paul was concerned about only one thing—obedience to the Lord Jesus. He was not interested in preserving his life or becoming rich and famous. He didn't plead with Jesus to grow old or live comfortably. Obedience was the top priority in Paul's life.

What is it that preoccupies you? Is it living in a nice neighborhood? Being able to live to see retirement? Making sure you have enough money so that the children can go to college? Or is it to see particular laws established or abolished? Unfortunately, none of these things will bring about the kingdom of God. Only one thing will bring about the kingdom, and that is obedience—obedience to proclaiming the gospel of the kingdom. But before one can proclaim the gospel of the kingdom, that person must know what the gospel is.

What is the gospel of the kingdom? It is the good news that God promised to the children of Israel, which he fulfilled in the form of Christ Jesus. The proof of this fulfillment is that God raised Jesus from the dead. What happens then when we believe that God raised Jesus from the dead? First, it is through that belief that we are reconciled to God; consequently, our minds are in a state of renewal, meaning that we don't think the way we have been conditioned to think according to this temporal world. If that is the case, then, how do we learn about this kingdom to which we now belong? In God's kingdom, the process of learning how to be a citizen of the kingdom is referred to as *discipleship*. It is through discipleship that one learns about the kingdom, then the person proves what he or she has learned by doing. In the kingdom, this is what it means to study. We have been conditioned to understand the concept of studying to mean reading and comprehending. Studying in the kingdom, however, means to learn and practice. When Paul instructs Timothy to "study to show yourself approved," he is instructing Timothy to practice, or put into practical effect, what he has learned. It is this act of practicing that proves that we are disciples. In religion, the process is for us to "get saved" and "go to church." In the kingdom, the process is to proclaim the kingdom and make disciples.

What Is the Church?

In our society, the word *church* has many meanings. One meaning is the building where people go to worship. For example, a person may ask the question, "Where is your church located?" The person is asking where the local body goes to attend services. Another meaning of the word church is the service that people attend. If a person asked the question, "What time does church start?" the person is asking what time the services begin. Still another definition of church is the denomination that espouses particular doctrines. For example, my family was part of the African Methodist Episcopal (AME) church when I was a child. That organization had a set of doctrines that made it distinct from other denominations.

While we are so accustomed to these definitions that they have become part of our religious lexicon, we may be surprised to discover that the word *church*, as it is used in the Bible, does not mean any of these things. The word *church* is a term used to describe the congregation of people who answered the call of the gospel by believing that God raised Jesus from the dead. In other words, the church is a nation of people. What this means is that the church consists of all of the believers from the time of Moses until this present day. If you read Paul's letters with care, you will see that he uses the term *church* to describe those assembled together (mostly in homes), and the body of believers in a particular city. These are the citizens that are ruled by the king. The church, then, is the body of citizens who are the kingdom of God. Put another way, we don't *go* to church; we *are* the church. Who is the body of citizens? The church is a nation of people, consisting of Jews and Gentiles who are neither Jews nor Gentiles according to the flesh. What do all of these people have in common? The belief that God raised Jesus from the dead. This belief is so essential to our citizenship, that Paul made this bold proclamation: "And if Christ is not risen, your faith *is* futile; you are still in your sins!" (1 Corinthians 15:17 NKJV). Think about the gravity of that statement—if God did not raise Jesus from the dead, your faith is futile. That means Christ did not die for your sins if God did not raise Him from the dead. It is this belief that is essential to our kingdom citizenship.

Kingdom Citizenship

But what happens *after* we believe? Why are we believing in this resurrection? Is it so we are able to go to heaven when we die? If that is the only reason, what is our purpose for living? There would be no need for us to be on this earth any longer; in fact, we may put ourselves in jeopardy if we stayed on this earth and gave in to temptation, right? Yet, this is precisely what we are to do: live out our kingdom citizenship in this earthly life. How are we to do that? In fairness, this life is the only life we know. But Paul admonished the saints in Rome not to be conformed to this world any longer but be transformed by the renewing of their minds (Romans 12:2). This transformation process is evidence of our kingdom citizenship. Is this process something that we can do on our own as individuals? In short, no. It is for this reason that God called us into the kingdom community. Life for the kingdom citizen is not working five days a week, getting a day off on Saturday, then going to church on Sunday. The life of a kingdom citizen is hearkening to the Holy Spirit on a daily basis. The Holy Spirit is the voice of Christ in the earth today. So how do we make these transformations? How do we learn to hearken our ears to hear? There is only one way—discipleship.

Discipleship in the Context of Kingdom Citizenship

Discipleship is the way that our kingdom citizenship is made manifest. What is discipleship? Discipleship is the process by which we learn to become kingdom citizens. Discipleship includes intimacy, instruction, and correction. It is more than learning, however. The other important component to discipleship is proving what you have learned by doing it. If you notice, Jesus had only twelve disciples He poured into. He spent time with them, teaching them and allowing them to observe His work. This process of discipleship requires a level of intimacy that one cannot get simply by attending a church. Discipleship is not a new member's class or a topical Bible study. In discipleship, there is a process that is taking place in the one being taught. That process is threefold: (1) revelation, (2) transfiguration, and (3) manifestation.[1] As a student, the first thing that must occur in the discipleship process is that truths or doctrines must be revealed to a person. This begins with the transmission of the gospel. Once a person hears the gospel and submits to it, this commences the discipleship process. The good news of the kingdom of God has now been revealed.

I remember when I first heard the good news of the kingdom of God. It was a message that was strange, but intriguing. It was something I had never heard before. I thought, *Why is it that I have never heard this message?* I had been in church all my life, and not one pastor or preacher that I could remember gave any emphasis to this message. Yet, every parable that the Lord Jesus spoke to His disciples pertained to the kingdom of God. I remember realizing that in reciting the Lord's Prayer, I mentioned the kingdom twice. Once the idea of the kingdom was revealed to me, I could not turn away. I could not ignore what had been revealed to me.

Transfiguration

The next step of this discipleship process is transfiguration. Transfiguration is the process of our minds being changed. It is more than just stating a belief. It is your mind now conforming to that belief. This is neither an easy process nor a single process. Our minds must be constantly renewed. Think back to the earlier part of this chapter when we discussed the fact that people living in the United States live in a democratic society. *Democracy* is a word that means "rule by the people." This is the mindset Americans have, a democratic mindset where the people are sovereign, and our legislators are elected. Contrast that with a kingdom mindset. A kingdom mindset recognizes that there is one ruler, the king, and that king is not elected; instead, that king gets his authority directly from God. The king is sovereign, meaning there is no higher authority in that kingdom than the king, and the only authority that is higher than the king is God Himself. Additionally, any edict that the king promulgates must be obeyed. In a democracy, people are encouraged to question authority. That is not done in a kingdom. Complete loyalty is the only standard, and that is expressed through obedience. This kind of transfiguration can occur only with submission to Christ and with the help of the Holy Spirit. This is where instruction and correction are necessary components to discipleship. Even with the best intentions, a believer will veer off course. When that occurs, a teacher must be there to help correct the disciple. This is why accountability is so important.

Accountability

Accountability is the act of giving an account or giving an answer. When I make myself accountable to someone, I am placing myself in a position where I am prepared to give that person an answer for any action I have taken. Discipleship requires accountability. If the teacher asks a question, the disciple is expected to give an answer. It is a combination of submission and discipline. As kingdom citizens, part of our citizenship is accountability. We practice our citizenship here on earth by being accountable to others, knowing that at some point we must give an account of our lives to God. In summary, I should be able to give an answer to man in this life, as I must give an answer to God at the end of this life. Accountability also provides us with a level of protection in this life. If I know I must answer to someone, I may not be as likely to commit certain acts. Accountability is like the security camera in the store. If a thief knows someone is watching, they are less likely to attempt to steal.

Manifestation

The last phase of the discipleship process is manifestation; exhibiting the change that has occurred in our lives. Put another way, manifestation is when your actions are consistent with your beliefs. At this stage, the disciple comes into full maturity. This is where the disciple not only believes the instruction "do not render evil for evil," but lives it out in his or her actions. It is at this stage of maturity that self-control is also exhibited. To be clear, this does not mean that a person will exhibit this self-control in all situations; for indeed, we will all be works in progress until the day we pass from this life. What it does mean, however, is that our practice, or habit, will be to exhibit the self-control that we have been taught as disciples. It is this self-control that proves our discipleship. This is especially challenging in a world where we have been conditioned to express our opinion on every matter or express our satisfaction or dissatisfaction with every event that occurs. In the United States, freedom to express one's opinion is something to be cherished and protected. Yet, in the kingdom of God, the only thing that God and Christ are concerned with is our obedience. For if we are not capable of exhibiting this obedience to God in this life, what would make us think we would obey Him in the life to come?

This is what our faith is all about. Faith, as it is used in the Bible, is not simply believing something is true; it is being so convinced that the believer is compelled to act on his or her belief. As an example, when one hears and believes the gospel of the kingdom, that person is so convinced that it is true that he or she is compelled to obey. Part of that obedience includes being discipled. Another aspect of the faith is the proclamation of the gospel itself. When we proclaim the gospel with boldness and urgency, we are expressing our faith. This is where our beliefs and actions are consistent with each other. Faith is not a denomination or a religion; faith is a belief that compels a believer to act. "Now faith is confidence in what we hope for and assurance about what we do not see" (Hebrews 11:1). How unusual it is for us to proclaim the good news of a kingdom when we live in a society that despises kingdoms! But this is just one of the extraordinary aspects of the life of a kingdom citizen.

A Kingdom Citizen

Think about that for a moment. You are a kingdom citizen. That is your true, eternal citizenship. You don't have dual citizenship; you are simply an ambassador of the kingdom of God in this life. God chose you to be an ambassador for His kingdom. He trusts you to reveal His kingdom in the lives of the people that you encounter wherever you go. His will is that you reflect His eternal kingdom in this temporal life. How awesome is that! This is why it is so important for us to understand that our faith isn't about a religion or a denomination; it is about a government. Ironically, this kingdom form of government is one that our American culture has taught us to hate. We are taught that kingdoms are bad because no one person should have that much authority over so many people. This was the reason the colonists rebelled against the British king during the American Revolution. This is why we must have a renewed mind. This is the reason that we cannot be conformed to this world. The life of a kingdom citizen is much more than walking down the aisle of a sanctuary and making a public declaration; it is understanding that we are part of a government completely different from what we have been conditioned to believe is one of the best in the world. Our citizenship is in heaven. That is our true, eternal citizenship. This means we are to live according to the instructions, rules, and edicts of the king. I encourage you to read this paragraph again, and let it take root in your mind. I assure you that the next time you pick up your Bible to read it, you will not read it the same way again.

Conclusion

Finally, if you are reading this chapter and you realize that you need to start doing something to learn more about your kingdom citizenship and discipleship, you may ask, "What do I do?" The answer will be different for everyone.

In 1991, I was a military officer living in New Jersey, and I was sure that God wanted me to stay in New Jersey. I was so sure; I asked God to bless my finances and help me secure employment on my discharge from active duty. Two years later, I was in my home telling God that if He got me back to Cincinnati, where I left to join the military, I promised Him I would not leave. It was in those two years that I realized I had asked God to bless a decision I made on my own, without His direction. Through an extraordinary sequence of events, I moved my family back to Cincinnati, Ohio, in 1995. After I returned to Cincinnati, I learned the truth of the passage that Paul wrote where he said God sets the members in the body as it pleases Him (1 Corinthians 12:18). Those words hit me with great power. God sets the members in the body as it pleases Him, not us. I realized I don't choose where I want to be set, I am set where it pleases God. I don't get to make the decision about where I want to live or what church or fellowship I will attend. I go where God sets me. This is the life of a disciple. This is a kingdom lifestyle, one that opposes the earthly freedoms we enjoy in this life. I am reminded of the words that describe Moses, written in the letter to the Hebrews: "He chose to be mistreated along with the people of God rather than to enjoy the fleeting pleasures of sin. He regarded disgrace for the sake of Christ as of greater value than the treasures of Egypt, because he was looking ahead to his reward" (11:25–26).

This is the type of life saints of God should desire to follow. Having the freedom of choosing, then choosing to obey God, regardless of the consequences. By doing this, we exhibit the kingdom rule in our lives while living in an earthly democratic society. In short, we render unto Caesar that which belongs to Caesar, but unto God that which belongs to God, which is our very souls.[2]

NOTES

1. Randy Shankle, *The Merismos* (New Kensington, PA: Whitaker House, 1987).
2. For further reading and another perspective on becoming a kingdom man in our Western society, I refer you to the book *Kingdom Man* by Tony Evans (Colorado Springs: Focus on the Family, 2012).

7

Health

Becoming an Expert on Our Wellness

MICHAEL R. LYLES SR., MD

> Do you not know that your bodies are temples of the
> Holy Spirit, who is in you, whom you have received
> from God? You are not your own; you were bought at
> a price. Therefore honor God with your bodies.
>
> 1 Corinthians 6:19–20

Introduction

Robert (not his real name) was an elder and Bible study leader in
his church. He believed in education and mentored many young
people for years. However, he did not believe in doctors. He did
not have a primary care physician, never received a physical, and
was militant about not getting a COVID-19 vaccine. Instead, he
was a vegan, took supplements to treat himself, and exercised.
One day, he did not show up for work. A week passed and nobody heard from him. The authorities were called to perform a
wellness check on him. He was found dead in his apartment at
fifty-eight years of age.

It is a fact that many men, like Robert, avoid going to doctors.
The Cleveland Clinic studied 1,174 adult males in 2019 and found
that 72 percent would rather do household chores than go to a
doctor. Twenty percent of these men admitted to not being honest
with their doctor. Fifty percent did not consider a yearly physical

to be important to their healthcare.[1] A US Centers for Disease Control and Prevention study found that men were half as likely as women to go to the doctor and twice as likely to have never had contact with a healthcare professional in their life.[2] Robert was not alone.

African American Men and Healthcare

Men, in general, tend to avoid doctors for several reasons. Healthcare visits are inconvenient and take too much time. There is a fear of finding out that something is wrong with you. There is the potential for embarrassing exams (such as prostate or rectal) or questions about lifestyle and habits. The costs of visits and medications can be an additional barrier. A male ego issue regarding not needing help can be an additional barrier to seeking care.

However, African American men may have additional factors that increase their reluctance to see a doctor. A health forum for men was recently held at a historic African American church in Atlanta. Most of the group admitted to not engaging with their doctors as they should. Some admitted to ignoring their health despite attending a health forum. Most of the group had a broad fear of healthcare systems. They expressed feeling like a powerless victim and that the healthcare system is there for doctors to make money. There was a widespread lack of trust that their doctor would truly care about them as a person instead of simply a diagnosis.

Some comments expressed at the forum were, "My doctor stares at the computer and talks instead of talking to me" and "My doctor does not look like me or understand my background. How could I be open with her?" Others had a lack of family role models for helpful medical care. Lack of access due to costs and insurance issues influenced medical care choices in relatives. "My parents couldn't afford to go to doctors. We took castor oil for everything and prayed a lot." Racism has been a driver of healthcare choices, as many doctors and hospitals restricted access to people of color. "My mother couldn't go to the local dentist because of racism. The White dentist would not see her. When she had a toothache, she went to the local vet to get it pulled."

As a child, I had asthma and remember the separate waiting room in the back for "colored people" that the pediatrician was willing to see. I remember sneaking a peek into the White waiting room to see what was different about it. To my amazement, they had an aquarium and magazines. We had an empty room with hard chairs. I cannot remember how my parents explained that to me.

The experience of racism in other areas of a person's life can influence the ability to trust a healthcare practitioner who does not understand the patient's cultural background. In the words of one of my African American male patients: "I try to have all Black doctors because I don't trust doctors who are not Black. I have been passed over for promotions at work, with these jobs given to White subordinates . . . and no one cared. My son was racially bullied at his predominantly White school by a group of White boys . . . and no one cared. My daughter was 'encouraged' not to rush for a White sorority at her college . . . and no one cared. So why should I assume that a doctor who does not look like me would truly care if I lived or died? At least if I have a Black doctor, I can reasonably expect them to care about me. At least, I hope so."

In these instances, the experience of medical care can trigger racially traumatic memories that discourage participation in and compliance with a treatment plan. "My doctor talked down to me like he thought I was too ignorant to understand him. He did not give me time to ask a question—after making me wait over an hour to be seen. There is no way that I am going to be honest with that guy if I go back." The low representation of African Americans in current medical research as participants and investigators leads some to mistrust whether the results apply across racial categories.[3] "That medicine may work for them, but I don't know what it will do to us. Those studies never include us."

This lack of trust in research is further magnified in the context of abuses of medical research in Black men in historical studies like the Tuskegee study in 1932.[4] In this rural Alabama study, Black men with syphilis were recruited to study the effects of untreated syphilis on the body. The participants were not informed when effective treatment, penicillin, became available in 1943. Instead, these men were left to suffer with the complications of a treatable condition until 1972 when an Associated Press story exposed the details of the study, leading to the study being stopped. Any remaining survivors were offered treatment but the effects of a system that allowed this to happen for forty years left a tangible imprint on men who are reluctant to enter a medical research trial or take a new medication. Their reluctance reflects a well-understandable lack of trust in the integrity of healthcare systems. Thus, these racial variables only complicate the usual variables that lead men away from healthcare systems.

Given all these variables, it is not surprising that African American men, like men in general, will pause before going to a doctor. Men of faith, like Robert, would understandably lean toward self-care with diet, exercise, supplements, and prayer rather than risk dealing with a healthcare system they do not trust. In the final analysis, some men of faith will use faith as their healthcare option. Robert was known to say, "If there is anything wrong with me, God will heal me. I don't need doctors! I have Doctor Jesus."

The Bible and Healthcare

The Bible teaches that our physical bodies are a "temple" inhabited by the Holy Spirit (1 Corinthians 6:19–20). Therefore, we are expected to care for our bodies like we would a physical church. This does not mean that no one gets sick. In fact, illness did happen often in Scripture and healing—when it occurred—happened in many ways. Consider that Jesus healed people miraculously using a variety of methods. He even healed blindness by spitting in the dirt and touching someone's eyes in two distinct manners (John 9:1–12; Mark 8:22–25).

Many men of faith minimize medical care as a vehicle by which God may heal them. Like Naaman (2 Kings 5:1–14), they have a preconceived idea of how they should be healed and reject methods, such as doctors, that they consider to be tedious, time-consuming, and inconvenient. A quick miracle is always better than the slow "miracle" of a medication working gradually over time or recovery from a surgical procedure. Like Hezekiah (2 Kings 20:1–7), many men don't fully understand the methods that God may use to heal them—but they still must comply to receive the healing God has provided. After all, Timothy apparently had stomach issues that disrupted his life enough for Paul to comment on it (1 Timothy 5:23). Paul told him to drink a little wine for his stomach because that was the accepted medical treatment of his day. In other words, Paul told Timothy to take his medication. Finally, the woman with the issue of blood did go to many doctors and spent a significant amount money on "co-pays." She was a good patient but still did not feel better. Jesus could have taken this opportunity to focus on the failure of the doctors to help her. He could have criticized her for going to the medical facilities of her day. He could have used her as an example of someone who placed her faith in those greedy doctors who took her money. He did not and used a physician to document it (Luke 8:43–48).

Mental Health

As a teenager, I sensed a calling from God to become a physician. My initial sense was that I was to go into primary care and serve in an underserved area. Psychiatry was not even on the list of possibilities. In fact, I would not have been able to spell *psychiatry* correctly when I started medical school, as mental healthcare was not an available option in my home community. In the junior year of medical school, students are required to "rotate" through all the major specialty groups—such as surgery, pediatrics, internal medicine, obstetrics and gynecology, radiology, and psychiatry. Near the end of that year, I began my required psychiatry rotation at an inner-city Detroit hospital. On this rotation, I began to learn that the brain was an organ, like the heart, that could get sick from infections, inflammation, nutritional deficiencies (for example, vitamin D deficiency), genetic variations, hormonal imbalances (for example, thyroid), traumatic injury, neurochemical imbalances, interactions with other illnesses (for example, diabetes or sleep apnea), and side effects from medications (for example, steroids or pain medications). I learned that the brain is often accurate in making decisions about how to get help when other areas of the body are ill. However, the brain is less precise in making decisions about getting help when *it* is sick. This would lead to many patients with illnesses of the brain avoiding getting help because of impaired perception of the nature of the problem. The most common misperception is the assumption that the causes of their emotional or behavioral symptoms are always related in some fashion to personal weakness or sin. At least, that was what I heard back in my home neighborhood and in churches that I attended. In contrast, I learned in medical school that these problems could be caused by a variety of triggers and that psychiatry specialized in helping people sort through them. After much prayer, I changed my career path from internal medicine to the even more underserved mission field of psychiatry.

This change to psychiatry was one of the most unpopular decisions that I ever made. A pastor friend told me that only non-Christians would need my services, and I would be casting my "pearls before swine" (Matthew 7:6 KJV). Many years later, he would need my advice when a member of his family developed behavioral problems that were related to menopause. Another pastor criticized my choice and preached from the pulpit against those who sought mental health services. "You don't need Prozac; you need pro-Jesus!" he said. Tragically, this same pastor committed suicide several years after he preached that sermon. A fellow small-group Bible study participant expressed shock that I was studying to become a psychiatrist. He stressed that Christians should not have emotional challenges and struggles. "After all, depression is not a fruit of the Spirit" (Galatians 5:22–24), he stated. I reminded him that it was not listed as a work of the flesh, either (Galatians 5:19–21).

Psychological and emotional struggles are common in the Bible. In fact, some have described the Bible as a book of trauma, suffering, and the response to it.[5] The Old Testament record of the nation of Israel is a real-world description of conflict, emotional pain, doubt, struggle, and suffering. All the prophets in the Old Testament lived hard and sometimes lonely lives. The book of Acts does not describe a comfortable, carefree life for the New Testament followers of Christ. In His last private, documented words to His disciples, Jesus warned them that life would be hard

(John 16:33). A concordance search for these words is just the start of the real world of the Christian life, from the first letter of the alphabet: *affliction, afraid, agony, alienated, alone, amiss, anger, anguish,* and *ashamed.* Whole books of the Bible, including Job, Psalms, Acts, Judges, Samuel, Kings, Chronicles, Lamentations, and Ruth highlight human struggles and suffering in life (and those are only some from the Old Testament). Every single character in the Bible, like Paul, had some "thorn in the flesh" challenge that they dealt with (2 Corinthians 12:1–10). Some were spiritual, some relational, some because of family or marital issues, and some physical. Some people suffered, as did Job, for reasons that were not clear to them at the time. Some crossed over from mild to moderate distress, to becoming impaired, to the point of committing suicide (Judges 9:50–55; 1 Samuel 31:1–6; 2 Samuel 17:23; 1 Kings 16:18; Judges 16:28–30; Matthew 27:5).

After four decades of psychiatric practice, I have learned that a "one size fits all" approach seldom works when helping people who are going through emotional crises. As someone who taught Sunday school for more than thirty years, I agree that spiritual resources and disciplines are important components of helping people. However, the problem occurs when we limit our diagnostic thinking, even on spiritual issues. Peter, Nehemiah, David, Jeremiah, Elijah, Job, and Ezekiel all had symptoms of sadness at times and for very different spiritual reasons. Symptoms can be misleading as they do not prove the underlying causes of the symptoms. For example, one may be depressed for physical reasons such as thyroid disease or a drug side effect—but the issue will never get properly evaluated if one never goes to the doctor for help. When we stop thinking and make assumptions about causation, we run the risk of missing other very important contributions to our emotional landscape. To illustrate this, the following list of issues that were seen during one day at my office comprises the variety of medical causes of significant depression:

- Uncontrolled diabetes
- Anemia (low blood count)
- Cancer (side effects of chemotherapy)

- Thyroid disease
- Prescription drug side effects
- Sleep apnea
- Traumatic brain injury from an automobile wreck
- Menopausal transition
- Low testosterone level
- Vitamin D deficiency
- Chronic low back pain

The concept of what leads a person to have mental challenges can be far more complicated than one might initially assume. In addition, illnesses of the brain can have a complicated effect on other body systems that interact with the brain. Thus, brain illnesses such as depression or anxiety can complicate the treatment of hypertension, diabetes, infertility, arthritis, stroke, or bone disease (osteoporosis). This would explain why the specialties that provide most of the care to patients with depression and anxiety problems are not psychiatrists. Psychiatrists are scarce and seldom located far outside of big cities or in financially challenged areas. Most people, especially people of color, are treated by OB-GYN or primary care providers.

However, the same variables that keep men from going to doctors are worse in terms of getting men to discuss emotional issues with anyone—let alone a doctor. As a result, men become at risk of acting out their feelings in anger and/or self-medicating with alcohol or addictive behaviors like food or sex. One of my patients described it perfectly. He said, "When my wife gets upset with someone, she gets sad and depressed. When I get upset, I get drunk and then I get even!" This man was referred to me by his cardiologist because his blood pressure was so high and unresponsive to medication that he was about to have a stroke. This patient's treatment plan illustrated the multiple variables that needed attention. He needed to stop drinking as a coping mechanism, develop a vocabulary for expressing his feelings, and take an antidepressant to turn down the level of stress hormones in his body that were driving his blood pressure up. He did have the spiritual need to apply his faith (he was a deacon) to forgiveness and reconciliation issues with his father, who had physically abused him.

Getting well physically or emotionally can be a long and complicated process sometimes. However, it always starts with honesty about your situation, openness to doing something different, and a willingness to listen to what that looks like in a treatment plan. In the book *Finding Hope in a Dark Place: Facing Loneliness, Depression, and Anxiety with the Power of Grace*, an African American man and his therapist have done a wonderful job of describing what that process looks like from a very personal point of view.[6]

Power to the Patient: Control What You Can Control

Men often feel paralyzed by a sense of hopelessness about getting well, physically or emotionally, like the man by the pool of Bethesda (John 5:1–9). There was no one to help him, so he assumed he would never get well. We assume that medical care may work for others who are rich or connected or the right skin color—but not me. Good healthcare is just not a possibility with this mindset. To that attitude, I challenge the reader to control what you can control. In other words, change your attitude. Do you want to get well or not? Then, focus on what you can do and not what others may or may not do in your healthcare world. "Take up your bed and walk" by controlling or at least influencing the things that you can control or influence. What does this look like? The following are a few suggestions about things you can control or at least influence—because they depend on you and no one else.

Preparation: Maximize your time with your healthcare provider by writing out a timeline of your current symptoms and previous history of medical problems and treatments. Have a list of your current medications and allergies available. Please document your family history of medical problems. Bring any previous lab results, results of procedures, or radiology studies. Focus on the top three things you want to discuss, as there may not be time for more.

Nervousness: Focus on your preparation and the top three

agenda items you want to discuss. Do *not* go alone. Have someone take notes or record the instructions on your phone. Have a notebook for recording notes from the appointments. Relax by taking a few deep, slow breaths as you wait and meditate on a Scripture or song. Pray as you put on that piece of a gown into which you will probably change.

Relationship development: Make it hard for your doctor to ignore you. Introduce yourself and tell something about yourself or your family. Look for an icebreaker—something that you have in common. If you research your doctor, you may find something about him or her to "break the ice." My cousin found that his doctor was trained at a school near our grandfather's house. He shared that geographical tidbit with her, and they immediately had a "connection." Share something about how your health affects your work or a hobby. You can control whether you become a diagnosis, a demographic, or a real person with relationships, dreams, and a life.

Active participation: Your doctor needs you and your family's involvement in your care. Your active participation will convey to your doctor the expectation of accountability. Expect to get help and do not act like a passive victim. Become an expert on your diagnosis by asking questions and reading reliable sources. Ask your doctor or nurse for suggestions about things to read or websites to visit for reliable information. Some practices will have reading lists on their website. If hospitalized, you must have visitors. Patients who have family visitors are treated better by the nursing staff. Please be kind to the nursing and administrative staff. I know the name of the grandson of the person who makes return appointments at my doctor's office. I ask about him every appointment, and "grandma" always finds me an appointment time I like. I brought donuts to the nursing staff every Wednesday while undergoing cancer radiation treatment. They were a bit sad to see me get better and "ring the bell." They were getting spoiled by the donuts.

Emphasize the basics: There are a few questions that every patient should have answered about their treatment. If your healthcare team refuses to answer these basic questions, consider changing your care provider.

- What is my diagnosis and prognosis?
- What are my options for treatment?
- Why are you recommending this treatment option over the other options?
- What are the common side effects of this treatment?
- Are there long-term safety concerns with this treatment?
- How long will I need this treatment?
- Will there be a need for periodic bloodwork to monitor this treatment?
- What are the lifestyle changes that will help the treatment succeed?
- Will this new medication interact well with the medications already in place?
- Are there ways to reduce the cost of this treatment if it is expensive?

Mercy and grace: Please be patient with your healthcare providers. They are people who have good days and bad days, like all of us. They may be running late because someone was sicker than expected and took far more time than scheduled. A family member may have called about an urgent situation about a patient who was at home. An abnormal lab may have come in that required immediate contact and intervention with a patient at home. The doctor may have literally been arguing with an insurance company about covering a medication or procedure that a patient really needed. He or she may be trying to get samples of an expensive medication from a pharmaceutical representative for patients who cannot afford their prescriptions. Then the doctor may have argued with a spouse or child or had to deal with all the usual stressors we all experience. A kind word and expression of understanding will go much further in relationship development than an angry word toward a doctor or staff member. Remember who you are ultimately representing—Jesus Christ.

Motivation: Taking care of ourselves requires discipline, time, and investment. What will be your motivation to do this? I suggest one of the "four Fs." Family—do you want to be around as long as possible? My grandkids are my motivation. Finances—do you want to spend all your money on health problems that could have been prevented? Future—Are there things you dreamed of doing that you want to be well enough to enjoy? Faith—Are there ministry opportunities you want to be healthy enough to participate in? For some men, having an accountability group or person you share this motivation with can be priceless.

Your toolbox: To fully participate in your care and become an expert in your diagnosis, some tools may be useful:

- All households should have a blood pressure cuff (arm preferred over wrist). Ask a nurse or someone from your church's health ministry show you how to use it.
- Sign up for access to your patient portal so you can communicate securely with your doctor.
- Develop a good relationship with your pharmacist, who can educate you about the proper use of medications and drug interactions.
- Become skilled in using healthcare apps (like iPhone Health), smart watches (to monitor sleep, pulse, activity level), and the Kardia mobile app for portable EKGs.
- A thermometer and weight scale are basic tools.
- A blood glucose finger monitor is useful for blood sugar checks.
- Digital resources from the Mayo Clinic or John Hopkins Medical Center are reliable places to gain information as you become an expert on your diagnosis.

Healing community: Have someone that you discuss your healthcare challenges with. Ask for prayer and pray for others. If at all possible, do not suffer with illness alone. Be a role model for talking about your feelings and discussing your process for getting help. One of my doctor colleagues encourages his patients to make a health presentation at family reunions. Research has shown that relationships are a main driver of happiness in life. Please invest in your health by involving healthcare relationships in your journey through life.

Conclusion: Nothing Changes between Us

In healthcare, we often talk about the partnership between patient and doctor or provider as a critical aspect for success. We have discussed how to think about your role as a patient in this partnership. I also encourage you to invite God into this treatment partnership. The ultimate Physician wants to be with us as we go through life's journey—including potential seasons of illness. I was diagnosed with cancer several years ago and will remember that day forever. I arrived at the doctor's office to get the results of the biopsy. I went alone because I knew it would be normal, and I did not want to waste my wife's time. I turned off the ignition and was about to step out of the car to enter the office when a quiet voice said, "You are not ready. Pray." I was quiet for a moment and then prayed, "No matter what this doctor says to me, nothing changes between You and me, Lord." After that confident prayer, I exited the car, confident that good news was coming.

An hour later, I staggered out of the doctor's office and walked to my car in horror. I was numb and confused at the same time. *This was not supposed to happen to me. I am a doctor. This happens to my patients, not me.* I sat behind the wheel of my car and reached for the ignition, my thoughts racing as to how I would tell my family that I had a life-threatening illness. That quiet voice again told me, Stop, pause, and pray. The Lord reminded me: As you said, nothing changes between you and Me. We will do this together. And He and I did. By the way, something did change. I learned to get up every morning and thank God for another day I had formerly taken for granted. I learned to look for His blessing in little things—like getting a prime parking space at radiation therapy. I learned to pray a prayer of gratitude every morning before doing anything else.

Like Job, my experience did not quickly change as I had a complicated treatment experience, and the cancer did not easily go away. However, I changed. I learned a tangible sense of the God who loves me through everything, especially the difficult and hard times. That's real life. That's real healthcare; walking through the promised difficulties of life while knowing that God cares, will not leave us, and will help us learn how to be an "expert" on our own health.

NOTES

1. "Cleveland Clinic Survey: Men Will Do Almost Anything to Avoid Going to the Doctor," Cleveland Clinic, September 4, 2019, https://newsroom.clevelandclinic.org/2019/09/04/cleveland-clinic-survey-men-will-do-almost-anything-to-avoid-going-to-the-doctor.

2. "Summary Health Statistics: National Health Interview Survey, 2014," National Center for Health Statistics.

3. Damon Tweedy, *Black Man in a White Coat: A Doctor's Reflection on Race and Medicine* (New York: Picador, 2015).

4. Elizabeth Nix, "Tuskegee Experiment: The Infamous Syphilis Study," History.com, June 13, 2023, https://www.history.com/news/the-infamous-40-year-tuskegee-study.

5. Diane Langberg, *Suffering and the Heart of God: How Trauma Destroys and Christ Restores* (Greensboro, NC: New Growth Press, 2015).

6. Clarence Schuler and Monique S. Gadson, *Finding Hope in a Dark Place: Facing Loneliness, Depression, and Anxiety with the Power of Grace* (Bellingham, WA: Kirkdale Press, 2022).

PART 2

MENTORING AND GUIDING THE NEXT GENERATION

8

Passage

Navigate Christ-Centered Covert Connections on Campus

KEVIN L. JONES, PHD

Brothers and sisters, I do not consider myself yet to
have taken hold of it. But one thing I do: Forgetting
what is behind and straining toward what is ahead,
I press on toward the goal to win the prize for which
God has called me heavenward in Christ Jesus.

Philippians 3:13–14

And I will ask the Father, and he will give you another
advocate to help you and be with you forever—the
Spirit of truth. The world cannot accept him, because
it neither sees him nor knows him. But you know
him, for he lives with you and will be in you.

John 14:16–17

Introduction

As many institutions of higher learning sustain an environment
that embodies a hostile and apathetic place for Black male students, fulfilling the dream of earning a college degree is still a
challenge for Black men.[1] Universities in America are stained with
a tradition of systemic oppression and exclusion that still have
lasting effects on students of color. In some schools, racial and
ethnic groups have been denied access, and, specifically, women

of color who do attend have been deliberately excluded.[2] These systemic assaults on the advancement of racial and ethnic groups from the past remain and have impacted enrollment of students of color for attendance in the nation's colleges and universities. Crystal Chambers and Loni Crumb state that the university space is designed to prepare students to succeed in a career, yet many Black men experience barriers they cannot explain.[3]

The road to challenging deep-seated ideologies that preserve racial inequities within educational institutions is obscure. Offering a safe and supportive environment conducive to the success of all students should be paramount at every educational institution. These environments hold our future and should treat students as precious cargo.[4] These environments can be developed through relationships, and Black men must cultivate "academic sneaky links" across campus.

Academic covert connections provide opportunities for Christian students to be their authentic selves where confidentiality is a priority. Academic covert connections are people who provide safe passage through a learning experience where Christian students can flourish in their educational achievements and social maturity. These Christ-centered opportunities aim to provide a physical and/or virtual environment for students to have candid and open conversations about Christ as well as obstacles they face and to navigate barriers on and off campus.

This chapter unpacks how a Christian Black man maximized his learning experiences in higher education to prepare for life. Exploring the lived experiences of a Black man in college can lead to understanding how to identify academic covert links on campus, the triumphs associated with his experience, and how institutions can better serve Black male students. Prayerfully, this will increase our understanding of how intentionally and aggressively cultivating relationships with Christians working within university settings, along with individuals of authority, can increase the likelihood of an individual's success both on campus and in life after college.

Identifying My Academic Covert Connections

As a Black man, I learned early in life that I cannot experience life on my own. I had to deconstruct Proverbs 3:5–6 to create a palatable conceptualization in my life: "Trust in the LORD with all your heart and lean not on your own understanding; in all your ways submit to him, and he will make your paths straight." My mom shared with me that the first place I visited after being born was church. I cannot remember a time when I did not hear gospel music playing in my home and on family car rides. My relationship with Jesus is the vehicle of inspiration and motivation that drives my innermost being.

My personal narrative thus far illuminates the role of music (band, choir, etc.) in the life of a young African American male whose family experienced significant trauma and changes not of our own making. In a way, my educational journey saved me from the fate of others in my subgroup population at school. I became the first man in my family and extended family to receive an advanced degree from one of the top fifteen research-intensive universities in the United States.

Scholarships and Hope

When I reflect on my senior year of high school, I do not remember having an official plan for my future. However, from a very young age I knew that the opportunities for a young Black man in Augusta, Georgia, were limited. In fact, I still remember praying for the Lord to give me a way out—and soon. Thankfully, the Lord heard my prayers and provided "a ram in the bush" (Genesis 22:13). I will never forget the night there was an evening rehearsal with the Central Savannah River Area community band under the direction of Dr. John Bradley. I had the opportunity to meet Mr. Eddie B. Ellis. At that moment, I had the chance of a lifetime: to audition for the Morris Brown College (MBC) band.

I never would have known about this opportunity, but I had high school peers who were already attending MBC, and they encouraged Mr. Ellis to visit Augusta and recruit more band students. When I asked them about their college experience, they described it as a place where they could also envision me thriving. I was ecstatic. My high school was limited in our ability to audition for university bands. My high school band director would not allow university band directors to visit our high school and audition students.

To my surprise, after auditioning for Mr. Ellis that evening, I would receive a letter in the mail that detailed a scholarship for the MBC band program. Thankfully, God had a plan for me to attend MBC. After graduating from high school, I was so excited about attending college and being in the band and pursuing my degree in music education. A few days later, I visited MBC to tour the campus and learn more about the university. I soon learned that you must schedule appointments in advance to meet with people on campus during a visit. Providentially, I visited the band room and found all the band directors as well as the owner of the bus company used for band travel.

This is where I began to develop lifelong relationships with these directors, especially Mr. Ellis. That day, and throughout my college career, we would have several meaningful conversations about expectations and how to prepare for the band as well as school. I will always be in debt to Mr. Ellis. Not only did he cultivate my potential but he also helped mold me into the musician and educated Black man I am today. I do not believe he will ever fully understand how he saved my life, as I was an adolescent who had no plan and no money—though I did have hope and a prayer.

Hope for My Future

The end of my junior year proved to be the most important time at MBC. I met Dr. Willie E. Jackson, one of the advisers for music students planning to teach. He motivated me to be greater at life and challenged me to grow as a student. Throughout my last year in college, we had many conversations about music, my classes, and my overall goals. However, there was one significant conversation that changed my life's trajectory.

I was nearing the end of my degree program and Dr. Jackson asked what I planned to do once I finished school. Naturally, I was so proud that I had everything planned out. I shared how I wanted to go back to my hometown of Augusta, Georgia, and start teaching at one of the high schools. In fact, I shared excitedly that one of my former teachers had promised me a job once

I completed my degree. I just knew he would be a principal by now, as he had told me he would be by the time I graduated. I was confident of that.

When I shared this with Dr. Jackson, he immediately burst into laughter and said, "What? Call him; let's see if this is really true." At the time I did not understand why he was laughing; I felt that I had serious plans. So, I called up my former teacher with enthusiasm and told him I was getting ready to graduate soon, and that I was ready to fill whatever position he could give me, just as we had discussed.

To my shock, he told me he did not have a job for me. In fact, he could not hire me because he was still a teacher. He apologized for getting my hopes up. As I hung up the phone, I told Dr. Jackson, who did not seem surprised at all. In fact, he told me that he already knew what I would be doing once I graduated, and it had nothing to do with going back home. He calmly shared with me that I was not ready to teach. I did not have a strong grasp of the many pedagogical approaches, classroom management methods, or a foundation of music theory.

I thought, Okay . . . so if I'm not going back home to teach, what am I going to do? He told me that first I was going to get my master's degree, and then afterward I would immediately get my PhD. Initially, I struggled with this idea. Like everyone in my community I knew at the time, I was convinced I should go back to school much later in life after I had experienced teaching. But Dr. Jackson concluded that my fate was sealed. He promptly made a call to his former adviser, a well-known and very well-connected professor on a southeastern university campus.

I am eternally grateful to Dr. Jackson. I mentioned earlier that there are several misconceptions about Black boys entering higher education, one of them being that we are *alone*. But my experience with Dr. Jackson is a perfect example of someone supporting me and believing in my potential. He made sure that I never felt alone, that I had a sound plan for success, and—even if he was not physically present—made sure there was always someone else to pick up where he had left off.

It was a rough road to even arrive at this southeastern university.

All the while, Dr. Jackson made sure I had everything I needed. When I arrived at my new campus, he continued to support me from afar. He would call me once a week. He helped me get all my percussion equipment, and when times were extremely challenging for me, he even gave me $500. Just thinking back on how much he invested in my future is extremely humbling and mind-blowing! I am still a firm believer today that this Christian, godly man was sent by the Lord to give me perseverance for the long road ahead of me. His work was not in vain, and his efforts are still bearing much fruit.

The "Big Man on Campus"

My graduate school experience began with racism right in my face. A particular instructor felt I should not have been in his program. The first meeting with all the graduate and undergraduate students (instrument studio) consisted of him asking me to play in front of the group. He did not select any other students to perform. After class, I recognized what was happening, so I immediately searched for someone who looked like me.

I was relieved to find a professor who was an eminent expression of friendship and mentorship. I shared the incident in detail, and he said that what had happened was not right and that I was being mistreated. Until then, I did not know that this was a common situation in this part of the university. It was amazing to see how he was truly confused by how this continued to happen. In hindsight, based on his response, this must have been commonplace.

I remember sitting in this professor's office as he phoned "The Big Man on Campus." As this professor shared his frustration with the situation I was experiencing, he yelled, "Why does this keep happening?" I didn't hear the response, but at the end of that conversation, the professor assured me that "The Big Man on Campus" would solve my issue of mistreatment. My initial conversation with him brought comfort in a high-tension environment. He treated me with dignity as a human and contacted another professor on my behalf to ask if he would be willing to work with me.

Unbeknownst to me, "The Big Man on Campus" would link

me up with one of the best percussionists in the world, Professor Leon Anderson. Professor Anderson was best known for performing around the world with several internationally known music artists. He was also the director of jazz studies.

I had experiences with people advocating for me and helping me throughout school, but they were limited to people who looked like me. "The Big Man on Campus" comforted me with his helpful words and actions—but I was surprised that he was an older *White* man with a long history at this southeastern university and an even longer history of being a man with power and influence. For a long time, I did not understand why someone like him would help me, a young Black person from Augusta whom he knew nothing about.

I will never forget the semester I took his class full of White students, with the exception of four Black guys. We were friends and always sat together in the front row of the classroom to make sure we did not miss any vital information. As the weeks went by, I guess the professor noticed that we always sat in the front row. He started calling us the "front five."

As time progressed, his relationship with us began to change. We had great discussions in class and after class. He told jokes and shared personal but impactful stories with us in class. It felt almost as if he was no longer teaching the class but talking directly to the five of us in a way that only we understood. The more interactions and conversations I had with "The Big Man on Campus," the more I learned that he was not just a man with influence; he was an advocate for the Black students at this southeastern university. In a short time, I grew to admire him and made a mental note that just because someone is White does not mean they are against me, or even a neutral bystander. Sometimes, you will meet others who do not look like you but understand the assignment at hand and are willing to advocate for you.

I will remember "The Big Man on Campus" in many different ways. and I truly appreciate him. I appreciate the fact that he picketed with Black people prior to the university adhering to the federal mandate to desegregate. I appreciate him using his power and authority as a catalyst to enroll more Black students into the institution. But mostly, I appreciate him for seeing others (like me) struggling with injustices and racism and doing everything in his power to help and assist, no matter the cost. Many people called him "god" on campus because he could literally do anything he wanted. I never referred to him in that way, but I firmly believe that God put him in my life to demonstrate advocacy and help me understand that mentors come in all shapes and colors and from all walks of life. Through him I learned that even when you have negative experiences where people say you do not belong or you are not supposed to be in a certain place, the Lord will bring someone you least expect to tell you that, yes, you *do* belong. In fact, this spot was created just for you.

Traveling with Harriet

My academic experience earning a master's degree created trauma regarding advanced degrees at predominantly and historically White universities. I waited several years to contemplate working toward a terminal degree. I frequently relived my experiences in which a professor worked to embarrass me in front of other students. In an attempt to move on, I found myself in an even more precarious environment—one that mirrored the landscape of the United States during the Underground Railroad in the South. It was an atmosphere laced with oppressive hidden agendas, racism, prejudiced ideologies, hegemony—and I could go on.

Thank God I had the opportunity to escape with the help of a twenty-first-century Harriet Tubman who was listening to the voice of the Lord! Throughout her career, she risked everything to bring scholars like me to freedom. In other words, her divine calling was to recruit, train, protect, and help Black students successfully complete their doctoral program. An advocate and warrior who navigated and won many battles in academia, throughout her career she led hundreds of Black people to academic glory and was responsible for helping over three hundred Black students to graduate in the record time of three years. To say I was excited to meet her and be mentored by her is an understatement.

I will never forget the moment I came into contact with "Harriet." At the time, this twenty-first-century version of hope was

Endowed Chair of Urban Education at Texas A&M University (TAMU). To many, she was the famous "Harriet." But initially, to me she was just Dr. Norvella Carter.[5]

One day as I walked into her office, she gave me a warm smile and asked me to have a seat. She told me how excited she was about my interest in the PhD program and that she would guide me through the application process for graduate school. Throughout our conversation, I also shared with her a little bit more about myself and my trauma with academia, vindictive professors, and how I would never allow myself to experience those encounters again. After much discussion, she uplifted me, affirmed me, and made it clear that if I listened to everything she said, I would soon arrive at the freedom I had been seeking for years. But first, I needed to complete my application.

The only problem was, when I learned about the program, the deadline for applications was literally three days away. My obvious concerns and question to Dr. Carter included whether I would be able to submit everything on time to gain admittance. Very calmly and confidently, Dr. Carter told me I would get in and to call a certain woman who worked at the university who would provide me with detailed instructions to follow for admittance into the TAMU system that day. Afterward, I was to return to Dr. Carter's office and tell her what happened. Her instructions sounded easy enough.

I immediately called and followed the script Dr. Carter gave me. However, when I spoke to the woman on campus, she told me the deadline had passed. I became confused. Why would she tell me the application period is closed when the deadline is three days away? So, I politely corrected her but before I could say anything else, she responded that she would not help me with anything because I was too late. As a matter of fact, she asserted that my *not* knowing the deadline demonstrated that I did not need or deserve to be in anyone's PhD program.

In that moment, my memory flashed back to professors who maliciously tried to ruin my future and slander my name. I became heated. After all, I promised myself I would never allow anyone to insult or disrespect me and cause me trauma when I had done nothing wrong. As a result, I lashed back at the woman on the other end of the phone to give her a piece of my mind. Thinking *I don't need her and will probably never meet her*, at that moment I decided to make sure she would never talk to me like that again.

Eating Humble Pie

I was so upset that I do not even remember walking back to Dr. Carter's office. It did not matter because she heard me talking on the phone in the hallway. Was I that loud? My eyes met Dr. Carter's piercing look as she told me, "Get in my office now!"

When I sat down, she told me she had heard me yelling on the phone and wanted to know exactly what was said. Now flustered even more, I told her everything about the woman and how she was rude, insulted me, and that I refused to allow anyone to speak to me with such disrespect.

Before I could say anything further, Dr. Carter told me to stop talking. The next few words she said to me would carry me through my doctoral program up until this day. In a very warm but firm tone, she told me that—despite what anyone says, no matter what—I could not lose my temper . . . ever. She went on to say that some people who seem to have minor jobs are always the most important people. She paused and then asked me whether I wanted my paperwork to be late or, worse, come up missing? As I recall, she continued: "That is what happens all the time when you mistreat people in charge of paperwork. You need her. You have to be kind to people and ask for help even if they are not kind to you, so you can get what you need. Remember, honey catches more flies than vinegar. Furthermore, honey can also make people remember your kindness and tell you information that you desperately need. Now, you will call back and apologize to that woman. Kindness, respect, and humility is the name of the game, Kevin, no matter what. Trust me, in the future there may come a time when they remember you treated them well at the lower level and reciprocate. If you kill them with kindness, you will always be victorious in the present and potentially the future."

So, in that moment, I had to eat humble pie, swallow my words, and apologize. When I called the woman back, the task proved to be very challenging, but Dr. Carter was right. Weeks later, on my first day of class, I was faced with the same woman I had told off months earlier. She welcomed me with a smile, never lost my paperwork and, in the future, helped me avoid threats that would have had a negative impact on my future as a doctoral student.

I will never forget all the tools and wisdom Dr. Carter taught me while I was in the PhD program. The story I just mentioned was only one highlight of her paving the way for my success. Now, years later, I am so blessed and grateful to be one of her many successors. As an assistant professor, my students do not call me "Harriet." However, I can proudly say I am boldly walking in her footsteps, teaching and advocating for my students so they, too, can navigate academia and reach the finish line to freedom.

Developing Your Links

Most Black men lack a significant number of family and friends who have been exposed to the higher education environment. As we know, the very existence of Black men on university campuses presents a threat to misconceptions of Black men in society. It is important that Black men employ the links available to be spiritually fit. Black men must find other Christians in their social sphere to help navigate campus life. These links may include professors, student-support staff, or Christian organizations or clubs. You must develop your academic sneaky links that inspire a Christlike love. These links should provide occasions for prayer, mentorship, and networking.

Conclusion

Navigating campus life is a crucial skill for Black men in higher education. Many institutions reinforce deficit-based narratives, marginalizing our students and limiting access to vital resources. We must develop strategic, covert approaches to seeking help that affirms our identity and aspirations. Cultivating relationships that deepen our faith and spiritual resilience—particularly a closer connection with Jesus—equips us to navigate these challenges with wisdom and strength, which prepares us for both academic success and the broader battles in the world.

NOTES

1. Terrell L. Strayhorn, "Measuring Race and Gender Differences in Undergraduate Students' Perceptions of Campus Climate and Intentions to Leave College: An Analysis in Black and White," *Journal of Student Affairs Research and Practice* 50, no. 2 (2013): 115–32, https://www.degruyter.com/document/doi/10.1515/jsarp-2013-0010/html.

2. Erin L. Castro, "They Sellin' Us a Dream They Not Preparin' Us For: College Readiness, Dysconscious Racism, and Policy Failure in One Rural Black High School," *The Urban Review* 53, no. 4 (2021): 617–40, https://link.springer.com/article/10.1007/s11256-020-00585-9. Ramon B. Goings and Qi Shi, "Black Male Degree Attainment: Do Expectations and Aspirations in High School Make a Difference?," *A Journal on Black Men* 6, no. 2 (2018): 1–20, https://muse.jhu.edu/article/706075.

3. Crystal R. Chambers and Loni Crumb, eds., *African American Rural Education: College Transitions and Postsecondary Experiences,* Advances in Race and Ethnicity in Education 7 (Leeds, England: Emerald Publishing, 2020).

4. Loni Crumb, Crystal R. Chambers, and Jessica Chittum, "#Black Boy Joy: The College Aspirations of Rural Black Male Students," *The Rural Educator* 42, no. 1 (2021): 1–19, https://thescholarship.ecu.edu/server/api/core/bitstreams/ba913262-b884-40e6-8896-11f4343d1b86/content.

5. Permission has been granted by the identified individuals to share the details of these personal interactions.

9

Relate

Choosing Role Models Wisely

TIM HERD, MSED, MA

> And let us consider how we may spur one another on
> toward love and good deeds, not giving up meeting together,
> as some are in the habit of doing, but encouraging one
> another—and all the more as you see the Day approaching.
>
> Hebrews 10:24–25

Introduction

Late nineteenth-century Irish playwright Oscar Wilde once re-marked that imitation is the sincerest form of flattery. Merriam-Webster's online dictionary defines a *role model* as "a person whose behavior in a particular role is imitated by others."[1]

I see two clear distinctions among the people I describe as such role models. The first group, *accessible* role models, consists of people we have direct contact with, such as family, friends, and mentors who model actions that inspire us in various areas. The second group, *aspiring* role models, consists of people that one has no direct contact with, such as celebrities like Michael Jordan or historical figures such as Dr. Martin Luther King Jr.

With new media such as TikTok and Instagram, there can sometimes appear to be an oversaturation of people to connect with, which can feel overwhelming. This chapter offers insights on ways to choose role models who convey the love of Christ

141

in a world that often feels inundated with negative images and ideas about being a man—especially a Black man. In the tradition of the Black church, I also share here my testimony and explain how developing a personal relationship with God has served as a guiding light in identifying my role models.

Growing Up in Detroit (Accessible Role Models)

As a young Black male on Detroit's east side for the first twelve years of my life, I looked up to Black people all around me. Growing up in a household with a mother who lovingly reared three boys and a father who served as both a probation officer and associate pastor, the ideas of faith and justice permeated our household. My parents were my first role models, and my father was and still is my ultimate role model on earth. Observing the loving ways my father treated my mother and vice versa left an indelible mark on the man that I am today and how I relate to women.

Other than my parents, my older brother served as my key role model; I wanted to be just like him. He would make people laugh and seemed to be popular. I admired him. I also admired aunts and uncles for different reasons, all of whom left a huge impact on me at a young age.

My grandfather was a professor at a community college, and I would often hear about how he was well-respected by his students and others in the community.

I had neighbors next door and across the street who cared for me, poured into me, and supported my endeavors. One next-door neighbor showed me bright smiles, and another watched out for my friends and me as we played in their backyard. The group of them served as accessible role models on this block in the East English Village section of Detroit.

I grew up not only feeling the love of my mother and father but also feeling love and seeing other Black people support one another. That is not to say that I did not have my own share of obstacles, but I had role models, starting with my father, who would show me the right way to go about doing things.

Outside of my neighborhood, accessible role models existed

within my church community. I noticed early on that they were kind and welcomed people into the church every Sunday with warmth and a positive faith message. Though I did not understand all of the preached messages at that point in my young life, I did understand and recognize the love that people conveyed to one another.

Sports also had a significant impact on me. My father placed a ball in my hand when I was a child and involved me in basketball. At the age of six, I was playing organized basketball through the Cannon League. There I began to develop role models within the sport—people whom I admired, including LeBron James. While LeBron was an inspiring role model for me, I felt more inspired by the people I had the most access to, such as some of my coaches. Growing up, a plethora of accessible role models in my family and beyond offered many blueprints to begin shaping my behavior.

Grosse Pointe Woods Aspiring Role Models

During adolescence, when I moved to Grosse Pointe Woods in January 2008, the role models that I had previously been connected with shifted tremendously. We were now in a completely new environment, albeit only three miles away. There was a significant difference that I observed when I moved to Grosse Pointe Woods, the starkest being that the neighborhood changed from majority Black to majority White. In fact, my family was the only Black family on the block in my new neighborhood, and I did not see many folks that looked like me. In part due to culture shock and the challenging experiences I had adjusting to being one of few Black students in my classes, I began to look elsewhere for role models. For example, while my parents were already my first role models in life, I began to lean more into aspirational role models I thought would help me navigate this new terrain.

Role Models outside of the Family

I found one new role model in my White fifth-grade teacher, Mrs. Kellogg. She showed me a lot of love and made me feel welcome in my new environment. As one of the first White people I interacted with frequently after moving to Grosse Pointe Woods, her kindness was invaluable. While I had grown up around some White people in my church, my interactions had often been limited outside of that space.

Some of the first aspirational role models that I began to model myself after included Dr. Martin Luther King and President Barack Obama, who was elected during the first year of my time in Grosse Pointe Woods. These two men of historical precedent served as my aspirational role models because I noticed how they were Black men able to overcome substantial difficulties to gain prominent positions that had an impact on millions of people of diverse ethnicities. I also observed how they were able to navigate Black, White, and other places and spaces. That was important to me.

Outside of my father who was my accessible mentor, I did not see other Black men in my immediate environment whom I wanted to model some of my behavior after. I looked at Will Smith in *The Fresh Prince of Bel Air*. I saw him as a young, fly guy to model some of my humor and fashion after as he appeared to be popular and also funny with all types of people.

As I began to get more involved in sports, I even began to model my basketball game after other aspirational role models such as Tracy McGrady and LeBron James. I was also inspired by the brashness of Muhammad Ali and the unfettered determination of Malcolm X, who inspired me to continue to lean into my Blackness in White spaces where I would frequently experience microaggressions and racism.

It was during this time, especially between twelve and fifteen years old, that I began to feel like God was testing me and developing my faith. While I knew God was real because of my parents telling me so and by demonstrating their faith in the ways they lived, I did not feel close to Him. Much of this frustration came from the fact that I did not want to live in Grosse Pointe any longer and was experiencing some difficulties associated with adolescence. If God loved me, why would I experience the anger and frustration that I had developed living in this city?

Making the transition from a loving community to a community that felt insular, and isolating was a difficult adjustment, especially at that age. This frustration caused me to look even more inward, and the only role models I had now begun to trust were my father and some of the aspirational role models I previously mentioned. That is, until my sophomore year of high school when I met one of the assistant track coaches, Diego Oquendo, who happened to be a younger Black man and former Michigan State University football player from Staten Island, New York. Outside of my father, Coach Oquendo became an accessible role model who would show me through his workouts how to attack a drill and other lessons about hard work and finishing strong. His consistency, the way he appeared to genuinely care about me, and the affirmations that he shared reminded me of characteristics I wanted to continue to build within myself.

Michigan State University Accessible and Aspiring Role Models

When I arrived at Michigan State University (MSU) as an eighteen-year-old undergraduate student in August 2015, I was bright-eyed and excited to be in a new place where there were more folks of color. For the previous seven years, I had lived in a majority White suburb, where Black people were few in comparison. My undergraduate studies at MSU provided an opportunity to be around more Black people—and experience a feeling that I had missed since moving out of Detroit.

I completed a one-month-long summer bridge program for incoming students through the Urban Educator Cohort Program. During this time, I was surrounded by Black faculty and staff, who served as accessible role models for me, including Drs. Sonya Gunnings-Moton, Marini Lee, Terry Flennaugh, and Dorinda Carter-Andrews. Dr. Flennaugh was the first Black professor I had seen outside of my family, and he was somebody I viewed early on as a role model. Dr. Gunnings-Moton was a role model to me because she was the first Black associate dean that I had seen, and she was an associate dean at one of the top colleges of primary and secondary education in the country. Dr. Marini Lee poured into me early and showed me that I could be a scholar, and Dr. Dorinda Carter-Andrews inspired me as I observed her leadership on campus in various capacities.

In my first year navigating MSU, I was hit with a range of feelings and emotions. I was outside of my parent's home, surrounded by people from all walks of life on a campus that consisted of fifty thousand students. They say that college is a time of exploration and growth, and while I continued to grow, I also wanted to surround myself with people who reminded me of home. Fortunately for me, I was blessed to have role models such as those listed above who reminded me of my parents and further inspired me that I was exactly where I needed to be at that point within my life. It was also during this time that I began to develop a personal relationship with God, which became the most important component of who I am today. Through this relationship, I was able to begin reworking a lot of the inner tensions and anger I held and use this energy in other areas outside of just sports. I exerted my energy in positive ways, such as joining different student organizations and meeting people I would now consider mentors, which I define closely as an accessible role model. I was blessed to participate in programs such as the Summer Research Opportunity Program, where I met other like-minded peers and prominent faculty and staff, who I would also consider accessible role models. Being around this group of people inspired a significant change in my life—I decided to develop a mentoring organization called Rising Black Men.

Rising Black Men

Rising Black Men serves as a pipeline of support for Black men from MSU to the Greater Lansing community. It is a space in which we aim to build and uplift Black men through mentorship and additional resources. During my first two years of college, I had begun to develop and deepen my personal relationship with God, and this played a significant role in the work that I began to do within this mentorship program. The biggest component for me was being able to take some of the characteristics that I have acquired from role models like my father and apply them in a way that felt comfortable and fitting to me. By doing this, I was able to develop genuine relationships with all types of Black men and communities while leading with love.

Man to Man

Having been blessed with amazing mentors and role models who continued to enter my life during my time at MSU, such as Dr. Chezare Warren and Dr. Lee June, I wanted to make sure I was paying it forward. This meant sharing the resources and information with other young Black men that accessible role models provided to me as I navigated MSU. Through Rising Black Men, we went to different schools and community organizations such as the Turning Point of Lansing, where we talked to young men and shared our stories of how we arrived at MSU. This was empowering because young Black men at MSU who were still finding their footing were able to discuss their trajectory with younger K–12 Black boys and detail how they made it all the way to MSU. It was mutually empowering because it affirmed to MSU students that they had a voice and value, which could sometimes be difficult to see in a university with such a large student population. Further, it was empowering for the young Black boys to whom we were speaking because they were encouraged and able to visualize themselves in the space by seeing others who looked like themselves there. This was important because it showed that we could be role models early in our lives and did not have to wait until we achieved a lifetime goal. We could be role models for others at eighteen just by taking care of our business.

Within the Rising Black Men program, we had biweekly learning objectives. I would invite accessible role models to share their career trajectory and some of the work they had accomplished. These role models included successful businesspeople, internationally renowned motivational speakers, and community organizers and leaders. The learning objective meetings lasted an hour and a half, and people from all across the country engaged with us because they knew we were spreading positivity and love. One of my biggest insights and continued thoughts is the belief that exposure is expansion. We do not know what we do not know. My job as the founder of this organization was to bring people who had successful lives to share and inspire young Black men who were continuing to find their footing and community on campus.

After our first year of the program, Rising Black Men was honored as the MSU Student Organization of the Year. However, more important than any awards or acknowledgment was the fact that we were able to create a space where young Black men in the organization had real-time accessible role models. These role models frequently joined our bi-weekly meetings as we achieved our learning objectives. Experiences gained from developing this mentoring organization have been extremely important both personally and professionally.

Strategies for Success in Choosing Role Models

As we choose our role models, it is important to think about where we are currently while also having a vision for where we want to be, both long-term and short-term. This can be as simple as writing out characteristics that we currently have and then taking time to find people who have the characteristics we want to develop. While social media can sometimes seem overwhelming, it can also be extremely beneficial if used intentionally to grow our connections and network. For example, a quick Google search of "young Black men in leadership" can lead to different websites that have information on Black men in leadership positions across various fields. There may be a short biographical sketch and/or contact information of this individual, and just reaching out to them via email could go a long way. These aspirational role models could eventually turn into accessible role models. For me, I would email people who made an impression on me and discuss the institution I was attending and some of the work I was doing and inquire about the possibility of scheduling a call with them, seeking advice and an opportunity to converse. I continued this strategy as a PhD student at UCLA.

Another helpful strategy has been writing out a list of people who inspire me to be my best self, then researching that person(s) to learn more about them. This can help navigate the daily grind, which can occasionally feel very robotic and mundane. Role models should bring us feelings of excitement and encouragement to continue persisting, as reflected in their own lives. We all experience challenges, and that is why it is important to identify and surround ourselves with people who are navigating these difficulties in encouraging and positive ways.

If we are not comfortable sending out cold emails, another potential opportunity to find mentors could come in the form of volunteering. I have found some of the most joy-filled people engaging in volunteer work who had a strong passion for serving their communities and spreading love. Those in these volunteer positions could also potentially serve as role models, as we observe how they interact with and engage people.

Role models can make a profound impact in one's life, whether it be through a personal relationship or one that we observe on television. For example, there are Black television fathers such as Uncle Phil from *The Fresh Prince of Bel Air* or even Carl Winslow in *Family Matters* who served as fathers and a positive representation of Blackness to millions of people across the country. For others it could be Nelson Mandela and noticing the way he led his life up until his presidency and through his post-presidency years. As Jesus forewarns us in Matthew 7:15–20, be wary of those who may come in sheep's clothing. We ought to know people by the fruit they bear. We must continue to think about individuals we want to model ourselves after based on the fruit or work they have produced. This becomes an important component in wisely choosing a role model.

The biggest component of choosing our role models is wisdom, which comes from God (Proverbs 2:6). This wisdom is God-given and allows us to distinguish between things that may be good or bad, and we want to use this in choosing our mentors as well. One commonality that I notice among people that I have viewed as role models, both accessible and aspiring, is that they have a heart for service and helping others. Additionally, when asked about the reasoning behind their service-oriented heart, many times they would discuss their faith and personal relationship with God.

Current Journey in Life with Role Models

As I write this, I am nearing the end of my doctoral studies in higher education and organizational change at the University of California, Los Angeles (UCLA). After completing my bachelor's degree in elementary education at MSU in December 2019, I pursued and completed a master's degree in higher education at the University of Pennsylvania. After completing this degree in May 2021, I began my PhD studies at UCLA in September 2021, which is my final stop in this educational journey. This journey would not have been possible without the blessings of God and the people that He has surrounded me with, beginning initially with my parents and then also with other mentors and role models who have entered my life over time.

Conclusion

The rich educational and service experiences that I have been blessed to accumulate since attending MSU have been phenomenal and continue to inspire me to do the work I am doing. As someone who takes mentorship seriously, I know that I would not be in this space if it had not been for my accessible and aspiring role models, starting with my father. Role models can be an invaluable part of our lives as they can help uplift us and the work that we do and aim to do. Under this idea of spreading a kingdom message and continued love, having role models rooted within their faith is an essential component of this work.

NOTES

1. Merriam-Webster, "role model," accessed February 3, 2025, https://www.merriam-webster.com/dictionary/role%20model.

10

Reflect

Developing Spiritual Self-Defense Tactics

PATRICK L. STEARNS, MFA, PHD

> Start children off on the way they should go, and even
> when they are old they will not turn from it.
>
> Proverbs 22:6

Introduction

Christian author and educator Dr. Jawanza Kunjufu once said that you cannot teach someone you don't love. I have this *agape* love for all, but especially for our young Christian African American men.

I sometimes find it fun to reminisce by looking at YouTube videos related to the Cincinnati, Ohio, I grew up knowing and loving—videos of the Coney Island and Kings Island amusement parks, the 1970s Big Red Machine Cincinnati Reds, and my hometown of Glendale, Ohio, a small village about sixteen miles north of downtown. One day, I decided to look up an old 1978 Halloween special filmed in Glendale, a made-for-TV special in which I was an extra. Much to my surprise and excitement, I found the footage. I fast-forwarded to the scene in which I could see myself riding my bicycle around Glendale's Village Square, the main center of town containing the shops and restaurants. The businesses are built around a circular area with an elevated garden surrounding a beautiful fountain. There I was, a slim, trim fourteen-year-old riding my Schwinn ten-speed bike around the square with two other neighborhood kids.

I remember riding my bike around pretty fast because I wanted to be seen on TV as many times as possible! As I was viewing my younger, much slimmer self, I felt compelled to pause the video and zoom in on my image. As I looked at my likeness, I remembered the mistakes I made at that age. I made some serious mistakes, mainly of the reckless, life-threatening, or juvenile delinquent type. My friends and I used to hop slow-moving trains to hitch rides to a nearby mall and other similar, reckless behavior, such as climbing very tall trees at night and jumping onto nearby commercial buildings and people's houses! It is only by the Lord God's grace that we did not sustain serious injuries or die!

The Healing Process: Looking at Your Younger You

As I looked at that still image of my youth, I wished that the fifty-nine-year-old me (as of this writing) could go back in time and warn his fourteen-year-old self what *not* to do. Thankfully, the Lord spoke to me through an immensely powerful Christian song titled *Dear Younger Me* by the Christian band Mercy Me. The song includes the lead singer and song cowriter Bart Millard singing about the way in which he could've spoken a forewarning to his younger self. His older self speaks to his younger self about regrets; he wishes he could have forewarned his younger self to avoid poor choices. I, too, wished the same. However, through it all, we are both reminded that we had to make mistakes because we were children. Scripture says, "When I was a child, I talked like a child, I thought like a child, I reasoned like a child. When I became a man, I put the ways of childhood behind me" (1 Corinthians 13:11).

The apostle Paul reminds us that our mistakes and miscues can be learning experiences, and any sinful choices we repent of are washed away by the precious blood of our risen Savior. The song by Mercy Me reminds us to cut ourselves a break, move on from the past, and change from our youthful wrongdoings. In Scripture, Paul shares this important truth: "Brothers and sisters, I do not consider myself yet to have taken hold of it. But one thing I do:

Forgetting what is behind and straining toward what is ahead, I press on toward the goal to win the prize for which God has called me heavenward in Christ Jesus" (Philippians 3:13–14).

Christian men are compelled to follow biblical truths consistent with being a real man in the body of Christ and the kingdom of God. We have our manhood instruction manual. It is the Bible, reminding us that we are to make the right adjustments as men in the kingdom of God and body of Christ. We must follow the positive examples of other men of faith who have had to make spiritual adjustments to live a fulfilling life as a believer. I cannot rewind to that day in Glendale. However, I can strive to be the best adult example to boys that age, all the way up to the young adult male students I try to lead and teach as a university associate professor. I can try my best to use the biblical principles taught to me by my spiritual role models.

That set of lyrics from the song Mercy Me and that Scripture remind me of my saved biological father, who would always say, "Son, that's water over the dam." My saved mentors would always quote Dr. Reinhold Niebuhr's serenity prayer to me, reminding me that a young man maturing in Christ must engage in the acceptance of past events, seeing them as a learning experience, and changing for the better moving forward:

> God, grant me the serenity
> to accept the things I cannot change
> courage to change the things I can,
> and the wisdom to know the difference.

We are going to make mistakes, and we are going to go through rough patches, trials, and tribulations in our young lives. Yet, during all this, it is important for us to seek other men in the body of Christ who have been through what we are going through.

The Man Looks at His Childhood Mistakes, Learns, and Grows Spiritually

I'm thankful to say that, at fifty-nine years of age, I am still here, and I've never had a criminal record. At the age of seventeen, I rededicated my life to the Lord. I stopped hopping trains, stealing quarters from video arcade machines, and criminal trespassing. I quit while I was ahead, thanks to the Lord God! I am also thankful for many other things in which the Lord has blessed me, including brother and sister mentors in the body of Christ who have reminded me of the Lord's protection.

The more I have continued to work on my relationship with Him, those personal feelings of guilt and embarrassment have lessened. Through studying the Bible, I have learned that I am not condemned by God for past things I've done because I belong to Him (Romans 8:1). I am thankful that the Lord loves me unconditionally, and that He loves me so much that He took my sins, and all the guilt and shame associated with them and tossed them into the sea of forgetfulness (Micah 7:19).

The Costly Mistake of Believing That Ignorance Is Bliss

Many of us are missing the blessings that the Lord wants us to experience. This happens when we don't know who we really are in the body of Christ. Although we are believers, many of us don't understand the truth of what the Lord God says about us. I continue to notice that not as many men have been attending Bible study as I have hoped. This has been the case even with numerous efforts to remind the men of the importance of coming to Bible study and growing in the Lord and learning just what He says about us. Despite such pleas, many still will not come to church.

After posing my question about the lack of male attendance at church and Bible study, one of the brothers stated that many men when they do attend church, don't hear messages directed toward them. Instead, they hear the pastor direct their sermon topics toward women's issues. I believe that many men allow their pride and ego to keep them from really seeking the kind of relationship that God wants all of his children to have—the kind of relationship where we are in total submission to Him, seeking help in all areas of our lives.

Many have bought into the world's belief that a man is supposed to have a rough, invulnerable exterior, to be a so-called "self-made man" who can solve his most challenging problems on his own. I believe that many men who are believers still have not totally "bought into" the truth that Jesus's yoke is easy, that His burden is light (Matthew 11:30), or that He will answer as long as we knock at the door and ask Him (Luke 11:9–10). Another brother mentioned that we as men must go outside the walls of the church and get the word out to other men about the good news of Jesus, introducing Him to those who don't know Him and reintroducing prodigal sons who are saved but who have drifted away from His grace and mercy.

Taking Mentorship and Outreach to the Streets

Perhaps one answer to reaching men is taking more ministry to the streets. When my wife, Karen, and I still lived in Maryland, I received the opportunity to do this. At our church in Baltimore, the men's ministry engaged in outreach. We would go into the heart of the inner-city neighborhoods and speak to the men, encouraging them to accept Jesus Christ as their personal Lord and Savior if they had not already done so. I have fond memories of doing this, because I finally was not engaging in any excuses that would convince me not to witness in this way. Jesus said we are to go forth and teach all nations (Matthew 28:19). This is something that I'm trying to discipline myself to do on a regular basis.

Another area needing focus is how some men view the church and the pastor. In Dr. Tony Evans's *Kingdom Man* DVD series, he tells a story about a time when he ran into a man in the community who was at one time attending his church. However, the man stopped attending church without any explanation. When Dr. Evans asked the man why he stopped coming, he replied that he "didn't want any man telling him what to do, especially God."[1]

Another reason given for why men do not attend church is that their wife or girlfriend focuses too heavily on the pastor, who then may be seen as a rival. Others feel that since more Black women are in churches than Black men, the church is too women-centered. In reaching men, one needs to be aware of these dynamics and understand the situation, realizing that there are men who feel this way and who don't realize that total submission is the answer to victorious living.[2]

It's Time to Step Up Our Training

The more I live, the more I realize that men in the body of Christ must step up to the spiritual self-defense training discussed in my book.[3] I believe that the biggest challenge many of us must overcome is fretting over and regretting past mistakes. I cannot go back and forewarn my fourteen-year-old self of the mistakes I am going to commit. Yet, I can realize this powerful tool that fortifies my self-defense training—the Lord God knew every mistake I was going to make and every test I was going to have to endure. Once I came back to Him, my tests became testimonies of the Lord's wonderful, enduring grace, mercy, love, and favor.

You Must Let the Past Bury Its Dead

My improvement in putting the past behind me has everything to do with improving my spiritual self-defense. The Bible says that since I've accepted Christ, I have become a new creature; so new that all of the old things of my life have passed away, and I have been given a great, new beginning (2 Corinthians 5:17). I'm convinced that many of us are going about life the hard way, trying to figure out life on our own, falsely thinking we can manage the challenges by ourselves. Sooner or later, someone has to let us know that we are not going to know true success, peace, or real, victorious living until we are in a proper relationship with the Triune God—our Father in heaven, the Son (Jesus, whose shed blood saved us), and the Holy Spirit (the wonderful friend and counselor, whose comforting presence shows us what to do and not to do and reveals to us life's correct choices).

As a man working to positively influence other Christian men, I encourage you to try this growth-oriented exercise: Identify the things of your past that are upsetting to you. Write them down. Afterward, look up Scriptures in the Bible that address how to deal with past hurts. I have had mentors advise me to engage in this activity, and it has been a highly effective tool of my spiritual growth process.

Count Your Blessings and Celebrate Your Tests Becoming Testimonies

One Saturday morning, as I stood in my kitchen cracking eggs and adding spices for breakfast while my wife cooked the sausage, I realized how blessed I am. Despite the challenges of daily life, the fact that the Lord has blessed me (with a wonderful wife, breath in my body, a roof over my head, more than enough to eat, and wonderful opportunities for increase) resulted in an overwhelming spirit of gratitude and praise. I shared this immediately with my wife, who agreed with me.

If there's one key thing that you get from this chapter, it should be this: some of the most powerful weapons of spiritual self-defense we must master are those of gratitude and praise. We can always find something to be thankful for and to give praise for. Think about it, and you will find something. No matter what situation we're in, once we realize this and claim it, we will find that this will give Satan, our enemy, a nervous breakdown—and that's a good thing.

Here's how this powerful weapon of spiritual self-defense also helps me successfully put my past to rest. The powerful weapon of gratitude and praise reminds me that the Lord God allowed me to get through the rough times. I can then literally shout out all of the wonderful things for which I can be thankful and give praise. However, I must keep my mind on them as the apostle Paul wrote in Philippians 4:8. I will continually be on the path to mastering spiritual self-defense and having a fulfilling, productive life.

An Athletic Analogy

Shohei Ohtani is a Major League Baseball player for the Los Angeles Dodgers. He is one of the best hitters in baseball; many consider him the best. When I've watched him hit the ball, especially when he hits a home run, he engages in a specific technique. Right before he sees a pitch he wants to hit, he literally aligns his feet, legs, hips, and arms in such a way that he is stepping and seemingly leaning the force of his entire body into hitting the baseball. The result is that he is transferring his weight in such a way as to provide optimum power for a positive result.

His hitting style reminds me of world champion mixed martial artist (MMA) Edson Barboza. He is acknowledged by many as the hardest kicker in MMA. He will quickly pause to plant his feet and position and throw his hips, then his leg and foot, throwing an effective technique such as a spinning wheel kick, turning his body in a 360-degree motion. On January 10, 2012, he knocked out opponent Terry Etim with this kick, scoring a "walk-off knockout." After he threw the kick and it landed, he simply walked away, knowing that his opponent was not going to be able to continue. Because of his technique and timing, many experts consider it one of the greatest mixed martial artist knockouts of all time.

Like Shohei Ohtani's batting technique and Edson Barboza's kicking technique, we African American Christian men must master the spiritual self-defense technique of letting go of and learning from our past. This technique frees us to be the most effective men we can be, by focusing on God's kingdom work. The Bible makes it clear that once we are in Christ, once we have accepted Jesus as our personal Lord and Savior, we are new creatures, newly appointed men in the body of Christ. Our old way of doing things, that person we used to be and that we no longer are is dead. The former self has passed (2 Corinthians 5:17).

Conclusion

Here is a powerful realization. When we bury our past and move forward, the devil has a nervous breakdown. We increase the devil's nervous breakdown by not dwelling on our past, instead using our past as a living testimony to how the Lord delivered us from past troubles. By initiating this powerful move, we demonstrate the truth that what the devil meant for evil, God means for good (Genesis 50:19–20). My fifty-nine-year-old self has learned to move forward, letting the past bury the dead and choosing only to refer to the past as a living testimony of the Lord's deliverance, grace, and mercy! This is a powerful spiritual self-defense tactic because it is the Lord God showing me that once I choose to submit to His will and have the necessary faith to do so, I latch onto the power to let go of the past and move forward toward my God-given destiny. This results in freedom, joy, and access to the most powerful force in the universe—the power of our eternal, all-powerful, all-knowing, always-present Lord God who has already given us this power to resist and overcome Satan, our already-defeated enemy!

Through these techniques of spiritual self-defense, we have power that we previously didn't know we had. Let's access that power! Let's move on and fulfill our destiny as mighty men of the body of Christ!

NOTES

1. Tony Evans, *Kingdom Man: Bible Study Book with Video Access* (Brentwood, TN: Lifeway Press, 2015).

2. This topic has also been discussed by Jawanza Kunjufu. See Jawanza Kunjufu, *Adam! Where Are You: Why Most Black Men Don't Go to Church* (Chicago: African American Images, 1994).

3. Patrick L. Stearns, *The Christian Man's Guide to Spiritual Self-Defense: Understanding the Lord God's Communications about the Real Holy Warrior in You* (Eugene, OR: Wipf and Stock Publishers, 2020).

Man to Man

Mentor

Serve Others' Success

CHRISTOPHER C. MATHIS JR., MDIV, PHD

Train up a child in the way he should go: and
when he is old, he will not depart from it.

Proverbs 22:6 KJV

Introduction

This chapter discusses how to maximize the mentoring process of
young African American men for later success. How one is mentored
and trained often is a precursor to determining one's contribution
and success in society and one's community. In this chapter, I review
the definitions of *mentor* and *mentoring*, discuss why mentoring
is needed, outline the challenges of mentoring, and then share my
personal experiences being mentored while giving tribute to those
who mentored me.

Definitions

Mentor is a distinctive boy's name of Greek origin, meaning "wise,
trusted guide." According to Merriam-Webster's online dictionary,
mentor is a word most commonly used to describe someone of
great importance who helps counsel others in the hopes of helping
them on their way.[1] Mentoring is a mutual and reciprocal learning
relationship in which a mentor and mentee agree to a partnership.

They work collaboratively to achieve mutually defined goals that will develop a mentee's skills, abilities, knowledge, and thinking.

Mentoring involves an experienced individual (a mentor) educating, guiding, and counseling a less-experienced person (a protégé) to help them develop skills and realize dreams.

Lillian Eby et al.[2] and Kathy Kram[3] identify several attributes of mentoring:

1. Mentorships are distinct and formed by the interpersonal exchanges and interactions that define and shape the relationship between the parties involved.
2. Mentoring relationships are learning partnerships in which the parties involved acquire knowledge.
3. As a process, mentoring is defined by the support that a mentor provides to a protégé.
4. A mentoring relationship is reciprocal, yet the protégé's growth and development is the primary relationship goal.
5. Mentoring relationships are dynamic, with an increasing impact over time.

Mentors provide advice and feedback to their protégés regarding interpersonal skills and career plans, as well as advice about academic, personal, and professional aspects of their protégés' lives.[4] The "Guide to Mentoring Boys and Young Men of Color" (BYMOC) also shows the importance of mentoring.[5] For the launch of My Brother's Keeper (MBK) initiative in 2014, President Obama, in focusing on BYMOC, stated, "I'm reaching out to some of America's leading foundations and corporations on a new initiative to help more young people of color facing especially tough odds to stay on track and reach their full potential."[6] The press release accompanying the launch of the initiative indicated:

> Data shows that regardless of socio-economic background, boys and young men of color are disproportionately at risk throughout their journey from their youngest years to college and careers. For instance, large disparities remain in reading proficiency, with

86 percent of Black boys and 82 percent of Hispanic boys reading below proficiency levels by the fourth grade—compared to 58 percent of White boys reading below proficiency levels. Additionally, the disproportionate number of Black and Hispanic young men unemployed or involved in the criminal justice system alone is a scary drag on state budgets and undermines family and community stability. These young men are more than six times as likely to be victims of murder as their White peers and account for almost half of the country's murder victims each year.[7]

Noted in America's Promise Alliance, research suggested that relationships play a very important part in mentoring and the ability to thrive.[8] They state that BYMOC show "negative or stagnant trends relative to others in high school graduation, college enrollment and completion, and employment and earnings."[9] Additionally, Eric Mata noted that the Schott Foundation presented statistics for African American male high school seniors which show that nationally, fewer than 50 percent graduate from high school, and the top 10 percent of low-performing schools graduate barely over a quarter of African American men.[10]

Exacerbating these difficulties is the lack of official assurance to provide Black males with the necessary educational support services (e.g., mentoring).[11] Hence, these factors, in turn, affect the matriculation rates of Black males, who are not only the least likely to enroll in college but are also the most likely to drop out without earning a college degree. Mentors help participants cope with their perceptions and views about attainment and stifling impediments, which improve graduation and retention rates. Mentoring can result in a more constructive approach toward school, helping students perform better scholastically, have greater self-assurance, and optimistically express their emotional state.

Mentoring is needed for Black males before entrance into a secondary program. W. M. Parker and J. Scott contend that for Black male students to flourish in higher education, an association must be made between the student and the school personnel (i.e., faculty and staff) to establish a sincere and nurturing environment.[12] Although, as I noted in an earlier book chapter, the African proverb "It takes a village to raise a child" captures this overall challenge.[13] Traditionally, the African American community has been group-oriented; hence, older Black males principally need to heed the clarion call to "man up" and take on the challenge of assisting in mentoring young Black males in our homes, churches, and communities so they can be effective in their future roles. Effective mentoring requires training in a particular manner, custom, or tradition to ensure that a certain outcome or order is continued and maintained.

Moreover, the mentor must also ensure that parents and guardians are treated as allies rather than hindrances in the mentoring relationship and bonding process. As noted by Christopher Mathis, Fredrick Douglass, a Black male leader in the 1800s, stated in an August 4, 1857, speech during the West Indies Emancipation for Freedom, "Those who profess to favor freedom and yet deprecate agitation are men who want crops without plowing up the ground. They want rain without the thunder and lightning, or they want the ocean without the awful roar of its waters. This struggle may be both moral and physical, but it must be a struggle, for power concedes nothing without a demand. It never did, and it never will."[14]

In this context, the point of this quote is that it takes conscientiousness to accomplish life goals and objectives. Impacting young Black males is an important goal and will take a lot of labor. As a Black male who has been mentored for leadership, I aim to encourage other well-trained Black males to mentor younger males and prepare them for a successful future in life and leadership.

Critical Elements in Effectively Mentoring Black Males

A pedagogy of authentic care, concern, and investment (mentoring) is critical for the optimum development of Black males in the classroom. Peg Tyre asserted that daily interactions and nuances in the classroom can be one of the greatest factors contributing to the education debt. In other words, the author suggests that many of our students drop out of school and do not become productive members of society.[15]

Man to Man

Several other educational researchers corroborated this notion and added that Black males also tend to disengage and devalue school by the fourth grade, known as "the fourth-grade syndrome." It is clear that positive or negative interactions between students and teachers at this stage of life are critical ingredients for schools that successfully graduate high numbers of Black males.[16]

In the future, one can assert that meaningful mentoring is another salient factor in addressing the education debt. Inquiries to improve classroom dynamics between Black males and teachers is a critical element that will be further examined. Mentoring can come in various forms, although it must come from sincere care for the student, genuine concern for the student's well-being, and a considerable investment of time, energy, and love toward the student's personhood. A critical element of mentoring a Black male is taking the time to strategically prepare our young Black men to be leaders and engage the earth. We must also challenge our leaders to adjust their practice of mentorship by shifting their paradigm to fulfill their calling for the present age.

Serious-minded, older Black males must develop specific answers in exercising the principles of our past and what we have been taught in order to find plausible solutions for today and the future. One challenge of mentoring Black males is to constantly strive for innovative methods to remain relevant and current with related issues. Older, grounded Black males must continue to use sound doctrine to aid in mentoring young Black males before college.

Likewise, we must understand the dilemmas of young Black males living in a technological, social, and educational reality through access, alienation, and authority. For example, as older adults, we need to look into the reality of young men's lives in relation to access; we see they have access to more resources and modern technology than we could even fathom. The formation of a mentoring program for young Black males can supersede human capital by providing Black men with the abilities, apparatuses, and means required to be fruitful inhabitants. The flip side of not having a college degree is that career choices are exceedingly restricted.[17] Thus, it becomes imperative to consider how the struggle to deliver mentoring for young Black males can be associated with the plight of the greater social justice objectives for all young people and their communities.

Additionally, the head of the mentoring program has to ensure that mentors of Black males receive suitable preparation and training to face issues of race, culture, and gender. All schools should be equipped with activities and strategies needed to recruit mentors with appropriate skills and the cultural competency to mentor Black males to adulthood effectively.

The difficult part is that each mentoring program needs to recognize that all young Black males vary in their needs; therefore, the specific type of mentoring program must be tailored to the appropriate type of mentoring support needed. If mentoring programs are not sound, problems such as vocational readiness deficiency, lack of workplace diversity, and low graduation rates will continue to exist.

Jeffrey Duncan-Andrade indicated that the types of roles and relationships that athletic coaches have with Black and Brown male youth can greatly benefit educators and stakeholders observing the dynamics between these relationships.[18] He further asserts that the struggle many teachers experience with some of the most uncontrollable students in the classroom differs from the relationships that athletic coaches establish with them outside the classroom. Therefore, one can state that the level of investment, commitment, and overall concern that coaches demonstrate toward young men is instrumental in their early development and that teachers, unlike many coaches, are often oblivious or nonchalant about the social and cultural realism many young Black men encounter. John Buchan stated, "The task of leadership is not to put greatness into people, but to elicit it, for the greatness is already there."[19] Effective and carefully crafted mentoring of Black males is essential to their overall development in life and should not be taken lightly by teachers who seek to educate them.[20]

Case 1: My Early Personal Experience with Being Mentored

My early stage of mentoring started with my upbringing in rural Newberry, South Carolina, under the protection and guidance of my father. He was a high school dropout who finished the eleventh grade, then served in the Army for six years as a paratrooper in the 101 Airborne Division during the Korean conflict. My grandfather on my mother's side worked at the sawmill and only completed the sixth grade before taking on a full-time job there, where he stayed for over thirty-five years. Although my father continued to work odd jobs to secure a future for the family, he also served faithfully as a civil rights activist during the late 1960s and early 1970s, advocating for social justice and equal pay for himself and fellow colleagues.

Reflecting on my childhood, I can clearly see the commitment of both of these men to mentor me, affording me the opportunity to form my racial identity and pride and develop my self-worth while understanding the environment surrounding me ("dual consciousness," as stated by W. E. B. Du Bois).[21] Growing up in the birthplace of Bishop Henry McNeil Turner, one of the African Methodist Episcopal Church's four horsemen, helped me understand the reasoning for projecting a positive self-image and seeing Jesus as a Black person, for such imaging allowed me as a young person to embrace my African heritage and lineage. Another ingredient was a stable home environment. My neighborhood was a kid's paradise. Most parents had only one rule: be home before it got dark (when the streetlight came on). I remember having to complete my chores before being allowed to go to the park and play with my friends, which taught me to complete tasks before pleasure. This experience in my parents' home and with my grandfather gave me the courage and confidence to face life's challenges and make good decisions and choices.

Case 2: Mentoring within the Church

Another salient factor in my later mentoring stages was my grandmother's church, where she was a member for more than twenty-five years. I was a constant summer visitor there in Winston-Salem, North Carolina, where the famous gospel singer Shirley Caesar attended. Attending and participating in various ministries (i.e., Sunday School, church choir, Junior Deacon Board, vacation Bible school, Baptist Training Institute, and midweek and night services) helped shape and mold my development.

Growing up at my home church in Newberry, South Carolina, and my grandmother's church was a true blessing, although I did not consider it so during my youth. Being mentored assisted me in clarifying and supporting what Peter Paris called the traditions of African peoples connected to their underlying spirituality.[22]

I am mindful to include my African view of mentoring and my cultural experiences from intergenerational influences into my psyche today. The final factor of my mentoring was my sense of community. Everyone seemed to know me and my family in every aspect of my existence, from my community, church, school, and even my summer travel to my grandmother's home in Winston-Salem, North Carolina. For example, my church families would acknowledge me as my father's son or my grandmother's grandson and shield me from any harm or danger that might arise. Although they advised me about what was right and wrong, I often made mistakes that were not cataclysmic to me or my character. Such a distinction existed until my late twenties. My father and mother stood for justice and God in the community, as well as my grandmother, who lived out her commitment to assisting others in need within the community and throughout the church, which she faithfully served until her death in 1980. Paris reminds us that separation from our community will create a void for us as African Americans if we do not rediscover who we truly are.

African theology of mentoring and ethics are practical sciences in the service of the community's well-being, and both are intrinsically political. For example, one of the key events that assisted me before attending an HBCU was working at Rose's Department Store as a night clerk in the stock room while participating in the varsity football and track teams. I earned a reputation at work for being an honest and punctual employee.

To my surprise, a colleague working there two years before my hiring decided to frame me for a stolen pair of underwear from the store. As fate would have it, cameras on the backside of the building proved my innocence, as well as the fact that this behavior was out of character for me. However, I was very upset and taken aback by the person's betrayal. This event sealed my mentoring moment that we have to be careful who we allow into our inner circle.

Man to Man

A second key event of my mentoring before attending an HBCU was deciding earlier in my life to attend college after seeing my Uncle Ervin and cousin Elvira graduate from college. My mother's youngest brother was the only one to graduate from Voorhees College and my cousin graduated from the University of Greensboro, North Carolina, a predominantly White college. At the urging of my paternal grandmother, I sought funding opportunities to support my endeavors to attend college. Knowing my father and mother were not financially able to fund me through college, my grandmother taught me to save up my earnings from an early age until my eighteenth birthday to assist in funding my college education. Having the good fortune of winning an athletic track, football, choir, and academic scholarship to Johnson C. Smith University in Charlotte, North Carolina, sealed my fate concerning my education.

Case 3: Mentoring during Graduate Programs

After working at Humboldt State University in Acadia, California, from 1991 to 1993 as the first African American complex director for Resident Life, I had the privilege to work at Michigan State University (MSU) as an assistant complex director, providing oversight to some twelve resident assistants and twelve minority aides. I also served as a fellow for the Master Program in Student Personnel Administration and Higher Education. While working and attending the MSU master's program, it was a delight to meet Dr. Lee N. June, who served as the associate provost of academic student support services, and eventually also as the vice president of student affairs and services. Dr. June became one of my mentors.

As an employee and graduate student, I had the unique opportunity to get to know Dr. June as my mentor and role model, both academically and spiritually. Knowing he was from South Carolina, a graduate of Tuskegee University, and that he attended the same church where he was a Sunday school teacher allowed me to connect with him on a much broader level. Dr. June has been my mentor since 1993, throughout my master's and PhD programs at Michigan State University. He guided me through both programs and afforded me various opportunities to learn and observe by attending high-level meetings at the university as his student intern. To my wildest imagination, he was sent to assist me in my academic and spiritual growth process, to prepare me for future leadership development while maintaining a Christian doctrine related to discipleship and understanding myself as an Afrocentric Christian Black male. This type of mentoring interaction and discipleship has led me to consider Dr. June as my godfather and mentor for the past thirty years.

Being the first in my family to obtain a master's and doctoral degree from a Division I research university (Michigan State) by the age of thirty-four and working at a historically Black college and university (South Carolina State University as an 1890 Research Associate and Adjunct Faculty member within the College of Education, Humanities, and Social Sciences) has allowed me to continue the process of mentoring at-risk young Black males and females. We have a collective past and a common understanding concerning cultural relevance related to obtaining a superior education, while being nurtured to advocate for the community one has departed from as well as the community that one has become part of. At SC State, my path crossed with Dr. Oscar P. Butler Jr., who also graduated from MSU in the late 1970s, and we formed a bond that existed until his death in 2017. Under Dr. Butler's guidance, mentoring, and direction, I grew and developed a solid platform, which I continue to stand on today.

Conclusion

Being mentored has been an integral part of my life and my ability to achieve what I have thus far. I encourage all young African American men to seek out mentors. Each stage of life presents different needs, and the right mentor can help provide those needs.

NOTES

1. Merriam-Webster, "mentor," accessed February 3, 2025, https://www.merriam-webster.com/dictionary/mentor.

2. Lillian T. Eby, Jean E. Rhodes, and Tammy D. Allen, "Definition and Evolution of Mentoring," in *The Blackwell Handbook of Mentoring: A Multiple Perspectives Approach*, ed. Tammy D. Allen and Lillian T. Eby (Malden, MA: Blackwell Publishing, 2007).

3. Kathy E. Kram, "Phases of the Mentor Relationship," *The Academy of Management Journal* 26, no. 4 (1983): 608–25, https://www.jstor.org/stable/255910.

4. Belle Rose Ragins and Kathy E. Kram, *The Handbook of Mentoring at Work: Theory, Research, and Practice* (Thousand Oaks, CA: Sage Publications, Inc., 2007).

5. "Guide to Mentoring Boys and Young Men of Color" (Boston: National Mentoring Resource Center, 2016), https://www.mentoring.org/wp-content/uploads/2019/12/Guide-to-Mentoring-BYMOC.pdf.

6. "Fact Sheet: Opportunity for All: President Obama Launches My Brother's Keeper Initiative to Build Ladders of Opportunity for Boys and Young Men of Color," White House Office of the Press Secretary, February 27, 2014, https://obamawhitehouse.archives.gov/the-press-office/2014/02/27/fact-sheet-opportunity-all-president-obama-launches-my-brother-s-keeper-.

7. "Fact Sheet: Opportunity for All," White House Office of the Press Secretary.

8. Robert D. Putnam, *Our Kids: The American Dream in Crisis* (New York: Simon and Shuster, 2015); Bruce Western and Becky Pettit, "Incarceration and Social Inequality," *Daedalus* 139, no. 3 (2010): 8–19, https://doi.org/10.1162/DAED_a_00019.

9. "Guide to Mentoring Boys and Young Men of Color," 4.

10. Eric Mata, "Reason for Hope: Mentoring Programs Prove a Crucial Resource in Minority Male Student Success," *Diverse Issues in Higher Education* 27, no. 25 (2011): 16, https://eds-p-ebscohost-com.proxy2.cl.msu.edu/eds/pdfviewer/pdfviewer?vid=5&sid=32626922-f8c5-45a0-a92a-e4c0526fb4c7%40redis.

11. Maristela Zell, "I Am My Brother's Keeper: The Impact of a Brother2Brother Program on African-American Men in College," *Journal of African American Males in Education* 2, no. 2 (2011): 214–33.

12. W. M. Parker and J. Scott, "Creating an Inviting Atmosphere for College Students from Ethnic Minority Groups," *Journal of College Student Personnel* 26, no. 1 (1985): 82–84.

13. Christopher C. Mathis, "Evangelizing and Discipling Youth and College Students," in *Evangelism and Discipleship in African-American Churches*, ed. Lee N. June (Grand Rapids, MI: Zondervan, 1999).

14. Christopher C. Mathis, "Preparing Young Black Males for Future Leadership," in *African American Church Leadership: Principles for Effective Ministry and Community Leadership*, ed. Lee N. June and Christopher C. Mathis (Grand Rapids, MI: Kregel Academic & Professional, 2013), 141.

15. Peg Tyre, *The Trouble with Boys: A Surprising Report Card on Our Sons, Their Problems at School, and What Parents and Educators Must Do* (New York: Crown Publishers, 2008).

16. Jawanza Kunjufu, *Countering the Conspiracy to Destroy Black Boys*, rev. ed. (Chicago: African American Images, 2004); Jawanza Kunjufu, *Restoring the Village, Values, and Commitment: Solutions for the Black Family* (Chicago: African American Images, 1996).

17. Michael J. Cuyjet, "Helping African American Men Succeed in College," *New Directions for Student Services* 80 (1997): 5–96, Doi:10.1002/ss.8001.

18. Jeffrey M. R. Duncan-Andrade, *What a Coach Can Teach a Teacher: Lessons Urban Schools Can Learn from a Successful Sports Program* (New York: Peter Lang Inc., 2010).

19. John Buchan, *Men and Deeds* (London: Peter Davies, 1935), 24.

20. John Buchan, *Montrose and Leadership* (London: Oxford University Press, 1930).

21. W. E. B. Du Bois, *The Souls of Black Folk* (New York: Signet, 1965, originally published in 1903).

22. Peter J. Paris, *Virtues and Values: The African and African American Experience* (Philadelphia: Fortress Press, 2004).

Engage

Stepping Up during Your Child's K–12 Journey

AMOD FIELD, MAS

> And a servant of the Lord must not quarrel but be gentle
> to all, able to teach, patient, in humility correcting
> those who are in opposition, if God perhaps will grant
> them repentance, so that they may know the truth.
>
> 2 Timothy 2:24–25 NKJV

Introduction

As I reflect on my life, it amazes me where I am and what I have achieved thus far. I was blessed enough to have completed a run with the National Football League (NFL), Canadian Football League (CFL), and the Arena Football League (AFL)—goals I had from my middle-school years. I have worked primarily in and around my hometown of Passaic, New Jersey as a school administrator, including roles such as dean of students, assistant principal, and principal for over twenty years. I can testify that "The LORD watches over the foreigner and sustains the fatherless and the widow" (Psalm 146:9).

While the experience of people of color is not monolithic, we share many similar experiences in our households and schooling. Although my father was present at times and we had a loving family, he perpetuated a dysfunctional home because he could not find work that was meaningful to him. This led him to commit petty theft, for which he was incarcerated several times. Consequently, my family suffered due to severe poverty and received welfare even while my mother worked. My mother, who was dedicated to the family, carried the load of raising three boys and one girl in addition to supporting and nurturing many in the extended family, including our younger cousins and children in the neighborhood. Despite the circumstances, because of her Christian faith and active church attendance, she raised productive children who all earned bachelor's degrees, and my younger brother and I earned our master's degrees. I believe that the extreme economic strain on my mother due to my father's absence and lack of employment led to her early death at the age of forty-eight.

I provide this context as I recognize that race and economics continue to be a systemic and exasperating factor in the outcomes of the K–12 educational system, especially for Black boys and increasingly for Latinos. I continue to confront many of the challenges that I grew up with and those faced by minority communities across the country: poverty, crime, gangs, single-parent or broken homes, domestic violence, poor school systems, shortage of teachers, and the absence of enriching extracurricular programs. My daily focus remains to develop and implement strategies to improve the K–12 education experience primarily for students but also for parents, teachers, and the many other stakeholders in the community.

Consider the wisdom captured in 2 Timothy 2:15, 20–21, 24–26 (NKJV):

> Be diligent to present yourself approved to God, a worker who does not need to be ashamed, rightly dividing the word of truth. . . . But in a great house there are not only vessels of gold and silver, but also of wood and clay, some for honor and some for dishonor. Therefore if anyone cleanses himself from the latter, he will be a vessel for honor, sanctified and useful for the Master, prepared for every good work. . . . And a servant of the Lord must not

quarrel but be gentle to all, able to teach, patient, in humility correcting those who are in opposition, if God perhaps will grant them repentance, so that they may know the truth, and that they may come to their senses and escape the snare of the devil, having been taken captive by him to do his will.

Dominant culture narratives continue to use a "deficit" model for boys of color, attributed to individual efforts instead of focusing on the structural impact of systemic racism. In my role as a principal for students in grades K–12, I still observe the intersection of race, economics, and expectations in working with boys of color. Yet, significant events from my past influenced my life and contributed to where I am today. This chapter is intended to give you an understanding of the intersection between parenting, schooling, and mentoring—and, in particular, how men can seize meaningful opportunities to directly influence and support our boys of color.

Parenting: Maximizing Your Parental Relationship (*Not Friendship*)

Despite how rewarding parenting can be, it can also be intense, complicated, and difficult—relationally, economically, and emotionally. Whether you are married, single, or otherwise co-parenting, being a parent comes with many inherent rewards, risks, and challenges. As a school principal as well as a father, I have found that being genuinely engaged, not just "present," is key.

"The share of all opposite-sex U.S. marriages with a breadwinner husband has fallen steadily, from 85 percent in 1972 to 55 percent in 2022."[1] Long gone are the days when fatherhood is relegated to being the sole "provider" in the home. Where does this leave us, as men, today? How else can (or must) we contribute to our families, particularly our children?

According to Maslow's hierarchy of needs, which is an idea used in psychology to study how humans are motivated, it is commonly accepted that immediately beyond meeting one's physiological needs such as food, water, shelter, and clothing, one must realize a sense of "safety." This must be realized before an individual can have a sense of "belonging and love" and continue to develop "self-esteem" or confidence along with respect for others.[2] This is true for us as adults as well as for children at every age. As I appreciate and embrace the God-given role of spiritual leader, I also accept responsibility for providing care, concern, and even empathy for my loved ones. This philosophy surely extends to my professional life, particularly to my role as a school principal.

In my professional and personal experience, many fathers and sons tend to develop a connection around one or more sports— typically a sport previously played by the dad. This may or may not be true for you. Nonetheless, in my professional capacity, I cannot tell you how many times I have routinely encountered fathers of my students at their children's sporting events—but they are nowhere to be found at back-to-school night, in report card discussions, or discipline conferences. I frequently take the opportunity at sporting events to counsel fathers about the value of getting engaged in other ways. For example, when I talk with fathers who attend several home and away games during the season, they freely emphasize that they attend because it is something that they really enjoy doing. Despite their attendance at afternoon and evening games, which is admittedly about their enjoyment, these fathers acknowledge that they have not made the time to get involved with what is going on in their son's or daughter's academic endeavors.

Parenting is not a science. It's an art! As with the "art" of medicine, fatherhood is also a bit of trial and error. So, brothers, let's get straight to the point. We can and must self-correct. Our direct involvement in our child's or children's academic life is crucial. The same thought process used to decide whether we will attend our children's extracurricular sporting events is the approach we should take in deciding to get engaged in his or her academic journey. As men, if we are going to be involved at all, we must be fully involved.

To help dads gain an appreciation for the value of making this shift, I routinely share some hard facts. As a former, passionate NFL, CFL, and AFL player, I truly appreciate the level of focus and commitment needed to excel in sports. Also, there is absolutely nothing wrong with dreaming and planning to go professional in any sport. As parents, we must guide and support our children. However, an element of our guidance and support must entail crucial reality checks. In relation to football and basketball, certain statistics tell a powerful story that you, as a thoughtful, wise, and courageous leader to your children, must first embrace before considerately conveying it to your child. *Being present is not enough; you must be engaged.*

Consider the laws of probability. The chances of making it into the NFL, for example, are very low. Merely 1.6 percent of candidates are picked, and not all of them make it onto NFL rosters.[3] Other sources rate the odds of ultimate success as even less, with as little as a 0.2 percent shot for any player to make it all the way to the NFL.[4] With more than one million high school players and only about three hundred NFL openings each year, the odds are astronomical.[5] My recollection is that the career lifespan of a professional football player is about three years. To many, including myself, the NFL stands for "Not For Long."[6]

In my case, I recognized that professional football was a way out of poverty, not the end goal. So, during the off-seasons, I continued to take college courses in pursuit of my bachelor's degree. I also volunteered my time to shadow school administrators and superintendents since I was interested in working in the educational system in some capacity. I spent my time in the off-season developing my "fall back" plan. The same was true for my son, Da'mon, who had a short stint with the NFL.

Unlike me, Da'mon had earned his bachelor's degree prior to joining the NFL. So, while recovering from an injury and contemplating his next moves beyond football, Da'mon seized an opportunity to become an academic adviser at Arizona State University. As you can see, it is imperative that each of us develop an awareness and sincere interest and involvement in our son's or daughter's academic life—to help him or her take the necessary steps to focus on the long game in life, such as a career or meaningful employment.

The reality is that your child spends more time each day dealing with his or her academics than playing a sport. Some questions you should ask are: What is he or she currently learning? What type of educational programs is he aligned with? What does she find easy? What is it that he finds difficult? What type of higher education or work is he or she interested in? How can I assist her in getting help and finding a support system, even in a small way? Does he know that I value his education? Have I shared my expectations? What are my expectations? *Being present is not enough; you must be engaged.*

Schooling: Meaningful Strategies to Get Engaged with Your Children

As an adult man, I am sure that you can look back on missed opportunities in your schooling years. I often do. Understanding our child's hopes and dreams is not enough. We also need to understand the many ways institutions and individuals diminish the most basic educational opportunities for Black students to learn core subjects such as reading, writing, mathematics, and sciences. We can and must engage with school systems to ensure our children receive a fair and meaningful education that will propel them forward in life. Tyrone Howard refers to "structural intersectionality" whereby Black males experience "political, economic, representational, and institutional forms of discrimination, oppression, exploitation, and domination."[7]

We could spend a great deal of time discussing the differences in educational outcomes between Black males and their peers and how Black boys are disproportionately impacted through various structural means, such as insidious academic tracking, high suspension rates, underrepresentation in educational leadership positions, and the perpetuation of cultural ideologies such as Black intellectual inferiority and athletic superiority. Instead, we will only focus on two major issues which I know we can immediately help to address in support of our children: (1) discipline; and (2) absenteeism.

Early childhood research suggests that the criminalization of Black boys' behavior begins in early childhood with high levels of scrutiny of behavior and punishment more severe than their peers. While Black learners in early childhood represent 19 percent of the preschool population, 47 percent of the Black student population is suspended or expelled.[8] These children are under the age of eight. Sadly, access to education is often denied to boys of color through the criminalization of behavior. Despite the evidence that students of all races misbehave at similar rates, many educators subconsciously associate Black students with misbehavior. In controlled studies, teachers were more likely to recommend more severe discipline, label students "troublemakers," and anticipate greater future misbehavior from Black students than White students, despite the behavior being described in identical terms. Another study, utilizing eye-tracking software, found that teachers spent more time observing Black students when told to look for "challenging behavior."[9]

In line with these findings, one analysis of middle school disciplinary referrals found that White students were referred to the office significantly more frequently for more observable, objective offenses (e.g., smoking, vandalism), while Black students were referred more for behaviors requiring subjective judgment (e.g., disrespect, excessive noise).[10] The result is that by fourth grade, Black males attending large city schools were three times less likely to meet reading or mathematics grade-level expectations.

What does all this mean? How does this affect a child's educational experience? The impacts of these disparities are profound and far-reaching. Black and Latinx students are deprived of valuable instructional time at a disproportionate rate compared to their White peers. Worse still, disparities in school discipline contribute to disparities in referrals to the criminal justice system. Some studies suggest that in schools with high levels of suspensions, there is a likelihood that the student will be arrested or jailed as an adult.

If boys of color are not pushed out of school through discipline, life experiences can also cause high levels of absenteeism. Poor health, parents' nonstandard work schedules, low socioeconomic status, changes in adult household composition (e.g., adults moving into or out of the household), residential mobility, and extensive family responsibilities (e.g., children looking after siblings)—along with inadequate supports for students within the educational system (e.g., lack of adequate transportation, unsafe conditions, lack of medical services, harsh disciplinary measures, etc.)—are all associated with a greater likelihood of being absent, and particularly with being chronically absent.[11]

So, men, you absolutely must get engaged with your child and his or her school experience. Here's some guidance for effective engagement:

1. Review your child's progress reports and report cards: In case you cannot rely on your child to give you regular feedback on how things are going in school, you should feel free to email or call the teachers to find out how your child is doing in school. You can also arrange to meet in person at designated times, before, after, or during school hours. What is my child excelling in? What seem to be areas of possible deficiency? What assignments are missing? What concerns does the teacher have? On what grade level is my child reading or achieving in mathematics?

2. Talk with your child about his or her school experience. Ask your child whether he or she is having any difficulties with comprehending what the teacher is asking them to do. What are her favorite subjects? What are the classes he does not like, and why? What type of progress does he or she think they are making? What makes him proud? Get to know what makes your child tick.

3. Back-to-school nights: *Show up!* Be sure to read your child's progress report(s) in advance so that you go with an understanding of what is expected of your child and of you. Seize the opportunity to meet each of your child's teachers. This is also a great opportunity to show your support to your child. You should be able to confirm whether or not your son or daughter is passing their classes and get an understanding of what is required, considering the school year calendar.

4. If there are disciplinary and/or attendance issues, it is imperative that you have conversations with your child and

his or her teachers. There will always be two sides to the story. School security staff and custodians can also provide great insight as to happenings outside of the classroom.

5. Based on my extensive experience in handling disciplinary matters, most behavioral issues are tied to the child's lack of a sense of engagement in the classroom. While school administrators must deal with teachers to improve the general level of engagement in classrooms, your son or daughter's lack of engagement may be connected to their own disengagement—which can happen for various reasons.

6. Again, *get engaged!* Work hard to build a rapport slowly but surely with your child about positive and fun aspects of their lives so that you can also tap in to discuss the more challenging issues. From my own experience dealing with a challenging time during my son's middle school experience, he jokingly (but also seriously) reminded me that, "I didn't ask to be here." So, you must maintain your sense of responsibility as a parent even when the situation becomes uncomfortable. Should it be necessary, you should be encouraged to seek support for coping with any dysfunctional family dynamics or interpersonal challenges that hinder your productive relationship with your child.

Mentorship: Give Him the Keys to Your Unconditional Support

With so many potential barriers to the academic and social success of boys of color, I strongly recommend the added layer of a mentor to benefit and enrich their K–12 experience. Effective mentors can help boys of color become empowered to maximize their potential and develop holistically to persevere through the multifaceted layers of contemporary social-emotional adversities. Based on my own K–12 experience, I know that mentors can support the academic growth and educational outcomes of young men.

Martin Luther King Jr. wrote, "The function of education is to teach one to think intensively and to think critically. Intelligence plus character—that is the goal of true education." My brothers, if you believe this profound statement to be true, each of us must recognize the crucial need to get involved in helping overcome and eliminate the destructive challenges and tragedies affecting the education of our young boys. Do you understand their difficult reality? What are they facing on a day-to-day basis? How are their future and our legacy at risk when our boys of color are prevented from receiving a relevant, robust educational experience? As we Black men walk in the light, it is imperative that we seek to be like Christ and "let the little children come to me and do not hinder them, for to such belongs the kingdom of heaven" (Matthew 19:14 ESV).

We have a role to play in the lives of our boys of color regardless of our position—as uncles, fathers, or mentors. Boys need to be heard, supported, and shown that they are loved by their fathers. They need to be supported by teachers, administrators, custodians, and coaches. They need to be supported by faith leaders and performing arts leaders. Boys need to be nurtured and developed by men from infancy and not rushed into adulthood or the "man of the house" role before their time. Both formal mentorship, that is, an organized, consistent relationship between the mentor and his mentee, and informal mentorship, which is without consistency or organization, can be powerful. Research suggests that among boys of color who are consistently mentored well, 98 percent stay in school, 85 percent stay clear of drugs, and 98 percent avoid connections with gangs.

As a mentor myself, I know that mentors must understand the time commitment. Time is determined by the relationship and driven by the student's availability. As a mentor, you can demonstrate the importance of the relationship through your consistent commitment to that time. With humility, as men of faith, we must strive to have a strong ability to listen and guide others. Notably, mentors of boys of color must be ready to engage in mentorship through a racial lens, having a keen understanding of systemic barriers and, through the needs of the mentee, seeking to problem solve and build a network of support to meet the goals of the mentee.

There are three foundations that we must help our mentees

understand. Mentees must: (1) be able to understand the systemic racism structural barriers, (2) believe and be empowered to learn of their own internal fortitude to change the outcome, and (3) engage in behaviors that counter the inequities to maximize the holistic benefits. To meet the three foundational requirements, research suggests that the mentorship must consist of the following five practices:

1. Self-Identity Awareness and Empowerment
2. Social Engagement
3. Academic Achievement
4. Postsecondary Aspirations
5. Managing Day-to-Day Racist Trauma

Self-Identity Awareness and Empowerment: This is a process with the mentee to identify their strengths and opportunities for growth through the "asset" lens. Mentees must gain an understanding of the expectations given to them as a society while identifying their holistic strengths. Having mentees identify their multiple identities such as sibling, athlete, Christian, and other attributes expands their vision of themselves beyond the narrow confines given to them through school and other organizations. An important aspect of this work also includes group mentorship sessions, especially during this identity stage to help mentees understand they are not alone, to dialogue about barriers in demonstrating their strengths against a system that is in denial and build a collaborative team to engage in challenging the system while each mentee becomes stronger and more empowered.

Social Engagement: Beginning with a group of mentees, one of the vital components of mentorship is to help mentees actively engage in social situations beyond themselves and in service to others. 1 Peter 4:10–11 says, "Each of you should use whatever gift you have received to serve others, as faithful stewards of God's grace in its various forms." Romans 12:11 says, "Do not be slothful in zeal, be fervent in spirit, serve the Lord" (ESV). While mentees have an affinity group with each other and another affinity group organized by the school, the mentee needs to participate in other programs, such as community service, volunteering, tutoring, or mentoring Black youngsters in elementary schools. These opportunities build esteem for the mentee and help them continue to strengthen their identity and utilize their gifts while building relationships beyond the confines of their schools.

Academic Achievement: For many youths of color, managing time and organizing for academic success is a challenge. Often working day-to-day, students miss deadlines for assignments as they do not plan well. This is not unique to boys of color, but heavy criticism and harsher punishments are given for assignments being late, incomplete, or missing as the underlying assumption is that academics are not important for boys of color. The penalties multiply and often, before mid-term, boys of color have no way to catch up and succeed. A mentor can help not just with the organization of deadlines for each course but as a friendly accountability partner. Effective mentorship should help mentees build academic work ethic, grow their skills in self-efficacy and advocacy, and develop effective and consistent study habits.

Postsecondary Aspirations: Mentors can expand the limited worldview of boys of color beyond the confines of the region where they live and help mentees use their strengths to unearth postsecondary possibilities. A guidance counselor should play that role as well, but often with their caseloads, they just approve courses that a student must take. With a mentor and their network of colleagues, the use of school tools may unearth career aspirations and postsecondary options that are well beyond the imagination of the mentee. This would lead to powerful goal setting, course planning, and perhaps internships and work programs to ensure the boys of color are fully prepared to meet their academic goals while aspiring to their postsecondary options.

Managing Day-to-Day Racist Trauma: Helping a boy of color manage the day-to-day racist trauma may be the most powerful impact a mentor can have. Microaggressions are generated by implicit bias and represent the insults, put-downs, and invalidations that happen daily. Whether in a classroom, in an open space with peers, or with teachers, boys of color experience this multiple times per day, representing "death by a thousand paper cuts."[12] Microaggression occurs in three different ways. Micro-insults, which can be conveyed behaviorally or verbally, are meant to insult and demean boys of color and their heritage. These comments are based on stereotypes of men of color and may include the pathologizing of language, culture, and customs, or assumptions of intellectual inferiority as "second-class citizens." A microassault is an intentional act, either verbal or non-verbal, to hurt the target through name-calling, avoidant behavior, or discriminatory practices. Finally, microinvalidation is any action of communication that seeks to negate the experiences of boys of color, including their feelings or thoughts regarding that experience. Effective mentors must be willing to listen to these stories rather than dismissing them, or worse coaching them to "man up" when these stories are told. The role of the mentor is to guide and build boys of color who can respond with impact to diminish the repetition of these events.

Conclusion

Ecclesiastes 4:9–10 reminds us that "two are better than one, because they have a good reward for their toil. For if they fall, one will lift up his fellow. But woe to him who is alone when he falls and has not another to lift him up!" (ESV). I realized the powerful and positive consequences of these verses as I reflected on my decision years ago to no longer play in the AFL but instead to coach, allowing me to be more available for my son, who at that time was in middle school. As a result, I was able to have a more active role in his day-to-day activities such as checking up on him at school, picking him up from school, enlisting in after-school academic programs, and attending the parent-teacher conferences. In my role as a father and as his chief advocate and mentor, I was able to guide him through high school, create goals and transition plans, and be an accountability partner with him. Some fathers may not have the experiences I've had, nevertheless, with a powerful mentor, great things can be achieved.

In-tune parenting, quality education, and effective mentorship help boys of color know their strengths, navigate the systemic racist world, and create goals and plans to reach career heights that may not seem imaginable. It's a powerful combination that leaves a positive legacy for the student and the mentor and establishes counteractions that the student can take to advocate and walk in their own power. Mentors must demonstrate strong relationships between themselves and their mentees and follow the wisdom espoused in 1 Peter 5:3, ". . . not domineering over those in your charge, but being examples to the flock" (ESV). Men of color have a legacy to fulfill to ensure that by our example, leadership, mentorship, and commitment, boys of color are not ensnared in our systemic racist system but rise above and thrive in this complicated world. Finally, in the words of my pastor, Reverend Dr. David Jefferson Sr., Esq., of Metropolitan Baptist Church in Newark, New Jersey: "Education is and continues to be a passport for men. . . . Learn the Word, Love the Word, Live the Word."

NOTES

1. Katherine Schaeffer, "Key Facts about Dads in the U.S.," Pew Research Center, June 15, 2023, https://www.pewresearch.org/short-reads/2023/06/15/key-facts-about-dads-in-the-us/.

2. Maslow's hierarchy of needs is widely referenced in psychology and is originally attributed to Abraham Maslow.

3. Adam Robinson, "NCAA to NFL: How Many NCAA Football Players Make It to the NFL?," The Juice Online, July 18, 2022, https://sujuiceonline.com/2022/07/18/ncaa-to-nfl-how-many-ncaa-football-players-make-it-to-the-nfl/.

4. Aaron Shields, "The Odds of Making It to the NFL," Casino.org, May 4, 2021, https://www.casino.org/blog/the-odds-of-making-it-to-the-nfl/.

5. "Getting into the Game," NFL Football Operations, accessed February 3, 2025, https://operations.nfl.com/journey-to-the-nfl/the-next-generation-of-nfl-stars/getting-into-the-game/.

6. Robert W. Turner II, *Not for Long: The Life and Career of the NFL Athlete* (London: Oxford University Press, 2018).

7. Tyrone C. Howard, "Examining Black Male Identity through a Raced, Classed, and Gendered Lens: Critical Race Theory and the Intersectionality of the Black Male Experience," in Tyrone C. Howard and Rema Reynolds, *Handbook of Critical Race Theory in Education*, 1st ed. (New York: Routledge, 2013), 45.

8. Brian L. Wright, "Black Boys Matter: Cultivating Their Identity, Agency, and Voice," *Teaching Young Children* 12, no. 3 (2019): https://www.naeyc.org/resources/pubs/tyc/feb2019/black-boys-matter.

9. "An Anti-Bias Vision for the Next Generation," Youth Bias Task Force, October 2020, https://www.nj.gov/oag/dcr/downloads/2020-ybtf-report.pdf.

10. Paraphrased from Russell J. Skiba et al., "The Color of Discipline: Sources of Racial and Gender Disproportionality in School Punishment," *The Urban Review* 34, no. 4 (December 2002): 334.

11. Susan Thomas, "Future Ready Learning: Reimagining the Role of Technology in Education, 2016 National Education Technology Plan," Office of Educational Technology, US Department of Education, January 2016, https://eric.ed.gov/?id=ED571884.

12. Derald Wing Sue and Lisa Beth Spanierman, *Microaggressions in Everyday Life*, 2nd ed. (Hoboken, NJ: John Wiley and Sons, 2020).

PART 3

STRENGTHENING RELATIONSHIPS WITHIN FAMILIES

13

Hear

Attending to Young Black Males' Voices

LEE N. JUNE, CTS, MML, PHD

Fathers, do not exasperate your children; instead, bring
them up in the training and instruction of the Lord.

Ephesians 6:4

Introduction

On August 3, 2023, I conducted a focus group via Zoom with
six young Black men. They were residing in New Jersey and participating in a youth summer program.[1] When asked why they
were participants in the program and what they were getting out
of being a participant, one young man responded, "It is helping
me to be a better man and to not get angry."

The purpose of the focus group was to hear the young men's
voices regarding some contemporary issues and for them to share
what they would like us to hear. The interview lasted for approximately one hour. Each of the participants is given a pseudonym.
Below is a summary of their views.

The Participants[2]

The participants were M (age fifteen), K1 (age fifteen), R (age twenty-
two), Z (age fifteen), T (age twenty), and K2 (age fifteen). R and
T are college students and the other four are high school students.

Question: Do you believe in God? (Strongly Agree, Agree, Disagree, Strongly Disagree)

193

Their Response: Three individuals strongly agreed, one agreed, one disagreed, and one was neutral.

My Reflection: Their response shows that while all of them do not believe in God, they are open to the Christian message and what a Christian-oriented program can provide when conducted in a caring manner.

Question: When you hear the word *religion*, what comes to mind?
Their Response:
- Christian
- Jewish
- Worship
- Church
- Something that represents you
- Something that represents your culture
- Unity

My Reflection: There is more of a positive response to the word *religion* than is often given.

Question: When you hear the word *spiritual*, what comes to mind?
Their Response:
- Ghost
- Holy Spirit
- Christ
- God
- Holy water
- Heaven
- Hell

My Reflection: Generally, when this question is asked, there tends to be a more positive response to the word *spiritual* than the word *religion*.

Question: Would you describe yourself as a religious person? (Strongly Agree, Agree, Disagree, Strongly Disagree)
Their Response: Two agreed, two disagreed, and two were neutral.

My Reflection: This response is not surprising and is consistent with research findings. The word *religion* typically carries a negative connotation to many people.

Question: Would you describe yourself as a spiritual person? (Strongly Agree, Agree, Disagree, Strongly Disagree)
Their Response: All six agreed that they were spiritual.
My Reflection: This response is not surprising and is consistent with research findings. Individuals in general tend to have a more positive reaction to the word *spiritual*.

Question: What are your thoughts about the church?
Their Response:
- Holy
- Help
- Brings people together
- Relieves anger
- Anxiety
- A place that makes you feel like a family
- Home
- Helps you find God
- Brings you closer to Him (God)

My Reflection: In general, these young men have a positive view of the church. This is encouraging and something that the Christian community can build on in its outreach activities.

Question: Do you attend church services?
Their Response: Four said no and two said yes.
My Reflection: This is consistent with research regarding church attendance among young people and specifically among males.

Question: Do you pray?
Their Response: Five said yes and one said not often.
My Reflection: This is consistent with research.

Question: What are your career aspirations?
Their Response:

Go to college

Nurse

College

Lawyer

Marine biologist

Truck driver

My Reflection: These are high aspirations. My prayer and hope are that each will achieve their personal goals.

Question: How optimistic are you about the future?

Their Response: Three individuals answered this question:

- Not optimistic at all.
- I don't think about it.
- Once I finish college, I will be optimistic.

My Reflection: Of all the responses, this one is most concerning. We need to work at helping our young people become more optimistic about the future. This means that as older adults we need to work to improve society and remove society's ills to generate a greater sense of optimism in what young people see around them.

Question: What are the issues that you are facing in life?

Their Response:

- Peer pressure
- Pressure to drink, do drugs
- To be a gangster type
- Stressed out
- Anger (When queried about what the response means or if they could expand on it, the response was "life in general.")
- Things going on at home
- Trust

My Reflection: As mentors, parents, guardians, and members of the older generation, let us help young people in whatever ways we can to deal with the pressures they are facing. Let us also keep them in our prayers.

Question: What things would you like older Black men to do for you? How would you like them to interact with you?

Their Response:

- Make better decisions
- Communicate more
- Give them more respect
- See where younger men are coming from—"This is our time."
- Passing on the baton
- More discipline

My Reflection: These responses represent a "tall order" for us. Nevertheless, the responses give us some marching orders as we work with the younger generation.

Question: Who are your role models?

Their Response:

- My parents
- My mom
- My coaches
- Mr. Westbook (head of the program in which they are participants)

My Reflection: It is instructive to see who their role models are. The fact that their parents are on the list is very encouraging. While in general, young people (including their parents) attend church and are involved in church activities less than prior generations, one of the key takeaways from this response is that to reach the younger generation, we need to influence the influencers. Additionally, their athletic coaches are seen as role models, underscoring the point that many of our Black males are involved with and influenced by sports.

Question: Who are the people you need to stay away from?

Their Response:

- Violent and aggressive people
- People that put me down
- Negativity
- Keep your friends closer

My Reflection: These are powerful responses. Again, let us hope and pray that their peers heed their voices and that they are successful in staying away from negativity.

Question: If you were president of the United States or a dictator for a day, what would you do to make the world a better place?
Their Response:
- Reduce taxes
- Add more shelter for homeless people
- Help the community
- Donate huge sums of money to nonprofits
- Ban some guns
- Set an age limit for elective office (When asked for an age, the age given was 65.)
- More funds for education
- Lower the age limit for people to work (When asked for the specific age, the response was 15.)
- Clean the ocean; it's filthy
- Protect the animals
- Reduce the smog
- Less fossil fuel

My Reflection: These young men are very socially conscious. We might even say that they are "woke." I see in their responses a deep sense of caring for their fellow human beings. They are very environmentally conscious and want to make the earth a hospitable place for us and animals. They are attuned to social and political issues, wanting attention to be given to issues of violence, education, and the homeless.

Question: What advice would you give to other Black men/your peers?
Their Response:
- You are the person you build yourself to be.
- Give back to your community.
- Us African Americans should have more respect.
- Never forget where you came from.

My Reflection: These words speak for themselves. I only ask that their peers listen to them.

Conclusion (Overall Reflections)

The goal of this focus group was to give voice to our young people. Thus, my reflections are brief. Their voices speak for themselves, which is why I presented their verbatim responses.

While this is not a large group and their responses may not be a representative sample, the responses give us some insight into how our young Black men are thinking. I encourage churches and communities across the nation to conduct their own focus groups to hear the voices of the next generations. There is a great need for their input and continuous cross-generation conversations. They are willing to talk to us. We must be willing to listen.

There is also a strong message in their voices for churches and great opportunities going forward. Churches must, in general, invest more time and resources into developing our youth. Our churches must budget for youth programs and, where financially possible, hire youth ministers to work with youth in a systematic way as they embark on this critical developmental phase of life. As can be seen in these responses, our youth are in tune with what is happening in society, know what needs to change, and are willing to engage in the change process. Let us thank them and furthermore ponder and implement their answers.

NOTES

1. Special thanks to Reverend Michael Westbrook, pastor of Greater Life in Newark, Jersey, for arranging the focus group and to the six young men for participating.
2. The names of participants are pseudonyms in order to maintain anonymity.

Not Alone

Parenting a Child with Special Needs

MICHAEL R. LYLES II, JD

KRISTINA J. LYLES, JD

Walking down the street, Jesus saw a man blind from birth. His
disciples asked, "Rabbi, who sinned: this man or his parents,
causing him to be born blind?" Jesus said, "You're asking the
wrong question. You're looking for someone to blame. There is
no such cause-effect here. Look instead for what God can do."

John 9:1–3 MSG

Introduction

I can't discuss my journey as a father to a child with special
needs—autism, in our son's case—without the viewpoint of my
wife, Kristina, both partner and mother. Through countless arguments and bitter tears, we've learned to lean on one another in
ways we wouldn't have imagined when we stood at the marriage
altar more than a decade ago and professed to do so. We truly
understand that "for better or worse" means for better *or worse*.

As such, there is no such thing as a chapter about our parenting
journey that doesn't bring in both of us; in as much as there's more
power in our collective—though sometimes conflicting —voices.
To help you follow along, we will indicate who is speaking at the
beginning of each section. We hope our story helps you.

"You're Pregnant"—What We Thought

Michael

It was a hot Friday afternoon at Howard University in April 2005, and I was enjoying my moment as one of eleven newly initiated members of my fraternity. Sweat poured from my purple-painted face, and I could feel my clothes sticking to my back. I probably smelled awful. None of that mattered to my twenty-year-old self. Hearing the boisterous crowd react to every move I made with my new fraternity brothers validated my decision to do something unexpected for the first time since I started college.

Through the sea of faces in the crowd, I saw my dad. He was not shouting or cheering, nor was he holding a big sign with my name on it, but his calm presence amid all those strangers posing as my friends was consistent with what my dad had demonstrated to me throughout my childhood.

He had made the ten-hour drive from our home outside of Atlanta up to DC the day before. You might expect him to do that as a Howard alum, or as a member of my fraternity, but my dad was neither. In fact, he was as out of place on Howard's campus that day as he was as a Black premed student at the University of Michigan in the 1970s.

Even though we have the same name, my dad and I have never had one of those "chip off the old block" father-son relationships. He introduced me to sports fandom, but beyond that, he was a math and science kid in high school while I was more into liberal arts. He liked sci-fi movies, while I preferred cerebral dramas and thrillers. In my adult life, I countered his golf and fishing hobbies with Peloton and cooking.

Despite our differences, my dad never allowed his own lack of understanding or appreciation for a legitimate interest of mine to stop him from actively supporting me. For him, the father-son bond was not about indoctrinating me with his same hobbies, academic interests, or career and life dreams. Instead, the father-son bond was ultimately about the two of us being able to rely on our unique relationship. I looked forward to establishing that bond with my own child one day. I never appreciated how much I would need to embrace that idea until I had a son with autism.

Kristina

We named our son Stone because his determined entrance into our lives (and my womb) was immovable, rooted, and tenacious. I can still remember the day that I learned I was pregnant, which certainly foreshadowed the miraculous ways God continues to move in our lives. I was scheduled to go in for my routine, annual checkup with my OB/GYN on May 6, 2016. A few weeks prior, I urgently visited a breast specialist given what appeared to be the presence of lumps on both of my breasts. Fear immediately set in when the specialist agreed that small lumps were present, but she needed me to wait a few months to monitor them before taking any precautions.

I was scared, and I was mad. I was especially mad at God—and I told God that I was mad. I was a fierce advocate for maternal health (I wear the "feminist" label proudly) and I'd always hoped to breastfeed my own children one day. But the presence of these lumps, which we feared were cancer, could not only take away that opportunity but could take my life. Together, and through tears and prayer, Michael and I waited.

Despite any trauma, anxiety, or depression we may experience in the seasons of our lives, Michael and I bring humor into our marriage and all the things we encounter. We call ourselves each other's "costars," and we often joke that even though we think we're funny, God has the best sense of humor and comedic timing. Cue the scene on May 6 during my annual gynecological exam.

After I provided my obligatory urine sample, my nurse came back into the room with a smirk on her face and said, "The doctor will see you now." Soon after, my doctor entered and stated plainly: *"You're pregnant."* Did I have lumps in both my breasts? Yes. Was my birth-control intrauterine device (IUD) still intact? Yes. But was I somehow pregnant even though the IUD we were using prevented pregnancy at a rate of over 99 percent? YES.

Our little embryo was part of the incredibly rare 0.3 percent of pregnancies that our doctor said occur notwithstanding the IUD. And because I was unknowingly several weeks pregnant, the lumps in my breasts were completely normal and of no concern for breast cancer. Ironically, the lumps represented my body's preparation of milk ducts to eventually feed a baby.

I know that 99.7 percent is not 100 percent, but I'm a firm believer that God listens, God answers, and God meets you where you are. God knew that the only way to catch our attention was to meet us right where it was evident we didn't truly trust Him. With the life-changing words of my doctor that day, I could feel the loving "smirk" from God which foreshadowed that there was so much more in store in this journey. Wide-eyed, Michael and I buckled up.

Postpartum/Newborn Stage: When What We Thought Clashed with How Things Were

Kristina

I knew my little guy was different at his three-month-old checkup. He was missing the milestones of a typically developing infant, like lifting his head. Even when I socialized with fellow new moms, I could feel that my baby boy was unique. When he walked late into his toddler months, not speaking when his peers were talking, and preferring solo play in a room full of children, I suspected autism, but I didn't have the words or the resources to plead my case. After raising these concerns to our pediatrician, to family, and to peers around me—and being met with skepticism—I lost sight of the inner wisdom that I know came from God. Isolation soon set in. And so did the postpartum anxiety.

Our marriage hit turbulence, as Michael and I didn't see eye to eye for some time. I became the defender of our son's late development, with Michael playing the gatekeeper of "everything will be all right." We would weaponize Bible verses like two spiritual lawyers proving that God was on *our* side. Me: "Stone is different." Michael: "Stone is going to thrive." In essence, we were both right—each of these statements were true. But what was really happening was that we were grieving in different ways. When I reflect on the time between Stone's birth through his autism diagnosis at age four, it ranks as the most challenging season in my entire life and in our marriage.

Michael

Before I had kids, whenever I thought about being a father, I thought about having a kid or a teenager, not a baby or a toddler.

It's easy to blame my own naiveté, but the overly patriarchal church environment I was raised in played a role in that thinking too. The prevailing view from my dad and many of his peers who taught us in Sunday school or coached our sports teams was that a father's primary role was to provide financial security to his family and that any meaningful emotional or personal connection to his children probably wouldn't come until they were school-age. Those men grew up in the 1960s and 1970s, and they were teaching what they knew. That did not make it right.

When I held Stone in the neonatal intensive care unit three days after he was born and looked into those big eyes of his, I was mesmerized. I can still see the same look he had in his eyes back then today when he sees something new. To me, parenting Stone was going to be a marathon. I heard all of Kristina's concerns about his developmental milestones, but I was trying not to be too much of a prisoner of the moment. Our pediatrician was not overly concerned yet, so why should we worry? Moreover, my dad, the psychiatrist and my mother-in-law, the speech therapist, did not share any concerns with us. Too bad they were biased grandparents.

I should have done a better job at validating Kristina's feelings and sharing my own feelings as her spouse and partner. The truth was, while my concern did not rise to Kristina's level, I had suspicions that something was going on with Stone too. I wondered why he never seemed to show much interest in other babies or kids and why he got so upset at his first birthday party when we sang "Happy Birthday." I did not know how to put words to what I was seeing until we put Stone in daycare when he was almost eighteen months old. I frequently saw him playing alone, and he never acknowledged adults or older kids entering the classroom the way his peers did whenever I would go to pick him up. I had heard about autism, but I did not fully understand what it was. I just wanted to connect with my son.

2020: Our Marriage under Attack

Michael

I am thankful to God that we did not become a divorce statistic in 2020. Our daughter, Stella, was born in July 2020, so in part to protect her, we had a very strict quarantine for over a year. At this point, we both knew that Stone was autistic, but we did not have a formal diagnosis, so we had no resources, and the people around us—family, friends, and others—were still in denial. Picture this: a newborn baby, an autistic toddler, a postpartum mom who works in Diversity, Equity, and Inclusion during the height of a racial reckoning, and a dad who works in a commission-based job at a time when business is grinding to a halt . . . and all are confined in their house for a year. What could go wrong with our marriage?

I remember one night when Stella was about four months old. Kristina and I had recently emerged into a better place after one of the worst arguments of our marriage had forced us to reassess our household and parental roles. We were waking Stone up from his nap to give the kids a bath when we realized that Stone, who was almost four at the time and not fully potty trained, had a potty accident inside the play tent he insisted on sleeping in for naps and bedtime.

We woke him up, cleaned up the mess, and took him into the bathroom when he suddenly stiffened up, resisted, and began crying and screaming uncontrollably. He did this for about ten minutes without ceasing as we tried to calm him down. Kristina began to cry out of exasperation, and even Stella had a look of concern on her face. Eventually we realized that Stone was looking for the remnants of his potty accident that he had left under the pillow in his tent (We later learned that this was not unusual behavior for a three-year-old on the autism spectrum.) I held Stone in my arms and silently wondered: *Why can't you just be normal?!*

Prayer, therapy, and self-reflection taught me that I was not angry at Stone in that moment. Instead, I was angry at the loss of my expectations of what I anticipated being a dad to my son would be like. It was important to acknowledge the pain that came from that loss. I also had to accept Stone for all of who he is and realize that we still could have our bond—but he had to lead, not me.

Kristina and I continued to repair our partnership and develop our parenting rhythm as we moved into the spring of 2021, still months away from a formal autism diagnosis. We were beginning to address our own pain related to Stone's inevitable diagnosis, but due to how we were navigating the pandemic in our house, we had not had much of an opportunity to observe how Stone's autism may impact how he was perceived by strangers.

That changed when we temporarily enrolled Stone in an online preschool class. The class was made up of three- and four-year-olds like Stone, and parents were supposed to stay off camera. Getting Stone to sit still for anything was a tough task, but on the afternoon of his first class I had somehow managed to get him seated in front of my laptop.

The teacher introduced herself and then proceeded to prompt each of the students to introduce themselves. After the first few kids took their turns, I got nervous because I knew that although Stone was four, he was not speaking in a conversational manner yet. He communicated primarily by giving simple commands or answering yes or no questions. We gave the teacher a primer about this before the program started. When she called on Stone, predictably, he was silent. I gave it a moment, and then I prompted him off camera, "Is your name Stone?" I'll never forget what happened next. One of the kids exclaimed in a skeptical tone: "He's four and he needs his dad to help him say his name?"

Have you ever seen a toddler make a grown man cry? A fire burned in my chest and up through my throat. I understood then that no matter how much progress Kristina and I made processing our own pain and becoming more effective parents for Stone, and no matter how much we educated our family and close friends, there was still a world of strangers out there who would never see Stone the way we did.

Autism Diagnosis Brings Validation

When we finally got Stone's formal autism diagnosis in September 2021, I was tempted to think, *It wasn't supposed to be like this*, but God eventually revealed something else to me when I looked closely at John 9:1–3. Eugene Peterson's Bible version, *The Message*, ends those verses with Jesus telling His disciples to "look instead for what God can do" as opposed to looking for a reason why a blind man they saw was born without sight. God chose Kristina and me to be parents to Stone, and He had a plan for Stone that was going to bless other kids and other families like ours. In addition, God reminded me about what really made my relationship with my own dad unique and how I could still have that with Stone, despite his autism.

Kristina

Every night before bed, Michael and I ascend to our children's bedrooms for our post–bath time ritual. With our now three-year-old baby girl and six-year-old Stone, we chase their naked bodies around, trying to get them into pajamas, then brush their teeth. We pray, read a book, sing our family song (complete with rap beats and sound effects), then we recite the passage from *The Message* that Michael referenced: "Walking down the street, Jesus saw a man blind from birth. His disciples asked, 'Rabbi, who sinned: this man or his parents, causing him to be born blind?' Jesus said, 'You're asking the wrong question. You're looking for someone to blame. There is no such cause-effect here. Look instead for what God can do'" (John 9:1–3).

Stella and Stone recite the last line as if they are cheerleaders at a pep rally: "Look instead for what God can do!" It rings in my spirit every single time. It's a reminder from their little voices that God is up to something in all our lives, and this doesn't exclude those of us with special needs. There's no cure I seek for Stone, myself, or our journey. There's nothing to be fixed. We're fervently creating a world in which other families like ours feel seen, affirmed, accepted, and understood, especially within communities of fellow believers.

Michael and I take active steps every day to counteract a world that's still not as accepting of families like ours. We brave judgmental eyes as we enter crowded restaurants, knowing that Stone is often triggered by wait times and certain foods. We avoid Fourth of July events out of sensitivity to fireworks, and we proudly announce "special ed" when the school attendant asks us which classroom we're picking up from. These may feel like small victories, but in the grand scheme, this is how we're advocating for Stone *and* taking care of ourselves throughout all that we encounter daily. There are no "small victories" when parenting a kid with autism.

The Present: Embracing How Things Are

Michael

As we write this, Stone is in first grade at our local elementary school within a special education class that is made up of kids on the autism spectrum. His teachers and therapists on the special needs staff at his school are truly "salt of the earth" type people, and we are thankful for them every day.

Most of all, we are amazed by how far Stone has come. He is still autistic and that is not changing, and some days are *hard*. Nonetheless, our family has found our rhythm and our joy in this season of his life. I am blessed to have a job that allows me to pick up Stone from school most days, and I love nothing more than to see his face waiting eagerly in the pickup line. I do not get a lengthy response when I ask him, "What did you do at school today?" But I know that he feels seen and accepted in his classroom.

Outside of school, Stone does gymnastics, participates in monthly activities through our local Jack and Jill chapter, and further engages his love of technology by taking coding classes. As I sit and watch him line up his toy cars, I do not always know what's going through his head nor do I always understand his interests. However, when Stone looks up and sees me beside him and requests a "squeeze" (a strong hug) from me, I realize by being present and showing willingness to embrace his differences, I am doing what my dad did for me that April afternoon in DC almost twenty years ago.

Kristina

My line of work centers on Diversity, Equity, and Inclusion (DEI), and a cornerstone of DEI is *belonging*; the feeling that you are supposed to be where you are and that the institutions you're a part of should do everything they can to make sure of that. For families with special needs, this is the role of the church: ensuring belonging for its believers. Whatever your difference is (perceived or otherwise), the church is for you, just as you are. Just like the Bible is the *living* Word that transcends history and the future, so too should the church show up for the uniqueness of the people who fill its pews.

Michael and I were actively involved in piloting a new children's church class for kids with special needs at our home church, Elizabeth Baptist Church in Atlanta. Therefore, we have the privilege of teaching Stone's class (with Stella) monthly. This is our attempt at creating belonging in our church. Rather than allowing Stone's sensory sensitivities to light and sound keep our entire family from worshiping on Sundays, we've created a class where he and his peers can learn about God in their own way, while parents and caregivers who may not have otherwise been able to attend the main service can do so with the peace of mind that their kids are with people who understand them. Stone and his peers with special needs belong in the community of believers just like other children.

Michael

We've spent this chapter providing you with a glimpse of our family's experience with autism, but it is very important to note that autism will show up differently in every person, so each family's story will not be the same. Moreover, we recognize that some of you reading this may have kids with other special needs that we have not addressed directly because we shared the story that we know best. If you are in this group, we see you.

For me, the shift in our family coincided with my decision to spiritually own my God-given role as a father to Stone and Stella and as a husband to Kristina. That's not to say I did not take my roles seriously, because I did. But as Life Church pastor Craig Groeschel pointed out in a recent sermon series titled "The Power to Change," I did not have a spiritual "Why?" behind my motivation to thrive as a husband and father. Yes, therapy helped, and I encourage other fathers to utilize it, but none of the joy we have learned to experience would have been possible without me embracing the spiritual purpose God had implanted in me long before I knew it. God was going to use our family to help other families, and for that to happen, I had to submit to God spiritually since I was ultimately going to be the one God held accountable for my family's spiritual well-being.

The day before Stone was born, Kristina and I took one last picture together of our family with just the two of us. If I could talk to the Michael in that picture, the version of me just about to start his fatherhood journey with a son on the autism spectrum *and* his journey of being a supportive husband to a first-time mother, I would say to him

- Embrace the new season in the marriage journey with Kristina out of love. Lean into supporting her emotionally. Communicate clearly which parts of the parenting and household responsibilities you will take ownership of so that she does not have to think about those tasks on top of her own job and being a new mother. For a practical resource, read Eve Rodsky's book *Fair Play*.[1] To corroborate this concept spiritually, see Galatians 6:2 and Ephesians 5:25.

- Let go of what your vision for what being a dad was supposed to look like. God's plan and vision for your life is better than your plan and vision. You will find a closer relationship with God, Kristina, Stone, and Stella by getting your own agenda out of the way.

- It is important to acknowledge that while you and Kristina are ultimately the experts in parenting your own kids and ensuring that your marriage is thriving under God, that is not a reason to isolate yourselves. You have a valuable contribution to make to the broader community of fathers, parents of kids with special needs, Christian parents who are dual earner couples, etc. God wants you to have community; the enemy thrives on isolating us.

Kristina

In the spirit of supporting others through the grief and triumph in this journey, here are a few things I'd do differently if you gave me a time machine:

- From day one, I'd embrace that Michael and I are on the same team. We took our vows over a decade ago, and we're better together, even if our approach to parenting differs.
- I'd read the Bible for myself. While spiritual advisers are critical to having a community and pathway to growing in Christ, so too is having a direct understanding of what's in the Word. I even teach my baby girl Stella to watch closely the power and stories of young women in the Bible, as evidence of her own strength that God has given to girls and women in the Word and world. Her favorite is Esther.
- I'd seek help and counseling right away. I believe in Jesus and therapy, both of which still are part of my journey of self-discovery and self-care.

Conclusion

The pandemic showed us that we have work to do within the church around how we discuss family roles and the gender division of labor within Christian households where both spouses work outside the home. We also have a lot of work to do to ensure families of kids and adults with special needs feel included in the work and mission of the church.

To that end, we are excited to see what God will grow from the new special needs children's church ministry Kristina mentioned at our church, and we are hopeful that more churches follow this example.

In addition, we hope that more church members will avoid saying things like, "I don't see a difference in your child, I will treat them like any other kid." This drove us crazy with Stone; the whole premise of his autism diagnosis is that you *do* have to treat him differently because he perceives the world differently than neurotypical people. Another poor communication is, "I'm going to pray that God fixes that baby."

Instead, be kind and validate the fact that God has not segregated kids or adults with special needs from His kingdom purpose, so we shouldn't do that as a church.

We pray that our story has provided some encouragement to

you. We know from experience that the enemy thrives on making you feel as if you are alone and that no one else gets what you're going through. If this chapter accomplishes nothing else, we hope our fellow Christian parents of kids with special needs trust us when we say you are *not* alone.

Acknowledgments

Our Parents: Karen Joye and Colonel Maxie Joye; Marsha Lyles and Dr. Michael Lyles Sr.; Dr. Craig L. Oliver Sr., Senior Pastor, and the God's Little Seeds Ministry Team at Elizabeth Baptist Church, Atlanta, GA
Pastor Michael A. Walrond Jr. and Rev. Dr. LaKeesha N. Walrond, First Corinthian Baptist

NOTES

1. Eve Rodsky, *Fair Play: A Game-Changing Solution for When You Have Too Much to Do (and More Life to Live)* (New York: G. P. Putnam's Sons, 2019).

Prosper

Growing Generations with Biblical Values

CLAUDE L. DALLAS JR., MS, MA

For we are God's handiwork, created in Christ Jesus to do good works, which God prepared in advance for us to do.

Ephesians 2:10

Introduction

Being a parent or grandparent is truly a high calling from God. This calling is such an honor and gift, both rewarding and challenging. As an African American, the social biases by those who are in positions of power and influence can make life for parents and grandparents seem difficult or even futile. But the Holy Spirit can give us the peace, patience, and perseverance to love ourselves and our enemies, as well as guide our children and grandchildren.

The home can provide fertile ground for the nurture and development of children. For example, a child uses language and grammar learned in their home. They also imitate behavior. The resolution of these aspects of parenting can be facilitated when the parents and grandparents accept the fact that since Jesus Christ created each child, He has a reason and plan for their lives and their individual purpose. The time, place, and family for each child was chosen by God. Helping children realize that they are part of a larger picture and plan is a privilege and opportunity parents and grandparents have.

We're Part of Something Much Larger Than Ourselves

My ancestors knew they were part of something much larger than themselves before they even learned to read the Word of God. They also testified to the Lord's providence and care as they proclaimed, "He, God, made a way out of no way!" Though they experienced many defeats as the children of slaves on American shores, they never accepted being defeated or hopeless. My parents told me that I was to take the family into the future stronger and healthier. I subsequently saw myself as a relay runner who grasped a sacred baton to pass on to the next generation. I also saw myself as a bridge, as reflected in one of my poems entitled "I Am a Bridge." A bridge has a point of origin and a destination. In our lives we understand that we're unable to go back entirely to our genetic origin, nor are we aware of the impact our lives will have on future generations. By faith we believe that our path will lead us forward. There are many parts of a bridge. The value of each part may be weighed differently. But there is an Engineer who looks at each part for durability and efficiency.

What Parents and Grandparents Can and Must Do: The Foundation of Parenting

Parents and grandparents can and must model the love of Christ with honesty, humility, vulnerability, and authenticity to their families. As we better understand the process of discovering God's purpose for our own lives, we can apply the same process and principles for parenting. And, yes, even grandparenting!

Most parents begin their parenting journey based on their own experiences as a child. Most receive no formal education or training in parenting. The foundation upon which a child is raised influences the child's entire life. It is important for parents to continuously help make the child understand that they are part of a plan much greater than their individual lives and those of their parents. The dual challenge is to become followers of Jesus

Christ and to love others as God has loved us. Such behavior must be observable. Children imitate what they both see and hear.

In our efforts to show children that they are part of something greater than themselves, parents and grandparents might use comparisons between smaller and larger objects. For example, a child is one member in a family, a student within a classroom, even part of their community and school. Each small neighborhood is part of a larger city, the city is part of the state, and the state is part of the country. The earth is part of a galaxy. We can integrate such comparisons into everyday life to help children see that they are part of a bigger picture. Note the African proverb: "It takes a village to raise a child."

One of my favorite examples is flowers. Just like the beautiful and plentiful variety of flowers, God made it possible for us as humans to multiply and express ourselves in a variety of ways. We are like God's human bouquet—beautiful and diverse. One honorable goal is for us as parents and grandparents to discover and grow into our best selves. Imitation of anyone else besides Jesus Christ is to be discouraged. God created us to be unique agents in the fulfillment and fullness of His kingdom. We must transmit this to our children and grandchildren.

Our collective actions and reactions help influence how other generations react. As parents and grandparents, we are stewards of our generation. We (our bodies) are a temple of the Holy Spirit (1 Corinthians 6:19–20). So be a steward of the kingdom of God on earth. We are a part of something big, so participate. Live it out. The tone, approach, and posture of Jesus should dictate our behavior. We determine how the church looks and acts in our generation.

Discovering the Purposes for Grandparenting

Being a grandparent is different from parenting. Some grandparents are placed in the role of parenting if the parents are not able to do so. Grandparents may fulfill several primary roles, including protector, childcare provider, encourager, and family historian. When parents are active in the lives of their children, grandparents can serve as coaches and counselors as permission is given. A more active parenting role can be assumed while grandchildren are visiting.

My Journey into Parenting and Grandparenting

Every child needs to know that they are part of something much larger than their own lives. Help them answer questions like, "Why am I here? What's my purpose?" My personal journey included questions related to my ethnicity. In my spiritual maturation, discovering the purpose of God for my life has been a continuous process and has become clearer each day, month, and year.

The evidence of our parenting skills and lessons become visible after our children are grown. The lessons learned by our children can be seen in the style and manner in which they parent their own children or those in their care. The transference of generational boundaries of faith and their guidelines are a blessing beyond description.

Each human being is a unique, unreproducible masterpiece of Jesus Christ. They are physically, mentally, and sexually as He desires, no mistakes! Children are gifts to parents by our Savior. The command of Jesus to love everyone as ourselves is not a suggestion (see Mark 12:31). It applies to the stewardship of our children. Failure to demonstrate kindness and love to others, especially our children and grandchildren, indicates a lack of love and respect for Jesus Christ.

Victims versus Victors

Jesus taught that the first and greatest commandment is to "love the Lord your God with all your heart and with all your soul and with all your mind" (Matthew 22:37–38). Our bodies are temples for the Holy Spirit (1 Corinthians 6:19–20). Our bodies may be chained as slaves, but our hearts and minds are to be focused on the Lord.

Parents and grandparents who teach their children to see themselves as integral parts of the body of Christ will lead them to believe that they are victorious by intent and content rather than victims by accident. We can help them to see the world from a rocket window rather than a peephole of a door in an apartment or home. They will be as they have been designed and created— victorious, well-functioning people who are only victims if they buy into the lies of Satan, the god of this world.

The Foundation of Parenting and Grandparenting

The foundation of parenting and grandparenting lies in providing a safe and nurturing environment that fosters a child's physical, emotional, and spiritual well-being. Parenting and grandparenting involve meeting basic needs, such as ensuring our child has access to nutritious food, adequate shelter, and quality healthcare. These are crucial for their development.

Building a secure attachment is also vital. Strong emotional bonds formed through responsive caregiving provide a sense of security and promote healthy social-emotional development. It is necessary to set boundaries and expectations. Clear and consistent boundaries help children understand acceptable behavior and develop self-control. Nurturing curiosity facilitates exploration and provides opportunities for learning. This helps children develop their cognitive skills and build confidence.

We must model positive values since children learn by observing. We must also be mindful of the values we demonstrate through actions and words. Depending on your beliefs, you can introduce your child to spiritual practices and traditions that provide them with a sense of purpose and meaning.

Here are some steps we can take to support the spiritual and physical growth of our children and grandchildren:

Physical Growth

- Involve them in physical activities: Encourage outdoor play, sports, or other forms of exercise that they enjoy.
- Promote healthy eating habits: Cook meals together, involve them in grocery shopping, and make healthy choices accessible.
- Ensure adequate sleep: Establish regular sleep routines and create a relaxing bedtime environment.

Spiritual Growth

- Expose them to different spiritual traditions: If you're comfortable, discuss your own beliefs and practices, or explore other traditions together.
- Encourage reflection and mindfulness: Practices like meditation

or journaling can help children connect with their inner selves and develop self-awareness.

- Engage in acts of service: Volunteering or helping others can foster compassion and a sense of purpose.

Remember, the most important thing in parenting and grandparenting is to create a loving and supportive environment where your child feels safe to explore, learn, and grow.

Here are some ways parents can empower their children to overcome challenges and embrace their inherent worth:

Foster a Strong Racial Identity

- Help children understand their cultural heritage and the contributions of family members as well as influential Black figures throughout history.
- Celebrate cultural traditions, holidays, and significant achievements to instill a sense of pride and belonging.
- Encourage open conversations about race, racism, and microaggressions, providing tools to navigate these experiences constructively.
- Take trips to cultural museums and historical places.

Cultivate Critical Thinking Skills

- Equip children with the ability to critically analyze media portrayals and societal narratives that perpetuate harmful stereotypes.
- Encourage questioning and discussion, fostering independent thought and challenging biases. Some schools refuse to teach slavery from a historical perspective.
- Nurture intellectual curiosity and a love for learning, empowering them to excel academically and pursue their aspirations.

Promote Positive Self-Esteem

- Counter negative societal messages by affirming children's unique talents, strengths, and intrinsic value.

- Encourage self-acceptance and appreciation for their physical features and cultural background. Dispel the light-skinned versus dark-skinned stereotypes.
- Provide opportunities to develop healthy coping mechanisms for dealing with prejudice and discrimination.

Build a Support Network

- Connect children with positive role models, mentors, and peers who share their identity and values. Drive to other neighborhoods to join congregations and social groups.
- Foster a sense of community belonging through engagement in cultural organizations, faith-based groups, or social justice initiatives.
- Encourage open communication and seek support when facing challenges or discrimination.

By nurturing a strong cultural identity, critical thinking skills, positive self-esteem, and a supportive network, parents and grandparents can empower their children and grandchildren to overcome racial barriers and thrive as equals in society. Remember, this is an ongoing journey, and open communication, validation, and unwavering support are crucial for guiding children and grandchildren toward self-assured and fulfilling lives. Understand that the growing awareness of racism and its impact varies amongst children of every racial group. Discerning signs of prejudice is vastly different from assuming that everyone has depraved beliefs.

The Veil through Which People of Color Often Peer (and Are Often Viewed)

Parents and grandparents influence the veil through which our children and grandchildren see. W. E. B. Du Bois's metaphor of the veil aptly captures the experience of many African Americans navigating a society steeped in racial bias. In *The Souls of Black Folk*, he combined history, philosophy, and music in an attempt to combat racism.[1] Du Bois used language and ideas to hammer out a strategy for political equality and to sound the depths of the Black experience in the aftermath of slavery. He set out to paint a vivid portrait of Black people in the decades after emancipation in 1863—how they lived and who they really were. His aim was to enlighten White America—still profoundly attached to the myths of Black inferiority—as to the true meaning of being Black in post–Civil War America. The "double-blinded veil" mentioned by Du Bois is a veil through which Whites often perceive African Americans. Such a veil can preclude them from being aware of the truth and beauty of other human beings.

Thus, parents and grandparents must learn to teach their children how to diagnose these misconceptions and determine the best ways to respond. In any case, we must understand that many Whites usually do not view us as equals but rather as a contemptuous reminder of the slavery that produced wealth for them. Some have a seared moral conscience (see 1 Timothy 4:2) from which they seek deliverance. The trend to omit slavery as a subject of American history seems to support this notion.

Conclusion

Though each individual must come to a personal knowledge of salvation, parents are given the opportunity to steward children and grandchildren, laying the foundation for a relationship with their Creator. Christian parents and grandparents must model the love of Christ to their family through demonstrating honesty, humility, vulnerability, and authenticity. As we better understand the process of discovering God's purpose for our lives, we can apply the same process and principles for parenting and, yes, even grandparenting!

NOTES

1. W. E. B. Du Bois, *The Souls of Black Folk* (London: Oxford University Press, 2008, originally published in 1903).

16

Balance

Balancing Family and Career

KEN STALEY, MDIV, DD

> But now your kingdom will not endure; *the LORD has sought out a man after his own heart* and appointed him ruler of his people, because you have not kept the LORD's command.
>
> 1 Samuel 13:14 (emphasis added)

> After removing Saul, he made David their king. God testified concerning him: "I have found David son of Jesse, *a man after my own heart; he will do everything I want him to do.*"
>
> Acts 13:22 (emphasis added)

Introduction

As men of God, we are to live lives aligned with sound biblical principles and priorities so that we may complete the assignments entrusted to us. As good stewards of the manifold blessings of the Lord (Proverbs 10:22), we must receive, accept, and perform the God-given assignments by submitting our will to God's will. We must become proactive in completing the commands, assignments, and purpose God gives us: "But as for me and my household, we will serve the LORD" (Joshua 24:15). "Keep this Book of the Law always on your lips; meditate on it day and night, so that you may be careful to do everything written in it. Then you will be prosperous and successful. Have I not commanded you? Be strong and courageous. Do not be afraid; do not be discouraged, for the Lord your God will be with you wherever you go" (Joshua 1:8–9).

Joshua was given an assignment from God (his life's purpose). He was to become the new leader of the children of Israel. His assignment was to lead the children of God to the promised land (Joshua 11:1–9). God spoke to him directly and told him what he needed to do to be successful. Understanding our relationship with God is the starting point. It's necessary to understand our assignment, and to have the power and wisdom to complete it (Romans 5:10–11; 2 Corinthians 5:14–15; Ephesians 2:8–9). We must come to the place where we accept the Bible as the Word of God and realize that as Christians, His Spirit lives within us. We must speak God's Word and meditate on God's Word, and God will be with us wherever we go.

Our Responsibility

Our responsibility as a "man of God," is to understand that God has given each of us an assignment. He has equipped us with every good thing to do His will (Hebrews 13:21). Our "core" assignment (encompassing our life and relationship with Christ) is to manage every area of our lives in a manner that will give Him glory and honor. To manage our lives means to be responsible for controlling and administering the performance of our lives to impact the lives of those God has given us leadership over in a loving (1 Corinthians 13:4–8), sacrificial (Ephesians 5), and God-honoring manner. The Bible has many examples of men submitting to the assignments God has given them, including Abraham, Moses, David, Joseph, and Paul. In the Word of God, Jesus commands, "Whoever wants to be my disciple must deny themselves and take up their cross and follow me" (Matthew 16:24). This requires self-denial of the natural man (only God can be the final authority in your life). We must understand that God has entrusted us with a "divine assignment" that has numerous parts and could affect many generations and people outside of our immediate influence.

Obedience Starts with Your Spiritual Growth

The most important aspect of our lives is to have a personal relationship with Jesus Christ, which includes the indescribable gift of being forgiven by His blood! A personal relationship means being connected by the blood of Christ (Romans 10:9–10; Ephesians 1:7–9; Hebrews 9:22). Matthew 22:37 commands us to "love the Lord your God with all your heart and with all your soul and with all your mind." Our love for Him must be complete. We can demonstrate this love through prayer, Bible study, meditating on the Word, service to God, our behavior, and having an attitude that honors Him (Matthew 7:12; Ephesians 4:29; 2 Peter 1:5–7). God's Word must become part of us. As we hide it in our hearts, we can speak it from the overflow and pray that it would become part of our everyday thought process.

Throughout the Gospels, Jesus pulled away from His earthly ministry to meet His Father in prayer (Matthew 27:46; Luke 6:12; 11:1–4; 23:34; John 17). How much more should we seek God in prayer for relationship, fellowship, purpose, forgiveness, supplication, godly love, and clarity of assignment? Our faith and trust in God must be based upon Jesus Christ and His finished work on the cross.

If we are managing these assignments as part of our daily and weekly lives, then we are becoming the kind of men God wants us to be. Through His Holy Spirit, God desires to transform us so that we may be equipped to advance His kingdom in our lives, our marriages, our homes, our communities, our churches, and our employment, and to use God's solutions to life's issues. In this world, we need to be reminded daily of Romans 12:1–2:

- Do not conform to the pattern of this world.
- Be transformed by the renewing of your mind.
- Offer yourself as a living and holy sacrifice, the kind God will find pleasing and acceptable.

Our Motivation Is to Worship Him

When we love God, we desire to please Him; we desire to be obedient to His Word and to complete our assignments in every area of our lives, as well as to honor and glorify God. John 15:10 says, "If you keep my commands, you will remain in my love, just as I have kept my Father's commands and remain in his love."

Psalm 128:1–2 says, "Blessed are all who fear the LORD, who walk in obedience to him. You will eat the fruit of your labor; blessings and prosperity will be yours." In our process of completing God's assignment, we will have self-control, make choices, and see the outcome of our decisions. The big picture of completing our assignment is how we desire to honor and glorify God.

Management of Others

Management of others involves creating an environment that allows each of those whom God has assigned to us to achieve their God-given purpose under our leadership, as directed by God's Word. We must exhibit servant leadership. According to Matthew 20:27, "Whoever wants to be first must be your slave" (in other words, a servant to others). Busyness is the enemy of God. It's a divided heart that does not walk in truth. A sheep can only have one shepherd (Psalm 23:1–3).

Workaholism

Workaholism refers to a behavioral addiction. It is a mental health condition that causes a compulsive need to work. This type of working leads to relationship and health concerns. There are 168 hours in a week: forty given to work, ten to travel, and fifty-six for sleep (most people don't get eight hours of sleep a night). This leaves sixty-two waking hours to complete God's assignment for our lives. This time must be managed to have a balanced life. J. Oswald Sanders has observed, "Time lost can never be retrieved. Time cannot be hoarded, only spent well."[1]

Marriage

The biblical model for marriage and family (husband, wife, children) was established by God. If you are a married man, you are commanded to love your wife as Christ loved the church and gave Himself for her (Ephesians 5:23–27). When we said, "I do," we covenanted with God and our wife to do all that we said at the altar, and that includes what is written in God's Word to define the relationship between husband and wife. In our society today, family is low on the priority list of most men. The covenant relationship has been altered by divorce (breaking the covenant), separation, children born out of wedlock, fatherless homes, "baby mama drama," government systems, single parenting, prison, and men who feel they have no responsibility for children they have fathered.

The Christian husband loves his wife like Christ loves the church. Keep a scheduled date night when she can talk with you alone, and you listen. Stevie Wonder's song "I Just Called to Say I Love You" could translate into a short phone call to your wife. Bring her flowers. Fulfill your role as the father and leader in the home. Make hard decisions for the family. Help your wife feel secure. Be considerate. Affirm her identity. Help her to fulfill her God-given purpose. Reverence her.

Children (inside and outside of the Home)

If you are a man with children at home or a man who has access to your children each week or month, your God-given responsibility is to evangelize and disciple each one of them. The goal is to help them understand who God is, what He has done for them through Jesus Christ, and the role of the Holy Spirit in their lives. As Christian fathers, we must teach our children the principles of the Word of God to live by and how they can live out God's purpose for their lives. We are to teach them to have a prayer life and to give service to God's church. This would require a minimum of two hours per child per week. Remember, no two children are the same. Each has their own individual needs, concerns, and issues that must be addressed with love (1 Corinthians 13:4–8).

Unconditional Love

Unconditional love is the standard within the family culture. Proverbs 22:6 states, "Train up a child in the way he should go: and when he is old, he will not depart from it" (KJV). Training takes time, patience, love, communication, verbal expectations, and in some cases discipline. Each child in the home has his or her own temperament, learning style, love language, emotional connectedness, and self–concept that you must understand and build on.

A Practical Assessment

Sit with a piece of paper. Write out what your priorities have been over the past three months, then the past six months. What are your top three items? Is your relationship with God first (not just going to church)? Does family fall in your top three priorities?

Our priorities reflect our value system. What is important to us and in what order determines where I put my time and energy. A disciplined man of God plans his week, giving priority to God's clear standards for his life, walking in those standards as he works to honor and glorify God. Our goal is to live a life of integrity, having the right priorities—honesty, truthfulness, strong biblical principles, dependability, loyalty, good judgment, decisiveness, respect, and love for the Word of God (1 Corinthians 13:4–8; Ephesians 5:25–27; 6:4).

Planning

Each day, each week, each year requires a plan from us to accomplish God's assignment. We must set goals for ourselves and every member of our family (with their input). Consider a "retreat" at home or away from home (January is a good month) where you plan activities and goals for the year. Every three months, review the goals to make sure you are still on point or if changes need to be made. Make sure to answer what, when, how, where, and why. This is called a "performance evaluation" to make sure you and your family stay on point with your January goals. As your plan, keep in mind the following:

- Establish a biblical standard for handling conflict (spouse, children, job, etc.)
- Have a Christian counselor evaluate your lifestyle and standards for your home.
- Remember that procrastination is the enemy of all good managers, and of the completion of godly assignments.
- Plan your day. Be realistic about what you can accomplish. Do not overload your day, don't commit to doing things

that require hours you don't have, and be sure to put tasks in order of priority.

Managing our time to complete God's assignment involves doing it God's way so we will have a balanced life. This requires that our life be transformed (Romans 12:1–2). God's will for us will make us more productive and we will be able to fulfill His purpose for our lives.

Conclusion

To be the manager and leader and complete our God-given assignments, there must be a change in our lives. Our lives must be pleasing to God, which requires obedience to His Word (John 14:15).

Change is a necessary part of living out God's purpose and assignment. Change requires submission to the Holy Spirit, repentance, and a life of obedience to God's Word. "Anyone who listens to the word but does not do what it says is like someone who looks at his face in a mirror and, after looking at himself, goes away and immediately forgets what he looks like" (James 1:23–24). Considering our personal time with the Lord, worship, and service, a good manager would still have at least twenty-five hours each week for other responsibilities in life, or to spend more time with his family's needs, concerns, and culture as well as time with God.

A good manager might wake in the morning and spend time with God to be refreshed for his day's assignment. In the evening, he gives thanks to God for the protection, blessings, grace, and mercy that kept him through the day. He also spends time in repentance, seeking God's forgiveness. In our management and in living a balanced life, we are stewards of everything God has given us. Our stewardship is to use our gifts to serve with humility, trust, forgiveness, and obedience. Most of all, we are to love those under our leadership, including our neighbors, communities, and churches.

NOTES

1. J. Oswald Sanders, *Spiritual Leadership: Principles of Excellence for Every Believer* (Chicago, IL: Moody Publishers, 2007), 95.

17

Love

Ways to Romance Your Wife

LLOYD C. BLUE SR., DMIN

Husbands, love your wives, just as Christ loved
the church and gave himself up for her.

Ephesians 5:25

Introduction[1]

Very few couples seem to be experiencing this thing we call *romance*—that uncontrollable sensation or feeling often caused by just a glance, a word, a greeting, or a smile. This feeling is usually very strong during courtship. After the wedding, however, the romance starts to fade. Most of us stop planning dates. We stop saying all those romantic words. We begin to take each other for granted, and it becomes easier to compliment others rather than our own mates.

Some people think romance is a myth, something that is entertaining in the movies, but not the way people live in real life. Some sincere Christians think romance is just not necessary in marriage. They love each other in the Lord and think that is what really counts. Others try to suppress romance because they are not interested in it. Some even reason that because they do not have it, it must not exist. Others believe that in their marriage, romance is just not possible. Before we consider the reasons why some people struggle in this area, let's dig deeper into the definition of romance.

What Is Romance?

Romance exists in a thrilling love relationship involving oneness. It is a deep intimacy with another person that is filled with joy and excitement. This wonderful, almost indescribable sensation is known as "being in love." Some people call it being on "cloud nine." They feel energized and motivated, and when they are apart from one another, they can hardly wait to be together again. There is a song that talks about having daydreams about night things in the middle of the afternoon. The song goes on to say that while his hands are making a living, his mind is on loving.[2] The person in the song wanted five o'clock to hurry and come so he could be home with her by six!

I believe that when God created Adam, He put in Adam the need for romantic love. The Bible says in Genesis 2:18–25

> The LORD God said, "It is not good for the man to be alone. I will make a helper suitable for him."
>
> Now the LORD God had formed out of the ground all the wild animals and all the birds in the sky. He brought them to the man to see what he would name them; and whatever the man called each living creature, that was its name. So the man gave names to all the livestock, the birds in the sky and all the wild animals.
>
> But for Adam no suitable helper was found. So the LORD God caused the man to fall into a deep sleep; and while he was sleeping, he took one of the man's ribs and then closed up the place with flesh. Then the LORD God made a woman from the rib he had taken out of the man, and he brought her to the man.
>
> The man said,
>
> "This is now bone of my bones
>   and flesh of my flesh;
> she shall be called 'woman,'
>   for she was taken out of man."

That is why a man leaves his father and mother and is united to his wife, and they become one flesh. Adam and his wife were both naked, and they felt no shame.

Of all the creatures God made, not one was suitable for Adam. In other words, the need in Adam for romantic love could not be fulfilled by any of these creatures; Adam was still lonely. So, God performed the first surgery. He took a rib from Adam's side and made Eve. When God brought Eve to Adam, Adam took one look at Eve and knew that his lonely days were over. Now, if you will allow me to use my sanctified imagination, I think that romantic love soared through Adam's total being and he said, "Wow, this is it! This is now bone of my bone and flesh of my flesh. Wow!"

In his book *Romance 101: Lessons in Love*, Gregory Godek makes this statement:

> It's just plain unrealistic to expect romance to last no more than a few years. "Romance inevitably fades in the face of everyday life." "Romance—it's just a passing phase we grow out of." I hear it in the Romance Class. I hear it in casual conversations. It drives me crazy every time. At least in the Romance Class I have the opportunity, if not the responsibility, to point out to people that they're strangling their own relationships with this kind of thinking. You see, romance isn't about flowers and candy and cute little notes. *Romance is the expression of love.* Without romance, love becomes just an empty concept. "I love you" becomes a meaningless, automatic phrase. Romance is not a thing separate from love. It's not something that you "grow out of" as you mature. If anything, one's love grows deeper as one matures, and the romance—the expression, the action of love—stays vibrant and creatively alive.[3]

Because romance is the expression of love, we must not allow it to die.

Why Romance Your Wife?

In Ephesians 5:25, the Bible states, "Husbands, love your wives, just as Christ loved the church and gave himself up for her." Thus, we are to romance the woman we vowed to love and cherish until separated by death. I believe there is a misconception about the true nature of romance and its relationship to love. People often remove the concept of romance from love, where it belongs, and connect it instead to other things—things like being single, being infatuated, being immature and irresponsible, being forever moving and searching and unsettled. When this happens, the surface expressions of romance—passion, intensity, excitement—become linked with those states of being. One then begins to believe, for example, that being single is exciting and being married is boring. Nothing could be further from the truth.

If you want a dull, boring marriage, however, you do not have to do anything to create one. The problem is that some people believe that all marriages are this way. Not so—your marriage does not have to be that way. You can change your relationship by changing your beliefs. I know many couples who have been married for twenty-five years and even some over forty years who "still have it going on" with their mates. They still date each other. These individuals all have one thing in common: they understand that they have control over whether or not their lives are filled with romance on a daily basis. A romantic marriage is not something that is reserved for a few privileged couples but is available to anyone who believes it is possible and is willing to work at it. Paul wrote in Romans 12:2, "Do not conform to the pattern of this world, but be transformed by the renewing of your mind. Then you will be able to test and approve what God's will is—his good, pleasing and perfect will." Proverbs 23:17 states, "Do not let your heart envy sinners, but always be zealous for the fear of the LORD."

The questions that we must ask ourselves at this point are

1. Do I believe that marriage has to be dull, boring, and routine?

2. Do I believe that marriage, yes, even mine, can be filled with romance—hot, passionate romance?

If your answer to question one is yes, I trust that before you finish this chapter you will change your mind. If your answer to question two is yes, then you are ready to embrace what is yet to come.

Ways to Be Romantic

Godek says, "Romance is a state of mind. Romance is a state of being. Romance is the expression of love."[4] I totally agree. While romance often starts as a state of mind, it must move beyond mere thoughts and intentions and be communicated to your wife, through words, actions, gifts, gestures, or sometimes just a tender look.

As men, we tend to think of romance as an event, when in fact romance is a process. It is not a onetime thing that is accomplished and then forgotten. In order to work, it has to be an ongoing thing, a part of the fabric of our daily lives, because women are motivated and empowered when they feel cherished. Let me suggest that you put your thinking cap on and come up with some ways you can make your wife feel cherished.

There are countless ways to do this. Here are a few suggestions.

Activity 1: Send a Romantic Card

Buy a card that expresses the way you feel, mail it to her, and when she thanks you for the card, take her in your arms for a moment and tell her, "Baby, I love you and I mean everything that card says." If you really want to get her going, send her a card every day for a week. Check with your post office to see if you can get next-day delivery, and if so, mail the first card on Saturday, then another on Monday, and so on. Make the Friday card a sexy one. She will love it, and you are going to have a weekend to remember!

Activity 2: Give Her Roses

Bring or send her roses. If she has a job outside the home, send eleven roses to her place of work. It does not have to be a special day. On the card, write, "If you want to see what a dozen roses looks like, take these and stand in front of the mirror." You will make her the envy of all her fellow workers. I know because I did it.

Activity 3: Spend Saturday Night at a Hotel

First, make sure she can be available. Tell her a week before the event that you are taking her on an overnight date. This is very important if you have children, and it will give her time to anticipate the date, which can be as much fun as the date itself. If she asks for more information, tell her, "It's a surprise. Just dress as if you were going out to dinner and be sure to bring your overnight kit." Second, make reservations at a four-star hotel, and if possible, reserve a suite. You are not going to do this every weekend so make the most of it, even if you have to save up for it. Third, on Saturday morning pick up the key and make sure you have romantic music and roses with a romantic card in the room.

Timing is important. If need be, you may want to secure the help of the hotel staff to turn on the music at just the right time. Either using your car's music system or your smart phone, select a song that says what you want to say and when you start the car, start the music also. When she looks in your direction, give her the most seductive look you can muster and tell her, "I love you, honey, and I sure hope you enjoy your day." When you arrive at the hotel, say to her, "I picked up the key when I went out this morning. I didn't want you to have to stand around waiting for me to check in." When you open the door to your suite with the music and the aroma of the roses flowing around the room, well, you can pucker up and get ready for a "mess" of kissing—and while you are kissing, be sure to do some slow dancing across the room with your queen. About that time, there should be a knock at the door—room service with your favorite beverage and snacks that you ordered when you were at the hotel earlier.

Now it's time to relax, relate, and enjoy the music and one another. This would be an excellent time to bring out the lotion and give her a foot massage. Then lie across the bed, touch, and talk. Tell her all the ways you love her and how much you need her—tell her, "Baby, I wouldn't last a day without you." About 7:00 p.m. there should be another knock at the door—room service again. In the dim glow of candlelight, she will enjoy with you her favorite meal. Well, partner, I'm going to stop now. You will have to let your feelings take you the rest of the way.

Activity 4: Play Love Songs

The market is filled with love songs. Think about what your wife wants to hear and find a love song that will express it. For example, once I went away for a week of preaching, and heard a song by Vince Gill called "Look at Us." That was back in the day, so I bought the cassette and set the tape on that particular song so when my wife picked me up at the airport, I could play it for her on the way home. Go online and check out the words of the song. When you have done this, you will see why after listening to it, she told me how much she loved it. But the look on her face had already said it.

Activity 5: Celebrate Valentine's Day

On Valentine's Day, send your wife a written invitation to dinner and a private concert to hear her favorite love songs. Some of my wife's favorites (old school music) are "When She Holds Me" by Larry Gatlin, "I'm Only in It for Love" by John Conlee, "Misty" by Johnny Mathis, "I Will Always Love You" by Whitney Houston, "I Believe in Love" by Don Williams, and "You Are So Beautiful to Me" by Kenny Rogers. But first, plan to take your wife to her favorite restaurant for dinner and then to a hotel suite for the concert and evening just for the two of you. You get the idea, right?

Activity 6: Focus on Her to Get Ideas

One way to generate romantic ideas is to focus on your wife. If you focus your attention on her, just think of her a little more often, then romantic ideas will simply pop up all around you! I guarantee it. Romantic gifts will jump off store shelves into your hands, and romantic opportunities will present themselves to you over and over again.

Activity 7: Take Action

Add these ingredients in any combination or measure to your next romantic gift or gesture: anticipation, intrigue, and surprise. Mix well, do not half bake, and serve with a flourish.

Activity 8: Remember That Little Things Mean a Lot

Do not just hand her the drink—open it first. Do not just hand her a stick of gum—pull back the wrapper for her. Pull out the chair for her, even at home. Open the car door for her and close it after she is seated.

Activity 9: Wrap a Gift

Get her a bottle of perfume, put it in a paper bag, twist the top, and tie it with a ribbon. Then put it in a larger bag and repeat the process until you have about three or more bags. When you present the gift, be sure to tell her, "Don't mash the bag, you may damage the goods." Now you can enjoy yourself watching her carefully open each bag. In the bag with the perfume, make sure there is a card expressing your love for her. This also works well with four or five boxes. Make sure each box is gift-wrapped. She will feel good about herself, and she will love you for it.

Activity 10: Practice Verbal Expressions

No matter how many things you do, it will not take the place of verbal expression. Your wife needs to hear you say how you feel about her. She needs to hear you say, "I love you" with your mouth, not just with things. Say it often—daily, even. This can be done when you leave for work or when you come home. Sometime in the middle of the day, call her and say, "Honey, I just called to tell you that I love you. See you later. Goodbye," and hang up before she can say anything. She also needs to hear you say things like, "I need you like the river needs the water," "I need you," or "I wouldn't last a day without you." She needs to hear you say she is beautiful in your eyes. When she asks, "How do you like my dress?" tell her, "It's great, and I am sure it would not look that good on any other woman on earth." She wants to know how she looks to you.

Consider the words of "The Master," King Solomon, when it comes to telling a woman how she looks:

> How beautiful your sandaled feet,
>   O prince's daughter!
> Your graceful legs are like jewels,
>   the work of an artist's hands.
> Your navel is a rounded goblet
>   that never lacks blended wine.
> Your waist is a mound of wheat
>   encircled by lilies.
> Your breasts are like two fawns,
>   like twin fawns of a gazelle.
> Your neck is like an ivory tower.
> Your eyes are the pools of Heshbon
>   by the gate of Bath Rabbim.
> Your nose is like the tower of Lebanon
>   looking toward Damascus.
> Your head crowns you like Mount Carmel.
>   Your hair is like royal tapestry;
>   the king is held captive by its tresses.
> How beautiful you are and how pleasing,
>   my love, with your delights!
> Your stature is like that of the palm,
>   and your breasts like clusters of fruit.
> I said, "I will climb the palm tree;
>   I will take hold of its fruit."
> May your breasts be like clusters of grapes on the vine,
>   the fragrance of your breath like apples,
>   and your mouth like the best wine.
>   (Song of Solomon 7:1–9)

Notice that Solomon describes his wife in many different ways. Give some thought to how you might describe these areas of your wife to her and watch her melt into your arms. Also, notice that Solomon selected the most beautiful and attractive objects of his time to describe his wife's body. You do not have to describe her whole body at the same time; you might just tell her how beautiful her eyes are, and at some other time tell her how beautiful some other part of her body is to you.

Activity 11: Date Your Wife

You should date your wife often. Do it weekly or monthly. You cannot overdo it, and it does not have to be expensive. The idea is to be alone with her, to talk about the things she wants to talk about. When you take the time to date your wife, it helps her feel special, and she needs to feel special.

Personally, I like to date my wife on Friday night because we usually sleep in on Saturday morning. We have gone to dinner, sometimes to a movie, sometimes both. Sometimes we have gone to a mall and just walked and talked and window shopped. There have been times when we have gone out for just a cheeseburger. Other times we have driven to a spot with a special view and just sat and talked. This is a good time for you to encourage your wife to talk about those things she has been wanting to talk about all week when you both were too busy. You might ask her some questions like, "How has it been going for you this week?" or "If you could, what is the one thing you would change about me?" This way you can learn what is on her mind and help her deal with any problems she might be facing.

Why Romance Your Wife?

Ephesians 5:28–29 states, "In this same way, husbands ought to love their wives as their own bodies. He who loves his wife loves himself. After all, no one ever hated their own body, but they feed and care for their body, just as Christ does the church." We should romance our wives because romance is a part of what love is all about, and we are commanded to love and cherish our wives as we love and cherish our own bodies. The apostle Paul believed that life was precious and that every care should be taken to preserve it. He was also confident that a healthy husband believed as he did and would value his body, doing everything possible to preserve it. Because of this, Paul commanded husbands to love their wives as their own bodies. Romance is not an option. We must do everything in our power to preserve a healthy relationship.

Wisdom Is Required to Romance Your Wife

Notice again how Solomon romanced his wife:

> You are as beautiful as Tirzah, my darling,
>   as lovely as Jerusalem,
>   as majestic as troops with banners.
> Turn your eyes from me;
>   they overwhelm me.
> Your hair is like a flock of goats
>   descending from Gilead.
> Your teeth are like a flock of sheep
>   coming up from the washing.
> Each has its twin,
>   not one of them is missing.
> Your temples behind your veil
>   are like the halves of a pomegranate.
> Sixty queens there may be,
>   and eighty concubines,
>   and virgins beyond number;
> but my dove, my perfect one, is unique,
>   the only daughter of her mother,
>   the favorite of the one who bore her.
> The young women saw her and called her blessed;
>   the queens and concubines praised her.
>   (Song of Solomon 6:4–9)

Solomon did and said it best. Briefly, let us consider how Solomon loved his wife. What were his secrets? A husband trying to follow New Testament admonitions in carrying out his role can find no better guidelines and examples of Ephesians 5 in action than those provided by Solomon in Song of Solomon 6:4–9, where we note, first of all, that he praised her for her physical appearance and her great character. He refrained from criticizing her. It was as if she did not deserve any criticism. Husband, your wife needs to hear similar praise from your lips. Every wife needs to be praised for her beauty by her husband. This makes her feel beautiful, gives her confidence, and builds her self-image.

Perhaps you have heard the words "not tonight" or "I have a headache." Well, do not feel alone; so did Solomon (see Song of Solomon 5:3). Now I want to call your attention to how he handled this most delicate matter. He extravagantly spread the door handles with perfume (myrrh). He did this so she would know that he was not angry and that he loved her as much as ever. Becoming an irate husband at times like these will not help you or your wife. Always seek to turn your negatives into positives. Why not say something like, "That's all right, honey, get a good night's rest, you'll feel better tomorrow. Would you like to sleep in my arms? I love you very much. Good night."

Despite being upset, Solomon behaved like a lover and so his wife realized she was loved and safe. Instead of rebuking her, Solomon reassured her of his love for her. Your wife should know that even if you do get a little angry sometimes, the one thing she can count on is your love for her. As Solomon the lover and king did, exercise wisdom in romancing your wife.

Welcome Romance from Your Wife

In Song of Solomon 7:11 and 8:2, the Shulamite woman does the talking and the initiating. After all, Solomon has been describing her physical attractiveness and sexual delights. He is ready, and according to the verses just preceding this section, so is she. She is ready to celebrate with him. Notice that in chapter 7:1–12, this is sex from God's point of view—explicit and intimate. It is filled with pleasure and enjoyment and there has never been a more beautiful description nor a more complete picture of romantic love. The words, "There I will give you my love," in verse twelve emphasize that the Shulamite is looking for a romantic and secluded place to enjoy their lovemaking. She feels the need for privacy, for a change of environment, for renewal, and for romance that will be remembered.

Take it from me, a man who has been married to the same woman for sixty-eight years as of this writing: no matter how much you enjoy sex at home, there is a need for romantic getaways with your wife. This does not have to be expensive or for a long period of time, it can be just one or two days at some romantic place. Or it can be just one night at a hotel, away from the children, away from the phone, away from the same environment. Believe me, it will do you good.

There is so much more to be gleaned from this passage, but I want to stress the point that in this case, it is the wife who is planning this getaway, and the husband welcomes the idea. Therefore, as men we must welcome romance from our wives.

Will to Romance Your Wife

God is love and He created humans to love Him back. Love cannot be compelled; it must be freely given by an act of will. Therefore, we must will to romance our wives and when we do, the Lord, who lives in us in the person of the Holy Spirit, will empower us to do so.

However, we have also been commanded to love our wives. "In this same way, husbands ought to love their wives as their own bodies. He who loves his wife loves himself. After all, no one ever hated their own body, but they feed and care for their body, just as Christ does the church" (Ephesians 5:28–29).

Notice that you are to nourish and cherish your wife as your own body. This means that just as you provide for the needs of your body, you must provide for the needs of your wife, and romance is a need. Because loving your wife is a command, you can by faith will to love your wife romantically and, according to 1 John 5:14–15, trust God to provide the power to get it done. Notice what it says: "This is the confidence we have in approaching God: that if we ask anything according to his will, he hears us. And if we know that he hears us—whatever we ask—we know that we have what we asked of him."

Conclusion

Now here it is in a nutshell: By faith, be willing to love and act lovingly. Then romantic love will come. It is so important that we understand this. As husbands, we must view romantic love as a *calling* from God on our lives and, as Paul writes, "The one who calls you is faithful, and he will do it" (1 Thessalonians 5:24). Paul also writes: "For it is God who works in you to will and to act in order to fulfill his good purpose" (Philippians 2:13). We have a faithful God who is at work in us, both to will and to do what He has called us to do. For this reason, we are without excuse. *Romance your wife.* I have been married for sixty-eight years as of this writing, and I am still romancing my wife.

NOTES

1. This chapter is an updated version of the chapter that appeared in *Men to Men: Perspectives of Sixteen African-American Christian Men*, ed. Lee N. June and Matthew Parker (Zondervan Publishing House, 1996).
2. This song is by Ronnie Milsap and is titled "Daydreams about Night Things."
3. Gregory J. P. Godek, *Romance 101: Lessons in Love* (Weymouth, MA: Casablanca Press, 1993), 197.
4. Gregory J. P. Godek, *1001 More Ways to be Romantic* (Weymouth, MA: Casablanca Press, 1993), 198.

PART 4

DEALING WITH THE CRIMINAL JUSTICE SYSTEMS

18

Survive

Avoiding Arrest and Prison

KENNETH L. MCDANIELS, LLM, JD

Everyone must submit to governing authorities. For all
authority comes from God, and those in positions of authority
have been placed there by God. So anyone who rebels against
authority is rebelling against what God has instituted, and they
will be punished. For the authorities do not strike fear in people
who are doing right, but in those who are doing wrong. Would
you like to live without fear of the authorities? Do what is right,
and they will honor you. The authorities are God's servants,
sent for your good. But if you are doing wrong, of course you
should be afraid, for they have the power to punish you. They
are God's servants, sent for the very purpose of punishing those
who do what is wrong. So you must submit to them, not only
to avoid punishment, but also to keep a clear conscience.

Romans 13:1–5 NLT

Introduction

The purpose of this chapter is twofold. First, I will discuss what
needs to be done in case of an arrest. Second, I will offer ideas on
how to avoid contact with the criminal justice system. I would
prefer not to discuss this first topic. Still, we need to because of
the high incidence of contact that African Americans have with
the criminal justice system, and our frequent deaths at the hands
of police, even at the hands of Black law enforcement.

Let us begin by assuming that on Monday morning, you go to your doctor, and the doctor looks at you and says, "You know you have a wart on your finger. Right now, we must take you to the emergency room and amputate your arm." Because of your knowledge and experience, you will look at that doctor and say calmly, "Thank you, but I will get a second opinion." We must have the same attitude about the legal profession as we do about the medical profession. African American people must know how the criminal system works to aid their families in times of need.

General Overview Regarding the Issue of Arrest

What to do if you are arrested:

It is two o'clock in the morning, and one of your friends calls to tell you (after watching the arrest) that John, a member of your family, has been arrested and taken away in handcuffs. Next, John will be taken into custody, fingerprinted, and photographed. There will also be other people at the police station who have been arrested. So, if you go down to the police station immediately, you will get little information. At the police administration building, there may be a public defender, an attorney, a district attorney, and a bail commissioner. They will summarize what your family member is there for, the charge, and the bail. Within three to five days of the processing, there will be a preliminary hearing. After the preliminary hearing, if evidence shows that a crime was committed and that John committed it, he will be held for trial. At that time, a bail request may be made. Weeks or months later, John (the defendant) will attend the pretrial conference. At the pretrial conference, the defense attorney will be given evidence to show what the commonwealth or state has against John. Eventually, there will be a trial. The trial may be a jury trial or a nonjury trial with only one judge. John will then be found either guilty or not guilty.

When a person is incarcerated, and while they are being processed, one of the things that will happen to them is that somebody from the service division of the court system will interview them in jail. Usually, this person is the one who will allow your family member to call home. These are court officials who are neutral, friendly, and polite. They will talk to the person while he is in custody. They will ask some questions because they need to know certain things about the person to have bail set on their behalf. They will ask for the defendant's name, address, employment status, and birthdate, which they will verify with a call to the home. If someone is not there, they will be unable to verify the information and will not be sure what kind of bail to recommend. Another critical factor when an arrest has been made is attitude. If you or some member of your family is arrested, you are naturally upset, but just because you are upset does not mean that you should lose your cool.

For example, a neutral person comes to you saying, "I'm here because the court wants me to be here, and I need to record some personal data on you because we need to report this to the bail commissioner so he can decide on your bail. What is your name?" You replied, "I don't want to tell you." Then they say, "Where do you live?" You answer, "That is none of your business." Guess what? When the officials see on the form that you did not cooperate and that they cannot verify an address, you are going to be in jail for a long time before a preliminary hearing. My point is that attitude does affect what may happen to you. When you go before the bail commissioner, your attitude is critical too. If you are hostile and uncooperative, they will set bail as high as they wish.

The Bail Process

Bail is the amount of money one must pay to secure the release of a person charged with a crime. Most offenses are bailable, except for first-degree murder. If bail is set, the person can get out of jail. A window is open twenty-four hours a day where you can pay the bail within most courthouses. You are required to pay 10 percent of the amount of bail. For example, if bail is $100,000, then 10 percent is $10,000. When you post bail and the case is over, the court system will take 30 percent of that bail, which, in this example, will be $3,000 of the original 10 percent you posted. Hence, you will get $7,000 back. One can also put up real estate as bail. Using real estate is a bit different. With real estate, you must deal with the actual value of your home. Say, for example, bail is $100,000. Your home must be worth $100,000, or you cannot use it for bail; if you live in a district where you can post bail through a bail bond agent, contact one as soon as possible.

Handling Being Arrested

The most important thing to remember is to be polite. Do not use profanity. Be the Christian you should be. Instruct your family and friends to be the same way. Have a cooperative attitude. Sometimes, people say that someone did not read them their rights when arrested. Let us say that the police caught you inside a safe. They brought you in and said, "We don't have to read you your rights because we caught you." You are not there to give a statement because the police do not know who committed the crime. They know that you did it. Therefore, if no information is provided or asked of you, your rights are usually not read to you. If you ask the officer, "Am I free to leave?" they might say, "No." Then you are under arrest. Is there a statement you want to make? If so, you have the right to remain silent. Anything you say can and may be used against you . . . In this case, you have just been read your rights. Faced with an arrest, you can do what you want regarding giving a statement. I tell my children they should never give a statement until they talk to a lawyer. When have you read in the newspaper that police officers, public officials, or judicial officials who were arrested have ever given a statement?

Finding a Good Lawyer

You should get a lawyer who knows their job, a specialist. I will not hire a dentist to do open-heart surgery on me. If I want a criminal lawyer, I will find criminal lawyers. This choice may start with contacting your state bar association by phone or online, requesting your state's free lawyer referral service, or your local free city or county lawyer referral service and asking, "Can I get ten names of experienced trial lawyers?" Additional ways would be contacting your friends and neighbors concerning attorneys they have heard of or hired. Some churches and other organizations also have lists of attorneys.

If available, use those resources. There are both excellent attorneys and poor attorneys. Therefore, it is crucial for you to ask questions when you go to see an attorney for yourself or with that loved one. Let me make a point about securing a lawyer by giving an example of buying a car. If you want to buy a car, you might go to a friend and say, "Look, I am too emotionally involved because I want this car so much; could you negotiate the price for me?" When you go to a lawyer's office, you may not be emotionally up to talking at first. So, you may want someone else to assist you in taking care of this business, someone who will help you keep your mind clear because many questions need to be asked. It is your life or your family member's life at stake. This arrest may result in jail and a permanent record; you need a clear head now.

One of the questions to ask a lawyer is: Do you try criminal cases? Other questions to ask include:

What is your success rate?

Do you win or lose? Do you negotiate?

Are your clients getting good deals? Can I check with your other clients? If you have anybody who went to jail, can I call them or find out about them? If people are walking around freely, can I talk to them?

Do you have any news clippings about yourself and what you have done? Is there anybody else I can call to check up on you?

It would be best to ask these questions because you are hiring a lawyer. Treat your session with the lawyer as a job interview. You are paying the bill. It is your life.

When you have found out about the lawyer's record, say, "Okay, here are the facts of my case. What do you think you can do for me?" Before you conclude your interview, ask if they practice appellate law. Let us be realistic about this. You will need an appellate lawyer if you lose and go to jail.

In addition to questioning the lawyer about their record, ask about first-time-offender programs. Suppose you or your family member is charged with drunk driving or drug possession, a first offense. There are programs for people who are accused of a felony, but who have no criminal record. It is at the discretion of the district attorney's office whether you get into such programs but at least ask about them. You may have to pay restitution or be placed on probation. You will have no record if you have no violations at the end of the probation time. These are things you need to consider because if you have no prior criminal record, chances are you will have no record when you finish doing the program.

Please leave if the lawyer does not know anything about such programs. You may be in the wrong place. Lawyers ought to be able to answer questions about first-time offender programs for you, which will reduce your lawyer expenses because you would be diverted into a program and spared a trial and a lot of other things. So, it is critical to ask about such programs.

Please Pay Your Lawyer

Once you get to the day of trial, judges will not let you fire your lawyer. An analogy may help. Suppose you are in the hospital for surgery and are supposed to pay the doctor's bill for that day. You did not do it and now you are about to have the operation. Do you think that the doctor will do their best work? It's the same thing with lawyers. It is terrible when you are sitting at the table fighting for your life, and your lawyer says to the judge, "Judge, please let me get out of this case. This guy hasn't paid me." The judge then looks at the lawyer and says, "Sorry, Mr. Lawyer, you know better than that; you are stuck with this case. You will try this case and have to represent him zealously." Appropriately negotiate the fee up front, have your attorney put your mutual agreement in writing, and pay what you agree to pay at the appropriate time. If your family pays for your attorney, do not expect your attorney to disclose information to your family without your written authorization. Remember, the lawyer-client privilege is between the client and not the client's family.

Public Defenders and Court-Appointed Attorneys

For years, defendants asked, "Shall I hire an attorney or get a public defender? Public defenders are lawyers, and most are some of the best criminal attorneys in this country. They can be some of the best criminal prosecutors' worst nightmares. Public defenders are trained similarly to prosecutors and have similar resources, such as private detectives, psychiatrists, and medical experts. Public defenders tend to hold prosecutors to a high standard of ethics and accountability.

Court-appointed attorneys are appointed by the courts to represent individuals in the court system who are indigent but, for some reason, do not qualify for a public defender because of a possible legal conflict, such as the public defender already representing a co-defendant. The court-appointed attorneys are highly qualified to represent defendants in any situation. They also have resources like public defenders, private detectives, psychiatrists, and medical experts.

Client Guidelines

Respect your lawyer. After the preliminary hearing, your lawyer will receive a discovery package—a list of the witnesses, the facts, the statements, the lab reports, and other proof that the prosecution has against you or your loved one. The lawyer will sit down with you and review everything the state may have against you.

Discovery is the disclosure of all the evidence the criminal prosecutor has against you and all the evidence that the prosecutor has that is exculpatory, that is, evidence beneficial to your case. Depending on the state that you live in, your attorney may be provided with your entire criminal record. When they receive your discovery, it would be best to ask your attorney several questions. These questions apply whether you are charged with a felony or a misdemeanor:

- What is the evidence against me?
- How does my criminal record affect my case?
- If I am found guilty and have no previous criminal record, is there any diversionary program I can participate in to avoid a criminal record and to obtain an expunged record?
- Based on the nature of the crime and my criminal record, what do you anticipate my punishment will be if I am found guilty at trial?
- Based on the nature of the crime and my criminal record, what do you anticipate my punishment will be if I plead guilty before trial?

Note that these fundamental questions give you an idea of what you may face if you or your family member are arrested.

- Be prepared for good news (that they may not be able to prove the case against you). But also, be ready for the sad news. Sometimes lawyers get information in the discovery package that points right at you—they have fingerprints, they have you on video, or they have eyewitnesses.
- Maintain a good attitude. Do not think the lawyer must get you off the hook. This is the wrong attitude to have. It would be best if you were prepared sometimes for the hard truth. Ask your lawyer what will happen if you do not get off. Ask how much time in prison you are going to get. Sometimes people don't do that. Then the trial comes and they are shocked because nobody prepared them for the worst.
- Pay your bill. Having a lawyer who is unhappy because you have not paid your account is a terrible situation. A divided house cannot stand, nor can a divided lawyer and client. A paid lawyer is a happy lawyer seeking to develop a good relationship with their client.

Who Selects the Jury

If a case goes to trial, how much influence does your attorney have in selecting the jury? The prosecutor and defense attorney select the jury with the defendant's assistance. If a juror is brought in, the prosecutor asks questions, and the defense attorney asks questions. The questions give you a feeling of what a prospective juror is like. Eventually, there is a meeting of the minds to determine if this person would be a fair and impartial jurist.

After the Trial

Let us assume that you or your loved one has been found guilty. You still may have another chance. For example, under Pennsylvania law, the person found guilty can have a postconviction hearing. At this hearing, the lawyer goes before the judge who tried the case and says, "I want a new trial for my client because of the following mistakes," which are listed in a petition. The judge looks at the petition, and your lawyer and the prosecutor submit briefs. The judge may grant you a new trial. The point is that the original trial may not be your last chance. There is sometimes another proceeding, and you need to be aware of it. This postconviction proceeding can also be called a "post-verdict motion." At this level, you can use the same lawyer if you have been satisfied, or you can hire a new lawyer to look at everything your first lawyer did at trial. If you are found not guilty, your lawyer can get the charges against you expunged—erased from your record as if they never existed.

How to Stay Out of Trouble

Tips on avoiding the criminal justice system:

Brothers (and all others), please read Proverbs 1:8–19, then read the following information.

While I have shared tips on preparing yourself or a family member in the event of an arrest, my ultimate hope is that you avoid the criminal justice system. Realizing this, I now share what can be done. I will speak particularly to young African American males, who are most at risk for involvement with the criminal justice system.

I am not a criminologist or a sociologist. However, after thirty years as a criminal rape, homicide, and fraud prosecutor and five years as a homicide defense attorney, I can offer a few tips that, if followed, will lessen the chance of your arrest or death. I share all this information with you, hoping it may save your life. I say "may" because there are no guarantees. However, if there is any possibility that this will save your life or the life of someone you love, wouldn't you agree that these things are worth knowing?

- Avoid so-called friends who commit crimes. Eventually, they will involve you. If friends commit crimes in your presence, make it clear to them and their victims that you are not involved.

- Control your temper. Thousands of people are killed and injured because of anger. Control your mouth in the presence of the police and your adversaries.
- Visit a court in session to see the criminal justice system firsthand.
- Tour a prison or a morgue. Ask questions about why some of the people are there.
- Avoid places where crimes occur. Why are you there if you know crimes happen in that particular area?
- Avoid alcohol and drugs. They will always control you. You will never control them.
- Avoid drug houses. They will either be raided by the police or by others, resulting in your arrest or death.
- Do not stick around if you get into a fight or argument with someone who tells you they will be back. They will come back.
- If you are in school, stay in school. It is rare to find people who regularly attend school committing a crime.
- Just because you feel disrespected, consider your actions carefully. Getting "revenge" will not make up for the years you spend in jail after shooting someone because they disrespected you.
- If there is an arrest warrant with your name on it, turn yourself in. Your family and loved ones may be arrested or harmed in their own home during a police raid, while they are looking for you.

Vehicle Stops or Personal Encounters with Law Enforcement

Tips on what to do and what not to do (or worse):

Brothers (and anyone else), please read Romans 13:1–5, then read the following tips.

- Pull over immediately, place the vehicle in a parked position, set the emergency brake, turn the engine off, and activate the hazard warning lights. If at night, turn on the interior dome light.

- Think carefully about your words, movements, body language, and emotions.
- Remain calm and tell all passengers to remain calm as well. Do not act like a fool.
- In many situations, you or the persons with you can talk your way into jail just as well as you can talk your way out of jail. By yelling, cursing, or threatening the officer, the best you can do is get yourself arrested.
- Please check to see whether the police officer is wearing a body camera.
- Do not get into an argument with the police.
- Remember that anything you say can be used against you in court.
- Keep your seat belt fastened and tell your passengers to do the same unless the officer asks you to exit.
- Remain in the car and lower the driver's window. Keep both hands clearly in sight on the steering wheel. Ask your passengers to keep their hands in plain view or on their laps. Wait for the law enforcement officer to give you instructions. An officer may approach from either side of the vehicle.
- Before reaching into your glove box or under the seat to retrieve your proof of insurance or driver's license, inform the officer of where the items are located and follow the officer's directions.
- Do not make any suspicious movements, such as looking in the back seat of your car or reaching under your seat or dashboard. Some officers might think you are trying to hide or search for something, for example, a weapon.
- If you have a gun in your car, it is crucial to inform the officer that you have a weapon and where it is located.
- If asked to exit the vehicle, check for passing cars to exit safely. Advise passengers to remain in the vehicle unless the law enforcement officer gives other instructions.
- Do not touch any part of the police officer. If you do, that will give them sufficient provocation to draw their weapon. This can only end tragically for you.

- Do not run! This will make the police think they were right all along and give them a reason to arrest you when they previously may not have had one.
- Remember that there are some bad police officers and some good police officers. The bad police officers want you to do or say something wrong. These police officers will use your defiance or disrespect against you and try to trick you into doing something that gives them reason to arrest or shoot you. Remember, bad police officers want you to escalate the situation so they can justify their conduct. This escalation always results in your arrest or injury. Remember that these types of police officers can be either Black, White, or other ethnicities.

Your Rights and Obligations When You Encounter the Police

- You have the right to know what you are being stopped for.
- You have the right to know how to identify the officer, especially if they are in plain clothes.
- You have the right to refuse to give consent for a search.
- You have the right to be treated with respect and dignity.
- You have the right to ask if you are free to leave.
- You have the right to file a complaint about mistreatment.
- You have the right to video your encounter.
- You can stop talking and request an attorney's presence.

Police Officers Also Have Rights as well as Obligations

- They have the right to ask for proper identification.
- They have the right to frisk you for their own safety.
- They have the right to search your car if they see something illegal or suspicious.
- They have the right to issue you a ticket, summons, or citation.
- They have the right to arrest you if you have committed a crime.
- They have the right to use deadly force if attacked.

- They are obligated to treat you with respect and dignity.
- They are obligated to stop you only for probable cause.
- They are obligated to respect your rights.
- They have the right to seek a search warrant if consent is not given.
- They are obligated to enforce the law fairly and equally.

Conclusion

We live in times when we need to understand and deal with the criminal justice system. Whether you or someone in your family are facing an arrest or any instance of an encounter with the police, you need to exercise wisdom. I hope you find this information helpful concerning the criminal justice system and how to act and conduct yourself in a trial. Also, just as critical for survival is learning how you or your family member can exercise wisdom during vehicle stops or personal encounters with law enforcement. It may save a life.

Thrive

Overcoming Prison like Joseph

JOSEPH WILLIAMS, MA

But the LORD was with Joseph in the prison and
showed him his faithful love. And the LORD made
Joseph a favorite with the prison warden.

Genesis 39:21 NLT

Pharaoh said to Joseph, "I hereby put you in
charge of the entire land of Egypt."

Genesis 41:41 NLT

Introduction

As I write, I celebrate more than forty years of freedom from crime
and addiction, after a stint in prison as a young man for robbery.
Prior to recommitting my life to Christ at the age of twenty-eight
and being delivered from addiction and crime, I lived as a career
criminal and hard-core heroin addict for thirteen years. At the age
of twenty-one, I was sentenced to two years of hard labor and a
dishonorable discharge by an Army court. I had accepted Christ
as my Savior at the age of nine and was baptized. I had regularly
attended church and Sunday school until I ran away from home
at the age of fifteen. At this young and tender age, I landed on
the harsh streets of my hometown, Detroit, Michigan.

Deliverance from Crime and Addiction

Being miraculously delivered from crime and addiction was the most joyous experience of my life. It brought to an abrupt end thirteen years of the type of misery that I would not wish upon anyone. My gratitude to Christ for divinely intervening in my miserable existence was matched only by my desire to serve Him and to see others I knew from the streets and prison experience the same freedom that I now know firsthand.

The members of my childhood church home warmly greeted me on my return. They were elated over my expressed commitment to live as a disciple of Jesus Christ. At the request of my mother, they had been praying for me all those years and were thrilled to see this stray sheep back in the fold.

Like the demon-possessed man in Mark 5, out of gratitude for deliverance, I wanted to hang out with Jesus 24/7 (Mark 5:18). I was, as they say, in the church house every time the doors opened. But Jesus told the man he couldn't just hang out with Him. He should go back and tell the members of his community what great things God had done for him (Mark 5:19). The man was obedient to Jesus and went back to his metropolitan area and began to testify about the goodness of God in his life (Mark 5:20). Having known the hopelessness of his previous condition, everyone was in awe. Like that man, I was diligent in testifying about God's goodness in my life to my own community.

My New Life in Christ

Some of the leaders in the church believed that because of my background, I would thrive in ministry to the incarcerated. They believed that incarcerated people would respond to a message coming from someone with my background—someone like them. So, like the demon-possessed man, I sensed a calling to community outreach, including ministry to the incarcerated and the formerly incarcerated and their families.

I began visiting the Wayne County Jail as a volunteer chaplain. I was so grateful to be able to serve in this ministry, to give back to God through serving others in need for all He had done for me. I became a regular fixture in the jail. I conducted one-on-one visits with men and participated in other religious activities in the jail, including conducting chapel services.

Those I visited in the jail appeared to be greatly encouraged and inspired by my visits. Many expressed that they had accepted Christ or recommitted their lives to Christ through my humble efforts. Some members of my church, including my pastor, Rev. Robert Joe Page, seemed to be very encouraged by my ministry. This was the first sustained effort by anyone in the congregation to establish and carry out a ministry to the incarcerated. Rev. Page was totally elated when I invited him to the jail to baptize some of the jail's residents who had accepted Christ. We both wept as he conveyed to the congregation the joy that he experienced by baptizing incarcerated men and women into the faith.

A few years after returning to church, an official from a nearby prison reached out to inform us that there were opportunities to facilitate worship services for the residents on Sunday afternoons. The leaders of the church, having embraced my ministry for several years, happily responded to this opportunity. I was part of the team that participated in worship services with men housed in the prison for several years. At that point, I switched from jail ministry to prison ministry.

Ministry in a prison was even more rewarding to me than ministry in the jail had been. The jail setting was more transitory. People cycled through at a relatively fast pace. Some were convicted and sent to prison. Others were released back to the community. I lost contact with most of them. It was difficult to form long-lasting relationships. In the prison, however, men were sentenced and remained at that prison for several years.

Participating in church services with incarcerated men has been one of the most awesome experiences of my life. However, something inside of me desired more. I wanted to have a more holistic ministry to those we served. I wanted greater impact. I met with the Assistant Deputy Warden (ADW) of the prison. She was delighted to learn of my desire to do more. In fact, she had recently been presented with a request by the men in that prison to start up a "lifers group" that would consist of those serving life in prison. Recently, laws have been passed that greatly increased the number of life sentences handed out. In many instances, teenagers who would have ordinarily been sentenced in the juvenile system were now being given adult life sentences. There were young men in this prison who had been sentenced to life as young as fifteen years old.

This shift in sentencing laws, which would be one of the factors that led to mass incarceration, was initiated at the legislative level. The courts and prison systems were caught flat-footed. The prison officials had no idea how to provide effective services to people so young but with life sentences. This ADW was thrilled to have someone like me, a young, African American, formerly incarcerated man, who was interested and willing to help her establish a program to serve this group of men. They would come to be known as "juvenile lifers," a new and horrible term added to the American lexicon.

About a year after recommitting my life to Christ, I enrolled in the local Bible college. I earned my bachelor's degree and went on to earn a graduate degree in Applied Sociology, concentrating on prison recidivism. The blessing of being able to continue my education provided me with a greater depth of understanding related to the incarcerated people I served.

Ministry with Prison Fellowship

In 1992 I was recruited by Prison Fellowship (PF), the largest prison ministry in the world. At that time, PF had a great deal of experience serving incarcerated men and women and their families. Their reputation as a premier prison ministry was growing. However, they had much less experience and success in serving people in transition from prison to the community. In those days we called it "prison aftercare." Today it is commonly known as "prisoner reentry." Even people returning to the community from prison who had participated in Christian programming, such as what PF offered, had extremely high rates of recidivism (the rate of return to prison).

At that time, approximately 70 percent of those released from prison were rearrested within three years. About half of those rearrested returned to prison. Black men suffered the highest recidivism rates of all groups. The assignment I was given was to create a program designed to reduce recidivism for those who participated in PF programs.

I became the founding director of the Transition of Prisoners Program (TOP). My mission was to "set the captives free" in a spiritual sense (Isaiah 61:1). And I became one person who would help to keep them free spiritually and physically after their release from prison. A 2000 evaluation report showed that those who graduated from the TOP Program were ten times less likely to have any further contact with the criminal justice system than a control group.

God has been very gracious to me in allowing me to engage in this level of prison ministry over such a long period of time. This experience has taught me a great deal about serving people in prison and those in transition into the community and their families. I must say that along with the knowledge I have been able to amass, my attitude toward this work has greatly shifted over the decades. I have seen God work in some amazing ways in the lives of people I had the privilege to serve directly and some men and women I observed from a distance.

When I first went into prison ministry, my attitude was much different than it is today. I went into this work like many others, thinking, *These poor souls need someone like me to come to their rescue. They need us!* I looked at those behind bars as people with significant deficits. My goal was to take Jesus to them. I hoped that they would accept Christ, shed their bad attitudes and habits, and begin to live crime-free, productive lives. And I worked diligently toward that end.

Mass Incarceration: Its Effects, Challenges, and Opportunities

As I continued in prison ministry, serving in just about every aspect of it at some time or another, I began to see incarcerated people differently. Earlier, I mentioned the term *mass incarceration*. Mass incarceration refers to the tremendous explosion of the prison population in this country. Beginning in the 1980s, the US prison population more than quadrupled. It went from approximately 500,000 in 1980 to over 2.3 million people in a twenty-year period. Many, including myself, see mass incarceration as a terrible evil inflicted on the most vulnerable people in the nation. African American men have borne the brunt of this staggering increase in incarceration.

It has been heartbreaking to witness so many poor people, including Black people and especially Black men swept up into this horribly unjust system. Most are caught up in this system at an early age. Many remain in the system throughout what should be the most productive years of their lives.

To a significant degree, mass incarceration is a Black issue. Approximately 12 to 13 percent of the American population is Black, but we make up 40 percent of the prison population. While one in thirty men between the ages of twenty and thirty-four is behind bars, the figure is one in nine for Black males in that age group. There are now more African American men in prison, on parole, or in probation than there were in slavery in 1850.[1]

The Good from the Bad

It is hard to imagine that anything good could come of such a terrible injustice inflicted on our people. But countless times in my life, I have witnessed God turn defeat into victory. I have seen Him turn victims into victors. Isn't that what the story of Joseph is about? Joseph's brothers sold him to enslavers for a profit. He was carried off from his homeland to Egypt where he was forced to serve in the household of a high government official, Potiphar. Even in enslavement, God's hand was on Joseph, and he excelled in his work (Genesis 39:2).

Joseph was so effective at his job, so faithful in his work, that he rose quickly through the ranks to become the chief servant in Potiphar's house. However, Mrs. Potiphar falsely accused Joseph of rape. He was wrongly convicted and sentenced to an undetermined length of time of confinement in the federal prison. Joseph's imprisonment was a terrible miscarriage of justice on all levels.

But the biblical text details that God was with Joseph, even in prison (Genesis 39:19–21). And because of his character and work ethic, Joseph once again rose through the ranks. He became the chief trustee of the prison. Joseph may have spent as long as twelve years in prison, between the ages of eighteen to thirty. God orchestrated his miraculous release from prison at the age of thirty. In a very short time, Joseph went from prisoner to prime minister of the most powerful country in the world at that time.

Years after Joseph became the prime minister of Egypt, his brothers, who had sold him into slavery, were forced to come to him for help. They were horrified when they learned that the person they had so grievously wronged was in a position to do them great harm, up to and including ending their wicked lives. As they stood helplessly before Joseph, he realized that God had used all the miserable circumstances he was forced to endure to put him in this tremendously powerful position. Joseph's words to his brothers were, "You intended to harm me, but God intended it for good" (Genesis 50:20).

Could it be that the evil of mass incarceration has not escaped the power and grace of God's hand? Writer Michelle Alexander, in her watershed book, *The New Jim Crow: Mass Incarceration in the Age of Colorblindness*, refers to this system as the greatest civil rights issue of our time. After decades of prison ministry, that is the conclusion at which I have arrived. Mass incarceration! They meant it for evil, but God uses this wicked system to work good in the lives of His children.

Amazingly, prison has become a university, a seminary for many. How did I come to this conclusion? I have realized over the years that many men who had no interest in academic learning while free on the streets of their neighborhood began to develop interest in reading and learning once they were incarcerated. I first witnessed this during my own incarceration many years ago. One of the things that surprised me when I was locked up was the voracious appetite that some of the men had developed for reading. We regularly recommended certain books to each other. A book in a jail setting would likely be read by twenty or more people before falling apart.

I have continued to witness this phenomenon through the years. When men go to prison, many of them develop a real interest in academic learning for the first time in their lives. I have seen men who would never dream of cracking open a book in free society end up in prison and become great scholars. Nathan McCall, in his book *Makes Me Wanna Holler: A Young Black Man in America*, writes about how, once landing in the county jail on his way to prison, he observed that many of his fellow incarcerated men had embraced the practice of reading volumes of printed materials.[2] Nathan himself embraced reading for the first time after going to prison. After his release, he became an acclaimed journalist, working at such prestigious publications as *The Atlanta Journal-Constitution* and *The Washington Post*.

Many men discover the Bible for the first time while incarcerated. Most people do not realize that there is a strong Christian movement behind the walls and fences of many prisons in this country. It's natural and actually biblical to turn to God when you are facing legal trouble. Thus, prison and jail ministry have yielded a great deal of fruit over the decades. In Psalm 50:15, the Lord says, "Call on me in the day of trouble; I will deliver you, and you will honor me." It doesn't say how a person's deliverance will happen.

The church is alive and thriving behind the walls and fences of this country's prisons. Some are hearing the gospel for the first time. Others are returning to the God of their youth. Church services in prison are livelier and more dynamic than many church services in the community. Go to a church service in a prison if you want to see men earnestly worship God. In many ways I've observed, Christianity in prison is purer than that practiced elsewhere in the community. Some Christians in prison have never attended a church service in the free world, so they are not infected by tradition. All they know is Scripture.

Christians in prison have a great deal of time to study and pray. Many take advantage of this time and apply themselves diligently to the study of God's Word and to prayer. I have found Christians in prison, for the most part, to be sincere and earnest in their pursuit of God.

Some of the most dynamic leaders in the community and the church today have come out of the prison church. Many made good use of the time, and whether justly or unjustly confined, found God in the darkness of prison and held on to Him for dear life. They have a level of faith, faithfulness, and commitment that I rarely see in the church today. And they are doing great work in the church and community. God is using them to address some of the toughest problems that have plagued our community for decades. Their approach to addressing problems is fresh and powerful. Some spend their time in the community addressing community challenges. Many are serving in church ministry, including in the pastorate.

Transformation of My Attitude toward Prison Ministry: Modern-Day Josephs

Yes, my experiences have greatly transformed my attitude toward prison ministry. I no longer look at people in prison and think, *They so desperately need us to come to their rescue.* I now see those who have used their time in prison to establish their relationship with God and grow spiritually and intellectually, and I think, *We desperately need them.* That is the Joseph effect. Many of them are Josephs in their own right.

Jerry's Story

I will share with you a couple of examples of modern-day Josephs I have come to know over the years. You may be able to think of others. I want to introduce you to my dear brother Jerry Blassingame.[3] Jerry is the founder and CEO of Soteria Community Development Corporation in Greenville, South Carolina. He grew up in Greenville and was raised by his grandmother after his mother was murdered by her boyfriend when Jerry was only five years old. He never knew his father. Jerry was raised in a low-income housing project in Greenville's inner city.

When the crack cocaine epidemic hit his small city in the mid-80s, Jerry began to sell drugs. He made a lot of money in the illegal drug trade. He had his own drug empire. Jerry was eventually arrested and sentenced to twenty years for several counts of distribution of cocaine.

While in the county jail, Jerry's sister, a Christian, encouraged him to read the Bible and pray regularly. He reluctantly did what she asked. He finally got to the point of submitting his heart to Jesus Christ. He thought, If I am going to do twenty years in prison, I need to do it with God. The first day that he got to the state prison, he found the chaplain's office. Soon he began meeting with the Christian men in the prison. They studied and prayed daily. The men in his group attended various church services.

Jerry began to write the plan for Soteria Community Development Corporation, a ministry he planned to start when released. He was inspired by Habakkuk 2:2: "Write the vision; make it plain upon tablets, so he may run who reads it" (RSV). Jerry was released from prison after serving three and a half years. He will tell you that it was God who brought him out after serving only a small portion of his sentence. Jerry joined a local church and began to lead the prison ministry. With the help of supporters, he launched Soteria in 1999.

Today, Jerry is a leading citizen in Greenville. Soteria is a vital organization that helps lift people from dire circumstances to become productive members of the community. It provides housing for people returning to the community from prison. Soteria also provides low-income housing for some of Greenville's most vulnerable residents through one of its social enterprises. Distressed properties are purchased and rehabbed by program participants. These newly renovated homes are made available to residents at a price they can afford.

Jerry has testified before Congress on behalf of faith-based organizations. He has been recognized as an outstanding social entrepreneur by the Aspen Institute. He has faithfully served in several church leadership positions and is a dedicated father to his children. He has also participated in several international ministry endeavors.

Darryl's Story

Now I want to introduce you to another friend who was a victim of mass incarceration. His name is Darryl Woods Sr.[4] Darryl grew up in Detroit, Michigan, during the crack epidemic. He was part of a group of teenagers who made their living by selling drugs. As a young criminal, he was very successful financially. He thought he had life figured out. He thought he had it made. This youngster, however, could not imagine how quickly life could change for the worse as he stood before a judge at the age of seventeen and received the sentence of life in prison without the possibility of parole.

Darryl grew up under very tough circumstances. His father made his living from the streets. His mom had gotten swept up by addiction to drugs and struggled greatly to raise her children in a tough Detroit neighborhood. Darryl grew up way too fast in a city that is as fast and hard as they come. Although Darryl's grandmother tried to steer him away from the allure of the streets by taking him to church and providing other positive influences for him, the song of the streets pulled him further and further into the deadly trap of street life.

While in prison, Darryl recommitted his life to Christ. He diligently applied himself to the study of God's Word. The prison chaplain recognized Darryl's genuine zeal and nurtured him in his faith. Darryl grew as a Christian within the prison church community of the various prisons in which he was housed.

Darryl's influence extended beyond traditional church services, Bible studies, and prayer meetings. He had a passion to help young people in the community. He wanted to reach them before they ended up in the awful place in which he found himself. Like Joseph, Darryl found favor in the eyes of his jailers. Somehow, this remarkable young man managed to create meaningful relationships with people outside of the prison walls.

He established relationships with leaders in law enforcement at the local and federal level. He became friends with judges and nonprofit leaders in the Detroit area. By leveraging these relationships in an amazing way, Darryl and a few of his fellow residents began to create youth programs focused on at-risk young boys. Judges sent boys who had begun to get into trouble into the prison. Law enforcement officers from local and federal agencies attended these sessions. The adults, both incarcerated and free, expressed to these youth how much the elders in the community cared for them.

Darryl described this program, which he named the Youth Deterrent Program, as a "cared straight" program, not a "scared straight" program. On a regular basis, in a prison located in Detroit, a group of incarcerated men and law enforcement officers ministered to young men at risk of arrest and incarceration. Their care even extended beyond the boys themselves but also to their families. The program was evaluated by the University of Michigan and found to be a successful approach to crime prevention.

The most impressive thing I learned about Darryl was that he actively raised his own son and daughter from prison. Darryl Jr. was only an infant when his dad was incarcerated. Darryl Sr. used all of the tools at his disposal to remain an active dad in his son's life. Contact was limited to letter writing, phone calls, and frequent visits. Darryl Jr. grew to become an outstanding student and citizen. He graduated with honors and received scholarships to complete his college education. Darryl Jr. is now a successful businessperson raising his own family in Florida. Darryl Sr.'s daughter Tiffany also benefited from Darryl's parenting from prison. She is a successful businessperson in the Detroit area.

On February 13, 2019, Darryl walked out of prison, having had his sentence commuted by then Governor Rick Snyder. Like Joseph, Darryl's faithfulness and gifts have caused him to rise as an important leader in Detroit and the state of Michigan. As I write these words, Darryl has access to the governor of Michigan, local mayors, and numerous other government leaders. He frequently serves alongside business leaders and is an adviser to several police agencies. Darryl's gifts have allowed him to create innovative approaches to solving persistent problems in the community. Since his release from prison, he has become one of Detroit's leading citizens and favorite sons.

Conclusion: The Way Forward

My friends Jerry and Darryl are not unique. There are Joseph-type men in various stages of development in prisons across this nation. You may not know their names, but perhaps you will someday. Many have reentered society over the past decade or so and are making great contributions to others. Some are pastors, bishops, and leaders in other positions within the body of Christ. Others are leaders in the for-profit and nonprofit worlds. Some are advocates for justice. Their time in prison did not destroy them. In the midst of a terrible plight, because of God's power, they discovered and tapped into their God-given potential. They used their time to learn, grow, and develop. They are an important part of the next great spiritual movement in this nation. Yes, they are the victims of mass incarceration, a terrible system of injustice that I pray will soon be dismantled. The devil meant mass incarceration for evil, but God is working in the midst of it for the good of His people. The children of mass incarceration are the recipients of God's blessing despite great adversity. This is the Joseph effect.

NOTES

1. Michelle Alexander, *The New Jim Crow: Mass Incarceration in the Age of Colorblindness* (New York: New Press, 2010).

2. Nathan McCall, *Makes Me Wanna Holler: A Young Black Man in America* (New York: Vintage Books, 1994).

3. He tells his story in his book entitled *Reclaimed: A History of Second Chances* (The Brand Leader, 2018); see also Jerry Blassingame, "Reclaiming the Man," TEDx Talks, Greenville, SC, May 10, 2018, 13 minutes, 24 seconds, https://www.youtube.com /watch?v=B088Z2tEMRw.

4. See further details on Darryl's life in the following article: Christine Ferretti, "Second Chance Granted: With Freedom Comes 'Great Sense of Responsibility,'" *Detroit News*, August 22, 2019, https://www .detroitnews.com/story/news/local/michigan/2019/08/23/second -chance-granted-darryl-woods/1922205001/.

PART 5

FACING CONTEMPORARY AND FUTURE CHALLENGES

20

Navigate
The World of Technology

REV. MICHAEL T. WESTBROOK, MA
BRIAN L. JUNE, MML, MS

And the Good News about the Kingdom will be
preached throughout the whole world, so that all
nations will hear it; and then the end will come.
Matthew 24:14 NLT

Introduction

In this chapter, we share our introductions to technology, the
subject of technology in the Black church tradition, and the
advantages and challenges of technology. We then discuss how
the COVID-19 pandemic caused everyone to pause. Finally, we
consider artificial intelligence and using technology to assist in
meeting our missions and some of our practical needs.

A Generation X Perspective: *Brian June*

I was born in the late 1970s and grew up just as computers were
becoming accessible to the general public. My first computer
was a TRS-80 from Radio Shack. It piqued an interest in learning more about what computers could do. In school, we were
exposed to educational programs through a computer book. The
book had sample programs to try that were written in the BASIC

programming language for the TRS-80. My curiosity and fascination with computers increased. It led me to eventually enroll and graduate with bachelor's and master's degrees in computer science.

Technology is increasingly important and used in all aspects of our lives. We see this in the business world and religious world. Technology is a particularly valuable tool, and we saw increased usage in churches during COVID-19. Historically, many churches incorporated sound system technologies (microphones, etc.) within church services. As technology progressed, churches added projectors, screens, and televisions to display songs, announcements, responsive readings, and sermon titles.

Several advantages of using technology in church became known over time. It broadened the outreach for the church because it enhanced the number of listeners who could hear the sermon and participate in collective worship. This furthered the fulfillment of the Great Commission (see Matthew 28:18–20). Technology was critical during the pandemic when church members were not able to meet in person. It was also used to reach and train. It presented the opportunity for people to try software they would not have otherwise had a chance to use. While Scott Thumma and Dave Travis define megachurches as those with two thousand or more congregants,[1] smaller churches also benefit from technology. The Pew Research Center[2] and the Hartford Institute for Religion and Research Center[3] have been highlighting the uses of technology during the COVID period and beyond.

My church experience with advances in technology includes seeing a change and update in the distribution of church bulletins, responsive readings, and other parts of the service. Prior to this, these items were generated laboriously with typewriters and copy machines. Later, computers, word processing software, and printers simplified the production and distribution of weekly church bulletins, announcements, and other materials. Displaying responsive readings and sermon titles on the screens at church, for example, became a training opportunity for adaption of technology by members across different age groups. Additionally, PowerPoint and other video software were used to display sermon titles and even sometimes sermon points or illustrations in the sanctuary. Members of our church were very appreciative of the changes and the ability to learn new skills. These changes, along with the changes experienced through the COVID-19 pandemic and beyond, have helped shape the technology landscape that our church utilizes today.

A Boomer Perspective: *Michael Westbrook*

Having been born in the late 1950s would make me a representative of the later part of the Baby Boom Generation (post–World War II). Growing up, I was always a curious kid. I wanted to see how things worked, so I would take toys apart, especially the toys that moved. I even wanted to see how music boxes made their sound. Unfortunately, I was not as good at putting them back together. To help satisfy my curiosity, my family would buy me Lincoln Logs, Legos, Erector sets, and similar building toys to help with my tinkering habit. One toy set I remember vividly was an electronic set where I could place the plastic pieces together to form circuits. I was able to build light displays and even a radio. I was an only child growing up with a single parent. However, I had great aunts and uncles, a grandmother, and great-grandparents. I say all of this to give you a glimpse of how good it was around birthdays and Christmas because of the gifts I received. For example, transistor radios I took apart. One Christmas I also received a small portable Panasonic television set, but I wasn't "crazy" enough to take that apart. What fascinated me about the television set was that it operated with electricity or battery power. This was the mid-1960s when most families who had a television had a big TV console in their living room.

This was also the beginning of the space program, when we could watch rockets launched on television. That opened a whole new world for me. I was not as fascinated with the astronauts as I was fascinated with the people who ran mission control. This was displayed on rare occasions when they gave a television view of the mission control room with all the people in this big room in front of screens. This was the point when technology really struck an interest in me, and the desire to follow technological advances was fascinating.

Black Church Leadership and Technology

One set of circumstances that vividly comes to mind regarding Black church leadership and technology is what happened in the 1990s. The church that I was attending had just built a new building. After construction, the pastor struggled with several minor technological processes, including a telephone system. The church had gone from a small building with one main telephone line in the pastor's office and a payphone right outside the sanctuary to a multilevel, multiuse facility requiring a more elaborate communication system.

A telephone representative was trying to convince the pastor to install a multiple-line phone system that would connect the church offices and rooms all over the building. The pastor was convinced once he saw the benefit of having various areas of the church connected with an intercom system, and that it would meet the needs of the church by allowing the different areas to communicate. He agreed because he saw its value and expressed a depth of gratitude for the unexpected conveniences it offered.

Another challenge came when the church secretary requested the purchase of a desktop computer and printer. Up to this point, the church office staff used a typewriter to type the Sunday church bulletin and recorded the church finances by hand, which was tedious. Once the pastor saw a demonstration of the potential benefit of the church's tithes and finances recorded electronically and available any time he needed them, he was convinced, by the secretary, of the potential benefits of a desktop computer.

The biggest challenge came, however, when the church secretary requested a fax machine. As the church grew, there became a need for a fax machine because of the increased need to file papers from entities requesting them to be faxed. Before long, an easier sell for a fax machine came when the secretary pointed out to the pastor that the closest and only fax machine near the church was the local liquor store. The pastor was speechless after coming back to the office and seeing the name of the local liquor store emblazoned across the top of the faxed page. It was not too long before the church purchased its own fax machine.

These seemingly small things led to an even more significant increase in the church's embracing of technology. For example, a couple of years after rebuilding, the church expanded its outreach. It began taping and rebroadcasting the pastor's Sunday sermons on the local cable TV access channel during the week. This also meant that the church became wired for cable television and other streaming services. These gradual changes ended up benefiting the church as those technological additions were made.

Advantages of Technology

There are advantages in the use of technology, as stated in the introductory examples of Brian's church and my own. As noted, technology can help churches run more smoothly by enhancing their day-to-day administrative functions. Other advantages include reaching a wider audience, which can increase opportunities for evangelism (Matthew 18:20). That is, it helps to fulfill the Great Commission. Technology's use can also lead to an increase in productivity, which can lead to better stewardship of time and finances.

As more members of the Millennial and Gen-Z generations assume greater leadership roles in the church, there has been an increased use of technology, as many grew up utilizing several forms of technology in their everyday lives. The same is true with the Black church members as well. A recent study published by the Pew Research Center entitled "Online Religious Services Appeal to Many Americans, but Going in Person Remains More Popular" surveyed a diverse range of people. They stated,

> Notably, usage tends to be higher among members of the historically Black Protestant tradition, who are, for example, more than twice as likely as the general adult population to say they ever use apps or websites for reading Scripture (47% vs. 21%). Close to a quarter of adults who belong to historically Black Protestant denominations say they use apps or websites *every day* for reading Scripture or for praying (23% for each activity). All in all, 59% of adults in the historically Black Protestant

tradition report that they ever use apps or websites in *at least one* of the four ways listed.[4]

The authors go on to state,

> Two-in-ten U.S. adults say they consume religious content through online videos, for example, on YouTube or TikTok, and 15% say they listen to religion-focused podcasts. (The question about online videos asked whether respondents watch online videos *other than religious services*. Other questions in the survey asked specifically about watching religious services online.)[5]

The study furthers states,

> Overall, adults in the historically Black Protestant tradition and evangelicals are more likely than other religious groups to say they ever watch religion-focused videos online (44% and 38%, respectively). And nearly one-in-ten (9%) Black adults overall (irrespective of religious tradition) say they watch religion-focused online videos *every day* (9%), compared with 4% of the general adult population.[6]

Challenges of Technology

One overarching reason many Black church leaders were slow to embrace technology in the past was the fear of the unknown. In many instances, older pastors were hesitant because they did not see the need, due to their own lack of use. Other factors come into play also, such as education level. Church leaders who have college and other advanced degrees have had more opportunity to gain experience and incorporate technology into their lives. As sources and articles point out, with the increase of technology, society has become more of a "high-tech, low-touch" world. Other church leaders have expressed fear that changes could lead to a lack of intimacy among church members, as they feel it could hinder in-person fellowshipping and the development of deeper relationships and interactions (Hebrews 10:24–25). One can have an exhaustive list of "friends" on social media, but relationships tend to be superficial. Another concern expressed is that it could hinder spiritual development such as worshiping, reading, discussions, and getting immediate answers to questions, as these are things that these are things that are more likely to happen when interacting face to face with people.

Erika Gault suggests that in addition to an aging Black church hierarchy, there is a technology gap in the Black community.[7] She states, "Nonetheless, studies suggest that racial and economic disparities could also be factors in why many Black churches struggled to go online prior to and during the pandemic compared to non-Black churches. On average, Black Americans face greater barriers to internet access and high-speed connection at home than do White Americans. This disparity extends to Black young adults."

In addition to the potential loss of real relationships, some pastors and church leaders question whether people who have the ability to read and even study the Scripture at their fingertips through their smartphones or tablets will still feel the need or desire to memorize Scripture, and to hide the Word in their hearts (Psalm 119:11)?

Pandemic-Forced Technology

In 2020, the COVID-19 pandemic took all of society by surprise, including churches. The sheer magnitude of instant change created an environment of potential chaos and confusion, and most churches were thrust into emergency mode all at once. If not addressed and responded to immediately, it could and sadly did result in many churches closing down permanently.

Before the pandemic, Black churches represented only a small percentage of online users. Kristal Brent Zook reported that "of the 30,000 member churches represented by the Conference [of National Black Churches], . . . only about 500 of those were streaming when COVID-19 hit. Most were forced to close completely, only reemerging months later after finding ways to pivot and reinvent themselves."[8] Churches were forced to unexpectedly seek new ways to worship and to provide the care and comfort that was desperately needed at that time. Asha Rivers and Steven Goldman state, "All ministries developed new perspectives on the importance of digital communications for their members and congregants. They had to become creative and imaginative, especially to reinforce the idea that their congregants were not abandoned."[9]

As a pastor, I (Michael) was looking at new ways to connect with my congregation as well. Since I also run a nonprofit organization, a local private foundation offered to purchase a Zoom account for my nonprofit so we could continue to function. From that connection, I was introduced to the world of Zoom. It was from there we purchased a separate Zoom account for the church and began to use it to reach our congregation for Sunday morning worship, Bible study, and other church-based events and activities. When other churches chose to move to streaming and/or Facebook Live for the experience they desired, we chose to remain on Zoom because it provided more direct interaction, which we desired. Also, we wanted to know who was online with us.

As the pandemic continued to ebb and flow, many other pastors closed their churches again and held their church services online using various platforms, while other churches remained in person and on a variety of platforms. One of the greatest challenges that pastors who remained online discovered was that their message delivery was different. The call and response that many preachers and pastors feed off in the Black church tradition was not as available when preaching to a camera or a computer screen. There was also the challenge of verbal responses on Zoom if too many member microphones remained on at the same time. However, the chat portion of the Zoom platform did fill up with digital "amens" and other responses on a group level, as well as personally with other members. Delays could also interrupt the experience if the internet became unstable. Either way, the positive outcomes of technology have been expressed to be considerably better than not being able to communicate visually or verbally at all. Some who were otherwise against technology prior to COVID-19 or against the advances of technology became grateful for the access at a relatively cost-effective level in a crisis.

The use of technology during the pandemic also opened the door to online teaching and learning opportunities. With the use of technology, platforms were established for Bible study and use of the breakout rooms to hold different classes at the same time. In my own case, I took advantage of online courses and was able to finish my master's degree on Zoom with a cohort of students, with live professors in the classroom. The methods of technology that we embraced during our virtual classroom presentations and exams actually afforded a sharpening of our skills and acceptance to change while growing. When we took what we learned back to our churches and ministries, our leaders and members were able to grow and embrace change much better. We were from various cities, thus enabling us to forge relationships virtually. Thankfully, when we all met each other in person when it was safer, our relationships were uniquely and closely bonded, particularly when we all met as a group for the first time at our commencement. We noted that we did not take each other for granted and are all continuing to forge relationships on a deeper level than would have been expected. We were able to listen to each other, share best practices, and help each other with referral resources to better enhance our growth personally and as church leaders. Furthermore, when I was hired to become an adjunct professor soon after, I was comfortable with technology, which allowed me to offer a course of study in real time for my students from all across the country in a virtual classroom setting. Students who would otherwise be unable to attend my Christian college are now able to participate "face-to-face" virtually.

Artificial Intelligence and the World of Technology

Since the pandemic, Zoom has become a common mode of virtual communication for many of us. On one occasion, I was signing up for a Zoom meeting with other Black church leaders, as we were all working on a national project. When I signed on, a little box popped up to let me know that the meeting was being recorded, and notes were being taken by an AI companion. I was ceremonially ushered into the world of artificial intelligence (AI).

At this point, I was no stranger to artificial intelligence. During the pandemic, I was finishing my master's degree, and the degree program required that all the research papers had to be put through a computer-based artificial intelligence program that would edit the paper and check for plagiarism. This AI writing program also offered various suggestions for drafting the paper. I soon saw that if I followed all of the changes that the program wanted me to make, the AI program would have redrafted my paper and it would look completely different from my original version. Thus, AI has become part of our lives, from talking to our phones or smart devices to speaking to devices in our homes and vehicles.

AI, having its origins in the late twentieth century, seems to have exploded in the early twenty-first century. There can be significant benefits to using AI in the church context, such as research for sermon preparation, analyzing biblical texts, and even helping to craft a sermon. I currently have software on my computer that I have yet to use that can help me put the Sunday morning message I'm writing in outline form. In addition to recording and taking notes in meetings, AI can be used for other administrative tasks as well.

Hlulani M. Mdingi states that AI is a major part of the Fourth Industrial Revolution, indicating, "The roots of AI are in the fields of philosophy, logic or mathematics, computation, psychology or cognitive science and biology or neuroscience (Kumar & Thakur 2012:58). Kumar and Thakur also assert that 'an important goal of AI research is to devise machines to perform various tasks which normally require human intelligence.'"[10] Mdingi goes on to say, "The Fourth Industrial Revolution includes the role of AI in the future. Artificial intelligence and biotechnology seem to be the most eyebrow-raising topics of 4IR for the church because of their connotation to human beings in relation to intellect and genes without the role of a creator."[11]

With the speed that AI has come into our lives, it does make one think of the images portrayed in recent science fiction movies where machines rise up and attempt to dominate and eliminate the human race. What should give us great comfort is to always remember that God sits on the throne. In preparation for this writing, I came across a PBS interview that contained part of a sermon in which the preacher spoke about that issue. The Reverend Cindy Rudolph of Oak Grove AME Church, Detroit, preached a sermon on AI in which she said, "AI can process information, but only God can provide knowledge and wisdom. . . . AI can answer questions, but only God can answer prayers. . . . AI can write papers, but only God can write names in the Book of Life."[12] In the Bible, the book of Psalms states, "The LORD has established his throne in heaven, and his kingdom rules over all" (Psalm 103:19).

While there are many benefits to using artificial intelligence, there are some cautions as well, including some things church leaders need to look out for. One caution would be the over-reliance on AI. While its use would make so many things such as research, sermon preparation, even various functions of church administration much easier, artificial intelligence cannot replace the human factor that is needed in ministry. Kenny Jahng states, "Integrating AI into ministry should be viewed as a partnership. Technology enhances the efficiency and reach of pastoral work while pastors maintain the depth of human connection that is fundamental to their role."[13]

Another concern of AI is the potential loss of human jobs for members of Black church congregations and the Black community as a whole. With AI having the ability to work faster and more efficiently, it may reduce the need for personnel, which would result in job losses. In May 2023, the Writers Guild of America, comprised of motion picture and television scriptwriters, went on a five-month strike. One of their grievances was the potential use of artificial intelligence that would replace some of their jobs. The strike ended with the screenwriters' winning concessions in that area and more.[14] As we can see from that example, it may be important to keep up the vigilance of AI as it relates to potential job loss.

Many parents, especially in the Black community, complain, "My child is always on the phone!" According to a report, African American children spend an average of four hours and twenty-seven minutes per day on all types of media—a number that was significantly higher than time spent on media by White and Hispanic children.[15] In the area of social media, there may be some persuasion involved in maintaining a high media use. Enter another part of artificial intelligence called persuasive technology. All of the social media platforms are built on persuasive technology.

In his book *Why Technology Should Matter to the Church*, Dave Brown says that "persuasive technology is the use of artificial intelligence technology to engineer digital tools that create addiction-based technology. Addiction-based technology exploits individual preferences, intentionally leading to over-reliance called technology addiction." The persuasive technology used in social media is designed to keep people coming back and spending long hours using the platform. Jonathan Haidt, in the book *The Anxious Generation*, discusses how when he first purchased a mobile phone in 2008, it just had basic features on it, with no addictive qualities. He likened it to a Swiss Army pocketknife, a tool with many features for basic use. Then various applications were added to the phones, and they were transformed into something else. Haidt notes, "By the early 2010s, our phones had transformed from Swiss Army knives, which we pulled out when we needed a tool, to platforms upon which companies competed to see who could hold on to eyeballs the longest. The people with the least willpower and the greatest vulnerability to manipulation were, of course, children and adolescents, whose frontal cortices were still highly underdeveloped."[16]

AI can both be useful and can cause some harm to the Black church and the Black community as a whole. The Black church needs to be in the conversation addressing both the benefits and the ethical concerns of AI. The church can use its influence to introduce and teach the parents in the congregation and the community the best uses and things to avoid. In addressing the issues of major impact on the Black community, the Black church should use its popular prophetic voice to weigh in on those matters that impact its membership and the Black community. The holy Scriptures compel the church to use its influence.

Conclusion

Currently, the world of technology provides us, as men in the body of Christ, the opportunity to spread the gospel through Zoom and the internet. These technologies allow people to access the gospel who may not have been able to access it before. Programs like Zoom allow individuals to hear messages and participate in weekly Bible studies. It was a particularly valuable tool used in churches during COVID-19. The internet allows ministries to reach people, stream services, and make their resources available around the world. Technology has been used in ministry seminars, conferences, scheduling, registrations, and collaboration. Through technological advances, more varied Bible versions are available with just a click. Moving forward, technology may make it easier for missionaries to translate languages for people faster than before. The use of technology can make resources more readily available. It can benefit church productivity, which can lead to better management of time and finances. It can help churches run more smoothly. It also offers the potential for online teaching and learning opportunities. Technology can be used to reach a wider audience, increasing opportunities for evangelism.

While the COVID-19 pandemic caught everyone by surprise, it forced us to do things differently. A positive outcome of that time period was the increased use of technology that enabled churches to reach people when the shutdown came. It was during that time, through the use of various virtual platforms, that churches were enabled to connect with and regain their members. Some even gained new followers locally and from distant places. As we are now on the other side of the pandemic, in what some have called "The Next Normal," we've seen how much technology can enhance our lives and livelihoods. One caution requires noting: The church still needs to maintain opportunities for people to physically connect. Realizing that technology is here to stay, providing a healthy balance is essential. The Black Church/The Black man's necessity for the use of technology is ultimately to enhance its mission to impact lives for Christ!

NOTES

1. Scott Thumma and Dave Travis, *Beyond Megachurch Myth: What We Can Learn from America's Largest Churches* (Hoboken, NJ: Jossey-Bass, 2007).

2. For instance, "Online Religious Services Appeal to Many Americans, but Going in Person Remains More Popular," Pew Research Center, June 2, 2023, https://www.pewresearch.org/religion/2023/06/02/online-religious-services-appeal-to-many-americans-but-going-in-person-remains-more-popular/.

3. "Congregational Research," Hartford Institute for Religion and Research Center, accessed February 5, 2025, https://hirr.hartfordinternational.edu/research/congregational-research/.

4. Michelle Faverio, Justin Nortey, Jeff Diamant, and Gregory A. Smith, "Online Religious Services Appeal to Many Americans, but Going in Person Remains More Popular," June 2, 2023, Pew Research Center, 48, https://www.pewresearch.org/wp-content/uploads/sites/20/2023/06/PF_2023.06.02_religion-online_REPORT.pdf.

5. Faverio et al., "Online Religious Services Appeal to Many Americans," 53.

6. Faverio et al., "Online Religious Services Appeal to Many Americans," 53.

7. Erika Gault, "Black Churches Have Lagged in Moving Online during the Pandemic—Reaching Across Generational Lines Could Help," The Conversation, July 2. 2020, https://theconversation.com/black-churches-have-lagged-in-moving-online-during-the-pandemic-reaching-across-generational-lines-could-help-132170.

8. Kristal Brent Zook, "Can the Black Church Return after Covid?," *The Root*, February 7, 2023, https://www.theroot.com/soul-survivors-covid-19-and-the-black-church-1849678515.

9. Asha Rivers and Steven B. Goldman, "Commentary: The Digital Stairway to Heaven, Black Churches and the Pandemic," MIT Professional Education, February 12, 2022, https://professional.mit.edu/news/articles/commentary-digital-stairway-heaven-black-churches-and-pandemic.

10. Hlulani M. Mdingi, "The Black Church as the Timeless Witness to Change and Paradigm Shifts Posed by the Fourth Industrial Revolution," *HTS Teologiese Studies/Theological Studies* 76, no. 2 (2020): 3, https://hts.org.za/index.php/HTS/article/view/5985.

11. Mdingi, "The Black Church as the Timeless Witness to Change."

12. Reverend Cindy Rudolph, "Artificial Intelligence's Impact on the Black Community," PBS WKAR Detroit, February 28, 2024,

https://www.pbs.org/video/artificial-intelligences-impact-on-the-black
-community-y73208/.

13. Kenny Jahng, "When AI Comes to Church," *Outreach Magazine*,
    May 7, 2024, https://outreachmagazine.com/ideas/80392-when-ai
    -comes-to-church.html.

14. "Writers' Strike: What Happened, How It Ended, and Its Impact on
    Hollywood," *Los Angeles Times*, May 1, 2023, https://www.latimes
    .com/entertainment-arts/business/story/2023-05-01/
    writers- strike-what-to-know-wga-guild-hollywood-productions.

15. "Zero to Eight: Children's Media Use in America," Common Sense
    Media, Fall 2011, https://www.ftc.gov/sites/default/files/documents
    /public_comments/california-00325%C2%A0/00325-82243.pdf.

16. Jonathan Haidt, *The Anxious Generation: How the Great Rewiring
    of Childhood Is Causing an Epidemic of Mental Illness* (London:
    Penguin Publishing Group, 2024), 115.

Interrogate

What to a Black Man Is a White Evangelical Education?

DR. KENNETH D. RUSSELL, MDIV, PHD

> To do righteousness and justice is more
> acceptable to the LORD than sacrifice.
> Proverbs 21:3 RSV

The title of this chapter may invoke varying responses. For some Christian men who are Black, the question may seem too "woke" and divisive. These Black believers, like some other Christians of color, may attend and work at White evangelical institutions and report few, if any, negative racialized experiences—as may other minoritized and marginalized individuals and groups. Then there are those who are, to varying degrees, vocal about their organization's exclusionary culture, climate, and practices, but who, for numerous reasons, decide to remain part of those institutions. These Black believers may regard the title as a necessary, though cautious, provocation of curiosity and inquiry. Then there are those who leave White evangelical institutions with several stories of marginalization and exclusion. They may be skeptical of finding a place for themselves in those communities and may regard engaging the title's question as a waste of time.

For me, few things in my life have demonstrated the veracity of racism and white supremacy more than my experiences in White evangelical educational institutions. In many respects, my experiences in those institutions lead me to similar conclusions as Frederick Douglass in his reflections on the Fourth of July. After roughly ten years in White institutions of theological education—earning a bachelor's degree in religious studies and a Master of Divinity degree as well as serving in several capacities in admissions, student affairs, and multicultural centers—like Douglass I might say,

> What to [a Black man] is [a White evangelical education]? I answer: [It] reveals to him, more than all other [educational institutions], the gross injustice and cruelty to which he is the constant victim. To him, your [institution] is a sham; your boasted liberty, an unholy license; your national greatness, swelling vanity; your sounds of rejoicing are empty and heartless; your denunciations of tyrants, brass fronted impudence; your shouts of liberty and equality, hollow mockery; your prayers and hymns, your sermons and thanksgivings, with all your religious parade and solemnity, are, to him, mere bombast, fraud, deception, impiety, and hypocrisy.[1]

At the same time, from a more charitable posture, my theological education helped me situate myself within the broad scope of Christian thought—though some may consider me too radical, while others might deem me too conservative. My experiences in White evangelical institutions also forced me to sharpen and defend my thinking, especially regarding matters of theology and race. Although I recently left Christian higher education, I attribute much of my passion for diversity, equity, inclusion, and justice to my journey through those institutions. Even now, as I pursue a doctorate in educational administration at a public predominantly White institution, I still draw upon my theological education. Thus, all has not been lost—which brings me to the purpose of this chapter.

The purpose of this chapter is threefold. First, I offer an overview of Critical Race Theory (CRT). Second, I use CRT to reflect on some of my experiences in White evangelical educational institutions. Third, I introduce readers to FaithCrit[2]—a burgeoning theoretical and analytical framework that incorporates CRT and faith in combating injustice. This chapter is an extension of Dr. Lee June's discussion of employing race-based epistemologies as Black men who are also Christian from *Men to Men*, the work from which this book serves as a completely revised edition.[3] However, where Dr. June centered Dr. Molefi Asante's *Afrocentricity*,[4] I take up CRT. My hope is readers will see that CRT provides helpful theoretical and analytical tools for naming, resisting, and surviving racializing experiences in White evangelical institutions.

Critical Race Theory

CRT is often misrepresented in the media and some popular press. In reality, CRT is a movement of scholars and activists who developed a framework, methodology, and epistemological orientation "for studying and transforming the relationship among race, racism, and power."[5] Examining those relationships, CRT focuses less on eradicating race as an organizing category and more on the conceptual and practical strategies to eradicate racism.[6]

CRT emerged during the 1970s as a critique of critical legal studies in response to the shortcomings of legal liberal rhetoric as a form of social change.[7] CRT came to the field of education in 1995[8] and has been used to study a range of topics in higher education, such as policy,[9] access,[10] and diversity initiatives.[11] CRT has also been employed to study the experiences of racially marginalized and minoritized individuals and groups in theological institutions.[12]

CRT is like a family tree with branches extending as other Crits[13]—branches such as BlackCrit,[14] LatCrit,[15] TribalCrit,[16] AsianCrit,[17] WhiteCrit,[18] Critical Race Feminism,[19] DisCrit,[20] and FaithCrit.[21]

There are five primary themes of CRT: (1) the permanence of racism, (2) challenging dominant ideology, (3) a commitment to social justice, (4) the centrality of experiential knowledge, and (5) a transdisciplinary perspective.[22] The permanence of racism refers to CRT's foundational premise that race and racism are permanent and endemic, and that race and racism are foundational for understanding how society functions in the United States and around the world. In a critical race analysis, race and racism are centered—yet they are assessed intersectionally with other forms of subordination including, but not limited to, phenotype, class, gender, sexuality, and immigration status.[23] Challenging dominant ideology refers to the way CRT challenges traditional claims of objectivity, meritocracy, colorblindness/race-evasiveness, race neutrality, and equal opportunity. In a word, CRT interrogates how these claims are laden with the self-interest, power, and privilege of dominant groups.[24]

A commitment to social justice refers to CRT's goal of offering a transformative response to oppression—raced, classed, gendered, etc. CRT seeks the empowerment of minoritized and marginalized individuals and groups.[25] The centrality of experiential knowledge refers to the recognition of the lived experiences of people of color "as legitimate, appropriate, and critical to understanding, analyzing, and teaching about racial subordination."[26] To that end, CRT draws upon the experiential knowledge of people of color in its research methods.[27] Finally, a transdisciplinary perspective refers to CRT's approach to studying race and racism in their historical and contemporary contexts by employing multiple disciplines.[28]

A Critical Reflection

As I reflect on some of my racialized experiences in White evangelical educational institutions using CRT, what follows are not my most provocative or painful experiences in White evangelical educational institutions. Rather, the following are some experiences that CRT has provided language to describe.

Growing up, most of my primary and secondary schools were predominantly Black. Similarly, although I occasionally visited some predominantly White and multiracial churches, my home churches were mostly Black. Black spaces were the norm. This changed after high school when I attended the local community college and helped start a hip-hop church with my cousin, who was partnering with a White denomination. During this time, I was encouraged to consider ministry as a full-time vocation. Skeptical but intrigued, I began looking at undergraduate programs. Because the denominational affiliation provided much-needed financial support, I transferred to this undergraduate university to study theology.

My academic coursework became a point of tension. Black churches taught me that the Christian God is a God of justice, that most of the people mentioned in the Bible were people of color, and that people of color, especially Black people, made profound contributions to the world and the Christian Church. However, these voices and contributions were regularly omitted from the coursework, and it became apparent that the curriculum centered on Western, White Christianity. Few classes incorporated work from scholars of color and fewer discussed matters of race and racism. Some professors included opportunities to engage these bodies of knowledge, but those opportunities were often minimal and frequently optional.

Church history classes glossed through the first few centuries of Christianity to the Great Schism of 1054, which led to the crusades that gave rise to the Roman Catholic Church and then the Reformations. We were taught that the monumental figures of the faith were White men like John Calvin, Jacob Arminius, George Whitfield, and John Wesley. Cursory remarks were made about the Black presence in church history, mostly limited to Black Liberation Theology and Dr. James Cone. Other classes were similar. Preaching courses allowed us to examine preachers of color, if we chose to do so, but there was little interrogation of the whiteness that was normalized and centered in the preaching those classes presented. Courses on biblical studies seldom included the perspectives of biblical scholars of color. Black approaches to spiritual formation and church leadership in those respective classes were nonexistent. I gravitated to historical theology, studying patristic theology to recover what Dr. Thomas Oden refers to as the forgotten African seedbed of Christianity.[29] Save that coursework on the early church, much of the discussions regarding Christians of color and matters that are important to us were relegated to a course on evangelism and global outreach.

For me, there was a resounding disconnect to the curriculum, as was the case for other students of color on campus. Beyond the broad language of sin or brokenness, my theological education did not provide adequate words or concepts to describe that curricular exclusion. However, CRT has.

One example is the concept of whiteness as property—a concept developed by Cheryl Harris, JD, to describe whiteness in terms of property rights, namely in terms of the rights of disposition, use and enjoyment, reputation, and exclusion.[30] In education, the curriculum represents a form of "intellectual property."[31] Dominant perspectives are given curricular real estate, while nondominant perspectives, especially those that challenge dominant perspectives, are minimized or omitted.[32] Looking at my undergraduate coursework, those courses upheld the rights of Whites to use and enjoy the curriculum to maintain their perspective, whereas Black voices (and others) were excluded and marginalized.[33] Relegating discussions of Christians of color to a few remarks in one lecture, to one chapter in a book, to one course on evangelism trivializes the histories and contributions of Christians of color. Whether intentional or not, it signals who is known and worthy to be known—who is seen as human with agency.[34] It can reinstantiate false, deficit-based narratives of minoritized communities as inferior and helpless souls in need of saving—that is, in need of the salvation offered by White evangelical Christianity. It assumes certain knowledge are objective and transcendent, when they should be particularized, contextualized, and challenged.[35] It renormalizes whiteness and reifies whiteness as property in the educational curriculum and beyond.[36] In this manner, as Dr. Gloria Ladson-Billings contends, CRT provides the theoretical and analytical tools to illuminate how the educational curriculum is "a culturally specific artifact designed to maintain a White supremacist master script."[37]

After my undergraduate studies, I attended a White evangelical seminary for their Master of Divinity program. Like my undergraduate institution, the curriculum was steeped in whiteness. But this time I was different. Like the late Dr. James Cone, "I was fed up with white theologians writing about the gospel as if it had nothing to do with . . . black people's struggle for cultural identity and political justice. . . . I was fed up with liberal white ministers condemning riots instead of the social conditions that created them. . . . I was fed up with conservative black churches preaching an otherworldly gospel as if Jesus had nothing to say about how white supremacy had created a world that was killing black people."[38]

Rather than be a passive recipient of a curriculum that was not created for me, I actively sought ways to center race and justice. I began asking questions during class discussions about how the course material addresses racism and oppression—to which responses frequently entailed dismissing the line of inquiry as a distraction to the gospel, exhorting the class to preach the gospel to get individuals saved and sanctified, or encouraging me to figure it out since it was a matter that impacted me and my community. Dissatisfied with those responses, I started asking professors to adjust class assignments and course materials. Some refused, but others were amenable. This led me to reading much of the work from the late Dr. James Cone, as well as other Black scholars—such as Drs. Willie Jennings, J. Kameron Carter, Cornel West, Eboni Marshall Turman, Traci West, Brian Bantum, and Christena Cleveland—whose scholarship informed my research papers and classroom discussions.

I wanted an education that not only resonated with my experiences as a Black man, but one that also challenged us all to grapple with understanding and addressing racism and other systemic injustices. CRT provided me with the language of race-based epistemology[39] to describe the educational orientation I was seeking during seminary to challenge what CRT would call the epistemological racism[40] of a White evangelical education. I was searching for an emancipatory epistemology that enabled me to problematize the whiteness of the Christian imagination[41] and fight for my own and our collective liberation.[42] Often disregarded as airing out my frustrations for being "a fly in the buttermilk,"[43] what was at stake was more than my "special pleading"[44] to color the curriculum. More fully, it was a call to examine our biases, practices, and policies that maintained the status quo[45]—a call to recognize that some members of the Christian Church were disregarded.

The experiences just mentioned and others like them shape my perception of race and racism in the world. These experiences inspired me to help change educational environments. Nearing graduation, I considered pursuing a doctorate in theology and race, but a White mentor at the time discouraged that because he worried my education would not be perceived as academically rigorous if I studied race as a Black person—a comment that, among many things, captured the reputation rights of whiteness as property[46] and the antiblackness[47] I had long sensed in White evangelical institutions. Instead, after graduation I returned home.

Following a brief stint in ministry, I became a diversity director at a small liberal arts college, and continued to consult with and guest lecture at various faith-based nonprofits and higher educational institutions on matters related to diversity, equity, inclusion, and justice. I wanted to share what I was learning about traversing White evangelical institutions as a Black man and how to challenge the whiteness I was experiencing in those spaces. I wanted to center racism and work toward equity and justice. My experiences as a diversity professional taught me that diversity work is deeply political and requires more than theology and a theological education. So, I started my doctoral degree in the Higher, Adult, and Lifelong Education PhD program in the College of Education at Michigan State University (MSU) with a focus on chief diversity officers and negotiation.

The education I received in White evangelical institutions was incomplete—often ignoring the work of Christians of color and failing to disrupt the whiteness of the curriculum, the institution, and the world at large. However, it provided a foundation and motivation as I continue my journey in higher education. Thankfully, my doctoral coursework at MSU has complemented areas where the curriculum of my previous institutions fell short. As I look across my educational journey, I would say that in undergraduate studies and seminary we talked a lot about theology and very little about race and racism and in my doctoral studies we have talked a lot about race and racism and very little about theology. What was needed was a way to bring them together.

FaithCrit

FaithCrit is one of the burgeoning Crits within the CRT family tree. Proposed by Dr. Larissa Malone and Dr. Qiana Lachaud,[48] FaithCrit extends CRT to explore "the role of faith in combating injustice, the extrication of prejudice and oppression from theology and spiritual practices, adopting religio-spiritual writing styles, and the invaluable role of hope while living in an unjust world."[49] While Drs. Malone and Lachaud draw from Christianity in conceptualizing FaithCrit, FaithCrit also invites interfaith dialogue, encouraging those from other religious and spiritual backgrounds to examine faith and race.[50]

There are five tenets of FaithCrit. The first "acknowledges critical race scholars' religio-spirituality as a part of identity and praxis."[51] The second "compels critical race scholars to engage in action against injustice."[52] The third "endeavors to disentangle religio-spirituality from white supremacy, prejudice, and oppression."[53] The fourth "aims to expand the practice of counterstorytelling through religio-spiritual writing styles."[54] The fifth "encourages critical race scholars to lean into their religio-spirituality as a source of hope."[55]

While some Christians reject anything CRT-related, others may question the necessity of FaithCrit when we have liberation theologies. However, FaithCrit is not an extension of liberation theologies.[56] Drs. Malone and Lachaud state that "while liberation theology informs our work, our conceptualization of Faith-Crit is distinct from liberation theology in that it is rooted in the foundational writings of CRT, not theology."[57] We can further FaithCrit by bringing together theology and CRT as complementary interlocuters.[58] Doing so expands FaithCrit and addresses some concerns of scholars who argue that CRT has insufficiently drawn from the religious sources of Black Christians.[59] It provides a space to complicate, challenge, and correct the racialized history and practices of Christianity, as well as offer a theological contribution to CRT.[60]

I introduce FaithCrit for two primary reasons. The first reason I present FaithCrit is to offer a theoretical and analytical framework for bringing together faith and commitments to addressing racism and other forms of discrimination. Contrary to some misrepresentations, CRT does not advance a religion of sorts.[61] While some CRT scholars do not identify spiritually, others come from various religious and spiritual traditions and draw from those traditions in their work. Furthermore, several CRT scholars are Christians who serve faithfully in their churches. In fact, Dr. Glenn Bracey argues that some of the founding scholars of CRT drew heavily from Christian traditions in conceptualizing CRT.[62] This foundation made CRT more than a scholarly project but also a spiritual work that sought to resist and correct the racist weaponization of Christianity in favor of more truthful understanding of Christianity. However, as CRT developed, CRT scholars focused on critiquing the law.[63] FaithCrit returns to that foundation and calls for further development.[64] In short, FaithCrit provides a theoretical and analytical framework to lean more explicitly into our religious and spiritual identities as we apply CRT personally and academically.[65]

Some may rightly argue that neither CRT nor FaithCrit are necessary to engage theologically in matters of race and racism. However, FaithCrit offers a space for those who want to couple theology and CRT in their personal and professional work. It challenges us to fully bring our religious and spiritual selves to the work of justice. It calls on us—Christians, and all who identify as spiritual—to live in the tension of leaning into our faith as a source of hope and truth, while engaging in the hard work of disentangling the histories and practices of our faith traditions from white supremacy and oppression. It encourages us to see theology and CRT as "reciprocal assets."[66] FaithCrit is one contemporary extension of Dr. June's exhortation for Black men to balance Afrocentricity and Christian identity.[67]

The second reason I present FaithCrit is to underscore FaithCrit's call to action. Some within the CRT community, like Dr. Marvin Lynn, are dissatisfied with critiquing for the sake of critiquing.[68] Although problem-posing on its own is necessary, I concur that it should be complemented with problem-solving, and I believe that theology can offer a needed, and frequently overlooked, contribution. In combining theology and CRT, FaithCrit can provide tools for addressing racism and other forms of oppression in Christian communities and challenge Christian communities that are reconciliatory in superficial ways.

Conclusion

Antiblackness and whiteness permeate higher education[69]—White evangelical institutions are no different.[70] My theological education was incomplete. It led to experiences that have shaped my understanding of race and racism; it also inspired my desire to pursue change in higher education. CRT introduced me to language and concepts that help me understand my experiences in higher education—language and concepts that also inform my work as a scholar-practitioner. CRT provides a lens and set of tools to study and transform higher education[71] in general, and Christian higher education[72] in particular—an opportunity also presented in FaithCrit.

So, what to *this* Black man is a White evangelical education? Reflecting on my theological education, I have learned we must always ask who the material is about, who the material is for, for whose interests, and at whose expense.[73] It was far from perfect, but through (and in many ways despite) my White evangelical education, I learned that my purpose in life is to love God, my Black self, others, and the created order—my purpose is not to be a White conservative evangelical in Black skin.[74]

NOTES

1. Adapted from Frederick Douglass, "What to the Slave is the Fourth of July?," in *The Speeches of Frederick Douglass: A Critical Edition*, ed. John R. McKivigan, Julie Husband, and Heather L. Kaufman (New Haven, CT: Yale University Press, 2018), 72.

2. Larissa Malone and Qiana Lachaud, "FaithCrit: Toward a Framework of Religio-Spirituality in Critical Race Theory," *Journal of Critical Race Inquiry* 9, no. 2 (2022): 93–109.

3. Lee N. June, "African-American, Afrocentric (Africentric), Christian, and Male?" in *Men to Men: Perspectives of Sixteen African-American Christian Men*, ed. Lee N. June and Matthew Parker (Grand Rapids, MI: Zondervan, 1996), 259–72.

4. Molefi Kete Asante, *Afrocentricity* (Trenton, NJ: Africa World Press, 1990).

5. Richard Delgado and Jean Stefancic, *Critical Race Theory: An Introduction*, 3rd ed. (New York University Press, 2017), 3.

6. Zeus Leonardo, *Race Frameworks: A Multidimensional Theory of Racism and Education* (New York: Teachers College Press, 2013).

7. Delgado and Stefancic, *Critical Race Theory*.

8. Gloria Ladson-Billings and William F. Tate, "Toward a Critical Race Theory of Education," *Teachers College Record* 97, no. 1 (1995): 47–67, https://doi.org/10.1177/016146819509700104.

9. Michael J. Dumas, "Against the Dark: Antiblackness in Education Policy and Discourse," *Theory into Practice* 55, no. 1 (2016): 11–19, https://doi.org/10.1080/00405841.2016.1116852.

10. Shaun R. Harper, Lori D. Patton, and Ontario S. Wooden, "Access and Equity for African American Students in Higher Education: A Critical Race Historical Analysis of Policy Efforts," *The Journal of Higher Education* 80, no. 4 (2009): 389–414, https://doi.org/10.1353/jhe.0.0052.

11. Susan VanDeventer Iverson, "Camouflaging Power and Privilege: A Critical Race Analysis of University Diversity Policies," *Educational Administration Quarterly* 43, no. 5 (2007): 586–611, https://doi.org/10.1177/0013161X07307794.

12. Benjamin D. Espinoza, "Understanding the Experiences of Racially Minoritized Doctoral Students in Evangelical Theological Education," *Christian Higher Education* 20, no. 3 (2020): 141–59, https://doi.org/10.1080/15363759.2020.1756529; C. Sotello Viernes Turner, E. I. Hernández, M. Peña, and J. C. González, "New Voices in the Struggle/Nuevas Voces en la Lucha: Toward Increasing Latina/o Faculty in Theological Education," *Journal of Hispanic Higher*

Education 7, no. 4 (2008): 321–35, https://doi.org
/10.1177/1538192708321649.

13. Tara J. Yosso, "Whose Culture Has Capital? A Critical Race Theory Discussion of Community Cultural Wealth," *Race Ethnicity and Education* 8, no. 1 (March 2005): 69–91, https://doi.org/10.1080 /1361332052000341006.

14. Michael J. Dumas and Kihana Miraya Ross, "'Be Real Black for Me': Imagining BlackCrit in Education," *Urban Education* 51, no. 4 (2016): 415–42, https://doi.org/10.1177/0042085916628611; Chezare A. Warren and Justin A. Coles, "Trading Spaces: Antiblackness and Reflections on Black Education Futures," *Equity and Excellence in Education* 53, no. 3 (2020): 382–98, https://doi.org/10.1080 /10665684.2020.1764882.

15. Daniel G. Solóranzo and Tara J. Yosso, "Critical Race and LatCrit Theory and Method: Counter-Storytelling," *International Journal of Qualitative Studies in Education* 14, no. 4 (2001): 471–95, https:// doi.org/10.1080/09518390110063365; Rosalie Rolón-Dow and April Davison, "Theorizing Racial Microaffirmations: A Critical Race/ LatCrit Approach," *Race Ethnicity and Education* 24, no. 2 (2020): 245-61, https://doi.org/10.1080/13613324.2020.1798381.

16. Nik Cristobal, "Kanaka 'Ōiwi Critical Race Theory: Historical and Cultural Ecological Understanding of Kanaka 'Ōiwi Education," *Contemporaneity: Historical Presence in Visual Culture* 7, no. 1 (2018): 27–44, https://doi.org/10.5195/contemp.2018.240; Bryan McKinley Jones Brayboy, "Toward a Tribal Critical Race Theory in Education," *The Urban Review* 37, no. 5 (2005): 425–46, https://doi .org/10.1007/s11256-005-0018-y.

17. Jon S. Iftikar and Samuel D. Museus, "On the Utility of Asian Critical (AsianCrit) Theory in the Field of Education," *International Journal of Qualitative Studies in Education* 31, no. 10 (2018): 935–49, https:// doi.org/10.1080/09518398.2018.1522008; Lan Kolano, "Smartness as Cultural Wealth: An AsianCrit Counterstory," *Race Ethnicity and Education* 19, no. 6 (2016): 1149–63, https://doi.org/10.1080 /13613324.2016.1168538.

18. Cheryl E. Matias and Colleen Boucher, "From Critical Whiteness Studies to a Critical Study of Whiteness: Restoring Criticality in Critical Whiteness Studies," *Whiteness and Education* 8, no. 1 (2021): 64–81, https://doi.org/10.1080/23793406.2021.1993751; Cheryl E. Matias, "Towards a Black Whiteness Studies: A Response to the Growing Field," *International Journal of Qualitative Studies in Education* 36, no. 8 (2022): 1431–41, https://doi.org/10.1080 /09518398.2022.2025482.

19. Adrien Katherine Wing, ed., *Critical Race Feminism: A Reader*, 2nd

ed. (New York University Press, 2003); Adrien Katherine Wing, ed., *Global Critical Race Feminism: An International Reader* (New York University Press, 2000).

20. Subini Ancy Annamma, Beth A. Ferri, and David J. Connor, "Disability Critical Race Theory: Exploring the Intersectional Lineage, Emergence, and Potential Futures of DisCrit in Education," *Review of Research in Education* 42, no. 1 (2018): 46–71, https:// doi.org/10.3102/0091732X18759041; Subini Ancy Annamma and Tamara Handy, "DisCrit Solidarity as Curriculum Studies and Transformative Praxis," *Curriculum Inquiry* 49, no. 4 (2019): 442–63, https://doi.org/10.1080/03626784.2019.1665456.

21. Malone and Lachaud, "FaithCrit: Toward a Framework of Religio-Spirituality in Critical Race Theory."

22. Tara J. Yosso, Laurence Parker, Daniel G. Solórzano, and Marvin Lynn, "From Jim Crow to Affirmative Action and Back Again: A Critical Race Discussion of Racialized Rationales and Access to Higher Education," *Review of Research in Education* 28, no. 1 (2004): 1–25, https://doi.org/10.3102/0091732X028001001; Solórzano and Yosso, "Critical Race and LatCrit Theory and Method: Counter-Storytelling."

23. Kimberle Crenshaw, "Mapping the Margins: Intersectionality, Identity Politics, and Violence against Women of Color," *Stanford Law Review* 43, no. 6 (1991): 1241–99, https://doi.org/10.2307/1229039; Yosso et al., "From Jim Crow to Affirmative Action and Back Again;" Michelle Christian, "A Global Critical Race and Racism Framework: Racial Entanglements and Deep and Malleable Whiteness," *Sociology of Race and Ethnicity* 5, no. 2 (2019): 169–85, https://doi.org/10.1177 /2332649218783220.

24. Yosso et al., "From Jim Crow to Affirmative Action and Back Again"; Solórzano and Yosso, "Critical Race and LatCrit Theory and Method."

25. Yosso et al., "From Jim Crow to Affirmative Action and Back Again"; Solórzano and Yosso, "Critical Race and LatCrit Theory and Method."

26. Yosso et al., "From Jim Crow to Affirmative Action and Back Again," 4.

27. Yosso et al., "From Jim Crow to Affirmative Action and Back Again"; Solórzano and Yosso, "Critical Race and LatCrit Theory and Method."

28. Yosso et al., "From Jim Crow to Affirmative Action and Back Again"; Solórzano and Yosso, "Critical Race and LatCrit Theory and Method."

29. Thomas C. Oden, *How Africa Shaped the Christian Mind:*

Rediscovering the African Seedbed of Western Christianity (Westmont, IL: InterVarsity Press, 2007).

30. Cheryl Harris, "Whiteness as Property," in *Critical Race Theory: The Key Writings That Formed the Movement*, ed. Kimberlé Crenshaw, Neil Gotanda, Gary Peller, and Kendall Thomas (New York: New Press, 1995), 276–91; Nolan L. Cabrera, Jeremy D. Franklin, and Jesse S. Watson, *Whiteness in Higher Education: The Invisible Missing Link in Diversity and Racial Analyses, ASHE Higher Education Report* 42, no. 6 (2016): 7–125, https://doi.org/10.1002/aehe.20116.

31. Ladson-Billings and Tate, "Toward a Critical Race Theory of Education," 54.

32. Lori D. Patton, "Disrupting Postsecondary Prose: Toward a Critical Race Theory of Higher Education," *Urban Education* 51, no. 3 (2016): 315–42, https://doi.org/10.1177/0042085915602542.

33. Harris, "Whiteness as Property;" Gloria Ladson-Billings, "Just What Is Critical Race Theory and What's It Doing in a Nice Field Like Education?," *International Journal of Qualitative Studies in Education* 11, no. 1 (1998): 7–24, https://doi.org/10.1080/095183998236863.

34. Gloria Ladson-Billings, "Racialized Discourses and Ethnic Epistemologies," in *Handbook of Qualitative Research*, ed. Norman K. Denzin and Yvonna S. Lincoln, 2nd ed. (Thousand Oaks, CA: Sage Publications Inc., 2000), 257–77.

35. Tara J. Yosso, "Toward a Critical Race Curriculum," *Equity & Excellence in Education* 35, no. 2 (2002): 93–107, https://doi.org/10.1080/713845283.

36. Cabrera, Franklin, and Watson, *Whiteness in Higher Education*; Harris, "Whiteness as Property."

37. Ladson-Billings, "Just What Is Critical Race Theory and What's It Doing in a Nice Field Like Education?," 18.

38. James Hal Cone, *Said I Wasn't Gonna Tell Nobody: The Making of a Black Theologian* (Maryknoll, NY: Orbis Books, 2018), 9.

39. Cynthia Tyson, "Research, Race, and an Epistemology of Emancipation," *Counterpoints* 195 (2003): 19–28.

40. James Joseph Scheurich and Michelle D. Young, "Coloring Epistemologies: Are Our Research Epistemologies Racially Biased?," *Educational Researcher* 26, no. 4 (1997): 4–16.

41. Willie James Jennings, *The Christian Imagination: Theology and the Origins of Race* (New Haven, CT: Yale University Press, 2010); J. Kameron Carter, *Race: A Theological Account* (Oxford University Press, 2008); Kristopher Norris, "The Theological Origins of White Supremacy," in *Witnessing Whiteness: Confronting White Supremacy in the American Church* (Oxford University Press, 2020), 31–53.

42. Tyson, "Research, Race, and an Epistemology of Emancipation."

43. Patton, "Disrupting Postsecondary Prose," 325.

44. Derrick A. Bell, *Faces at the Bottom of the Well: The Permanence of Racism*, 1st ed. (New York: Basic Books, 1992), 111.

45. Patton, "Disrupting Postsecondary Prose"; Ladson-Billings, "Racialized Discourses and Ethnic Epistemologies."

46. Cabrera, Franklin, and Watson, *Whiteness in Higher Education*; Harris, "Whiteness as Property."

47. Dumas, "Against the Dark:"; Dumas and Ross, "'Be Real Black for Me'"; T. Elon Dancy II, Kirsten T. Edwards, and James Earl Davis, "Historically White Universities and Plantation Politics: Anti-Blackness and Higher Education in the Black Lives Matter Era," *Urban Education* 53, no. 2 (2018): 176–95, https://doi.org/10.1177 /0042085918754328.

48. Malone and Lachaud, "FaithCrit."

49. Malone and Lachaud, "FaithCrit," 93.

50. Malone and Lachaud, "FaithCrit."

51. Malone and Lachaud, "FaithCrit," 100.

52. Malone and Lachaud, "FaithCrit," 100.

53. Malone and Lachaud, "FaithCrit," 100.

54. Malone and Lachaud, "FaithCrit," 100.

55. Malone and Lachaud, "FaithCrit," 100.

56. Malone and Lachaud, "FaithCrit."

57. Malone and Lachaud, "FaithCrit," 97.

58. Robert Chao Romero and Jeff M. Liou, *Christianity and Critical Race Theory: A Faithful and Constructive Conversation* (Grand Rapids, MI: Baker Academic, 2023).

59. Brandon Paradise, "How Critical Race Theory Marginalizes the African-American Christian Tradition," *Michigan Journal of Race & Law* 20, no. 1 (2014): 117–211.

60. Malone and Lachaud, "FaithCrit"; Romero and Liou, *Christianity and Critical Race Theory*.

61. Glenn E. Bracey II, "The Spirit of Critical Race Theory," *Sociology of Race and Ethnicity* 8, no. 4 (2022): 503–17, https://doi.org/10.1177 /23326492221114814.

62. Bracey, "The Spirit of Critical Race Theory."

63. Bracey, "The Spirit of Critical Race Theory."

64. Malone and Lachaud, "FaithCrit."

65. Malone and Lachaud, "FaithCrit."

66. Malone and Lachaud, "FaithCrit," 94.

67. June, "African-American, Afrocentric (Africentric), Christian, and Male?"

68. Marvin Lynn, "Moving Critical Race Theory in Education from a Problem-Posing Mindset to a Problem-Solving Orientation," in *Understanding Critical Race Research Methods and Methodologies: Lessons from the Field*, ed. Jessica T. DeCuir-Gunby, Thandeka K. Chapman, and Paul A. Schutz (New York: Routledge, 2018), vii–xii.

69. Patton, "Disrupting Postsecondary Prose"; Sharon Stein, "Universities, Slavery, and the Unthought of Anti-Blackness," *Cultural Dynamics* 28, no. 2 (2016): 169–87, https://doi.org/10.1177/0921374016634379.

70. Alexander Jun, Tabatha L. Jones-Jolivet, Allison N. Ash, and Christopher S. Collins, *White Jesus: The Architecture of Racism in Religion and Education* (New York: Peter Lang Publishing, Inc., 2018); Espinoza, "Understanding the Experiences of Racially Minoritized Doctoral Students in Evangelical Theological Education."

71. Patton, "Disrupting Postsecondary Prose."

72. Jun et al., *White Jesus*; Espinoza, "Understanding the Experiences of Racially Minoritized Doctoral Students in Evangelical Theological Education."

73. Ladson-Billings, "Racialized Discourses and Ethnic Epistemologies."

74. Frantz Fanon, *Black Skin, White Masks* (New York: Grove Press, 1952).

22

Closing

A Letter to Young Black Men

LONNIE J. CHIPP III, MA, HONORARY DOCTORATE

Now that you have purified yourselves by obeying
the truth so that you have sincere love for each
other, love one another deeply, from the heart.

1 Peter 1:22

I greet you in the name of our Lord and Savior Jesus Christ. As a pastor, I want to share my view of some of the obstacles affecting our young Black males. I have experience working within a variety of programs within the church and community. I often share my own life experiences in order to assist them with their personal struggles, encourage young men, and direct them to resources both within the church and in the community. Currently, I serve as the pastor of New Mount Calvary Baptist Church in Lansing, Michigan, and have since 2009.

When I was a member of the New Ebenezer Baptist Church in Detroit, Michigan, I served in the capacity of a mentor in a weekend program that was designed to educate, motivate, and instruct young men on how to make a positive impact in their communities, and to give them the tools to be successful. At the onset, these young men were encouraged to develop a personal relationship with the Lord. Our goal was for them to understand a relationship with the Lord as the building block for them to have someone they could trust. Our theme Scripture was Proverbs 3:5–6: "Trust in the Lord with all thine heart; and lean not unto thine own understanding. In all thy ways acknowledge him, and he shall direct thy paths" (KJV).

Many of the young men were from homes without a father or mother and were searching for something to believe and trust in. During our session, we tried to instill within them how the Lord could bring stability in their lives. During this program and conversation, the subject of the lack of leadership (father or strong male figure) and love in the Black household were always leading topics.

Although I had a strong father in my home, many of the young men I tutored did not have this father figure in their homes. I discovered through the life of those young men that life without the stability of both a father and mother was very challenging. We reflected on how they made decisions based on their situation at the time, doing whatever might be necessary to survive. All options were on the table from their perspective. They engaged in activities that were of questionable standard; in the "hood," we referred to it as "getting your hustle on." The absence of a father or male figure in the life of an inner-city male often transforms his mind from a boy into trying to be the man of the house. I do want to send love to those single mothers who gave everything to raise their sons by themselves; many of them have done so with much success.

Too many Black young men miss the love from a father, so they seek love and brotherhood that leads them to gang activity, surviving by selling drugs, robbing and stealing within their communities. Throughout the years, those pursuits have caused a deterioration in our communities and led to a continuation of prisons packed with young Black males. As churches, we love you, but we need to and can do more to combat this trend and to help our young Black males strive for a life in Jesus Christ, to gain success in life.

Let me close this brief letter by indicating that, as important as human love is, there is a greater love. The Bible tells us that

God so loved the world that He gave His only Son, Jesus Christ. And whoever believes in Jesus Christ will not perish but will have everlasting (eternal) life (John 3:16–17). So, I urge you to confess (say and agree) with your mouth that Jesus Christ is Lord and believe in your heart that God has raised Jesus Christ from the dead (Romans 10:9–10). This is what I have done. As a result of this confession, I now live a new life in Jesus Christ (2 Corinthians 5:17). You can also begin this journey now if you have not done so already.

About the
Contributors

Henry (Hank) Allen

Henry (Hank) is a retired sociologist who has served at several postsecondary institutions of higher education, including the University of Rochester and Wheaton College. He has a degree in biblical studies from Wheaton College and a PhD from the University of Chicago. He is married to Juliet Cooper Allen, and they are the parents of eight children.

Karl I. Bell

Karl Bell is president and CEO of Diverse Capital Solutions, a capital advisory and consultancy firm, and managing director of GAA New Ventures, a private investment company led by Dr. William F. Pickard. Karl completed his undergraduate work at Morehouse College, graduate work at University of Wisconsin-Madison, and several industry-related certificate programs. He and his wife, Pamela Bell, reside in Metro Detroit and have three adult children.

Lloyd C. Blue Sr.

Lloyd Blue is a native of North Carolina, a former pastor of Israel Baptist Church (Ohio) and Prosperity Baptist Church (California), and former CEO of Church Growth Unlimited. He is currently the senior associate minister of the Cornerstone Baptist Church of Arlington, Texas. He received his bachelor of theology degree from the Institutional Baptist Theological Center, Houston, Texas; master of arts degree from Union University in Los Angeles, California; and his doctor of ministry degree from the University of Central America. Lloyd has been married to his wife, Tressie, for sixty-eight years and counting. They are the parents of one son, Lloyd II.

Lonnie J. Chipp III

Lonnie is a member of the Baptist, Missionary, and Education Convention of the State of Michigan and the Lansing (Michigan) Ministerial Alliance. He has been awarded an honorary doctorate. He and his wife, Loretta, have been married for twenty-two years and have two daughters, two granddaughters, and two godsons. He has been pastor of New Mount Calvary Baptist Church in Lansing, Michigan, since 2009.

Claude L. Dallas Jr.

Claude earned a bachelor of science degree in zoology from Ohio State University, a master of science degree in cellular biology from the University of Cincinnati, and a master of arts degree in religion from Liberty University. Claude is married to Sheilah Ferebee Dallas, and they are the parents of four adult children, nine grandchildren, and five great-grandchildren. Most recently, he has been adjunct professor at National College of Cincinnati, Ohio, where he teaches medical, surgical, and pharmaceutical technology.

Amod Field

A native of New Jersey, Amod is a former elementary, high school, college, and professional athlete and multisport coach. Amod was assistant principal of the International High School, Paterson, New Jersey, and is now principal of Paterson Adult and Continuing Education School, where he oversees the adult multilingual school and the New Jersey youth core program. He is also cofounder and program director of the Garden State Scholars. Amod is the father of one son and is married to Karen June Field.

Tim Herd

As of this publication, Tim is in his final year of his PhD program and a Wasserman Fellow in the Higher Education & Organizational Change Program at the University of California, Los Angeles (UCLA). Outside of his studies, Tim serves as a creative consultant who partners with different nonprofits and other organizations around the areas of governance, culture, and student success. He has a bachelor's degree from Michigan State University, a master of science in education from the University of Pennsylvania, and a master of arts from UCLA.

Kevin L. Jones

Kevin earned a bachelor of arts degree in music education from Morris Brown College, a master's degree in music education from Florida State University, and a doctor of philosophy in curriculum and instruction with an urban education emphasis from Texas A&M University. He is currently assistant professor of Education Studies at Stephen F. Austin State University, where he champions equity, inclusion, and fugitive pedagogy in teacher education. His teaching philosophy centers on honoring diverse backgrounds, encouraging students to bring their full selves into discussions, and preparing them with strategies that amplify underrepresented voices.

Lenroy Jones

Lenroy is a servant leader with a career advising, coaching, and ministry background. Born and raised in Detroit, Michigan, he began his service journey early and continues to guide others on both spiritual and professional paths. A retired captain from the U.S. Army and Michigan Army National Guard, his leadership is grounded in discipline, purpose, and a deep commitment to helping others pursue their life calling. Lenroy holds a bachelor's degree in communications from Central Michigan University and a master's from Michigan State University. He currently serves as the director of career services at Columbus State Community College and resides in Westerville, Ohio.

Brian L. June

Brian holds a bachelor's degree in computer science from Tuskegee University, a master's degree in computer science from Michigan State University, and a master of arts degree in ministry leadership from Grand Rapids Theological Seminary. He is a member of the media team at New Mount Calvary Church in Lansing, Michigan.

Lee N. June

Lee is a native of Manning, South Carolina. He earned a bachelor's degree from Tuskegee Institute (now Tuskegee University) in biology and a master of education in rehabilitation counseling, master of arts in clinical psychology, and doctor of philosophy in clinical psychology all from the University of Illinois Urbana-Champaign. He also has a certificate in theological studies from the Interdenominational Theological Seminary, Atlanta, Georgia; did sabbatical study as a special student at the Duke University Divinity School; and earned a master of ministry leadership degree from Grand Rapids Theological Seminary (Cornerstone University). He is a licensed psychologist in the state of Michigan. Lee has previously served as director of the Counseling Center; Associate Provost for Racial, Ethnic, and Multicultural Issues; Vice President for Student Affairs and Services; and most recently as professor in the Honors College and Department of Psychology—all at Michigan State University. Recently retired, he is now professor and vice president emeritus at Michigan State University. He serves as the dean of the Lansing Area Ministerial Alliance, a member of the Advisory Council for Our Daily Bread Ministries, a member of the Board of Directors of Free International Mission, chair of the Board of Directors for the Institute for Black Family Development, and a Commissioner for the Dr. Martin Luther King Jr. Holiday Commission of Mid-Michigan.

Lee is married to Shirley Ann Spencer June, and they are the parents of two sons, Brian and Stephen.

Michael R. Lyles

Michael completed his undergraduate and medical school studies at the University of Michigan, Ann Arbor, and a psychiatric residency at Duke University School of Medicine. At Duke, he was an American Psychiatric Association/National Institute of Mental Health Minority Fellow and North Carolina Neuropsychiatric Association Resident of the Year. He was assistant professor of psychiatry at the University of Kentucky. He is married with three adult children and four grandchildren. He is a Fellow of the Townsend Institute for Leadership and Counseling at Concordia University.

Michael R. Lyles II and Kristina Joye Lyles

Michael and Kristina are "recovering attorneys" and former New York City residents who have called Atlanta home for the past seven years. They are parents of Stone and Stella. Michael is a legal recruiter with a national attorney search firm and Kristina is vice president of equity and impact at a large nonprofit in the education space. They are proud historically Black college and university alums (Spelman for Kristina and Howard for Michael). Kristina earned a law degree from Georgetown University, while Michael graduated from Mercer Law School.

Christopher C. Mathis Jr.

Christopher received a bachelor of science degree in biology from Johnson C. Smith University and a master of arts in educational administration and higher education and a PhD degree in agricultural and extension education from Michigan State University. He also received his master of divinity degree from Payne Theological Seminary, Wilberforce, Ohio. An ordained and itinerant elder of the AME Church, he has served as the pastor of Beulah African Methodist Episcopal Church in the Kingstree district and the Palmetto conference and is currently the pastor of Mt. Olive

AME Church in Kinards, South Carolina. Christopher serves as professor and assistant dean of research for the University of Arkansas at Pine Bluff School of Agriculture, Fisheries and Human Sciences. His research interests include the attitudes of students, faculty, and extension personnel regarding issues of diversity; factors affecting student persistence and graduation rates; effective mentoring of racial/ethnic males; and effective models and methods of racial/ethnic identity formation. He is married to Gossie H. Mathis, MD, and has four children, Courtney, Tamilia, Sterling, and Christopher.

Kenneth L. McDaniels

Born and raised in Asheville, North Carolina, Kenneth received a bachelor of science degree in chemistry from North Carolina Central University, a Juris Doctorate from North Carolina Central University, and an LLM in trial advocacy from Temple University Beasley School of Law. He was admitted to the North Carolina Bar, the US District Court, and the Pennsylvania Bar, and has been adjunct professor at Temple University and West Chester University of Pennsylvania. Ken is married to Anita McDaniels.

Ron Mosby

Ron Mosby, an elder in Cincinnati, Ohio, was born and raised in Cleveland, Ohio. He attended college at the University of Cincinnati. Ron served in the U.S. Navy as a Supply Corps officer. He currently serves as executive director of Norwood Together, a nonprofit community development corporation. Ron has been married to his wife, Cynthia, for over thirty-eight years. They have four children and eight grandchildren, seven of whom are living.

Matthew Parker Sr.

Matthew, a leader in the Christian community, has worked with a variety of Christian organizations, including Zondervan, Moody, and Our Daily Bread Ministries. The holder of an honorary doctorate, he is president of the Institute for Black Family Development and founder of the Global Summit, a consortium of leaders throughout the world. He is married to Karon Parker, and they are the parents of five children and have one grandchild.

Rodney S. Patterson

Rodney is a native of Chicago, Illinois. In 1989, he founded New Alpha Missionary Baptist Church, the first Black church in the state of Vermont. He also established Ebenezer Baptist Church of Lansing, Michigan. Rodney was also instrumental in establishing Olivet Institutional Baptist Church in Stockton, California. He most recently pastored Shiloh Missionary Baptist Church in Chicago, Illinois. Rodney is the diversity resource for Farm Credit bank and the CEO of The Learner's Group consulting firm. Rodney is married to Dr. Charlene Humphrey Patterson.

Kenneth D. Russell

Kenneth earned his PhD in the Higher, Adult, and Lifelong Education program at Michigan State University. He also holds a Bachelor of Arts degree in religious studies and a Master of Divinity degree. He resides in Cambridge, Massachusetts, with his wife, Lisa Russell, while he completes a research fellowship with the program on Negotiation at Harvard Law School.

Ken Staley

Ken is president of the Philadelphia Center for Urban Theological Studies. He is an author, lecturer, clinical marriage and family therapist, adjunct professor, former pastor and assistant pastor, and chaplain for the Philadelphia Police Department, and he sits on numerous boards. He received a bachelor of science degree in civil engineering from Villanova University and a master of divinity degree and a doctor of divinity from Miller Theological Seminary. He is married to Sheila Staley.

Patrick L. Stearns

Patrick has a bachelor of fine arts degree from Ohio University, Athens, Ohio; a master of fine arts degree in film from Howard

University, Washington, DC; and a doctorate of philosophy degree in mass communication from Bowling Green State University. He is an associate professor in the Mass Communications Department at Claflin University, Orangeburg, South Carolina. Patrick's research interests include ethnic images in film, audience reception in film, and visual media's portrayal of people of color.

Michael T. Westbrook

Michael has a master of arts in Ministry Leadership from Pillar College, Newark, New Jersey. He is currently a PhD student in Christian Leadership with a concentration in Emerging Generations at Liberty University Rawlings School of Divinity. Michael serves as an adjunct faculty member at Pillar College. He is a U.S. urban missionary, serving youth and families, as cofounder and president/CEO of Greater Life Inc/Community Outreach Center, and as cofounder and pastor of Greater Life Christian Fellowship Church, both in Newark, New Jersey; alongside his wife, Maria Westbrook, who is his cofounder, vice president, and assistant pastor. Michael is also president of The Global Summit, an African American leadership development group, which also includes managing The Matthew Parker Study Center located at Greater Life Community Outreach Center in Newark, New Jersey.

Joseph Williams

Joseph's mission is to restore the lives of those affected by crime. His passion for helping the incarcerated, formerly incarcerated, and their families reach their God-given potential is born from his own personal battles. He currently serves as senior training and technical assistance consultant with American Institute for Research, where he serves as a core coach for the National Reentry Resource Center. Joseph is married to Sharon Marie, and they have four adult children and two grandchildren. He has a bachelor's and master's degree in religious education.

Permissions

VOICES
from Our Daily Bread Ministries

See Us.

Hear Us.

Experience VOICES.

VOICES amplifies the strengths, struggles, and courageous faith of Black image bearers of God.

Podcasts, blogs, books, films, and more . . .

Find out more at **experiencevoices.org**